The Freelance Editor's Handbook

The Freelance Editor's Handbook

A COMPLETE GUIDE TO MAKING YOUR BUSINESS THRIVE

Suzy Bills · *In Consultation with Aaron Ostler*

 UNIVERSITY OF CALIFORNIA PRESS

University of California Press
Oakland, California

© 2021 by Suzy Bills

Library of Congress Cataloging-in-Publication Data
Names: Bills, Suzy, 1981– author.
Title: The freelance editor's handbook : a complete guide to making
   your business thrive / Suzy Bills.
Description: Oakland, California : University of California Press,
   [2021] | Includes bibliographical references and index.
Identifiers: LCCN 2021005241 (print) | LCCN 2021005242 (ebook) |
   ISBN 9780520381322 (hardback) | ISBN 9780520381339
   (paperback) | ISBN 9780520381346 (ebook)
Subjects: LCSH: Editors. | Self-employed—Handbooks, manuals, etc.
Classification: LCC PN162 .B554 2021 (print) | LCC PN162 (ebook) |
   DDC 808.02/7—dc23
LC record available at https://lccn.loc.gov/2021005241
LC ebook record available at https://lccn.loc.gov/2021005242

30   29   28   27   26   25   24   23   22   21
10   9   8   7   6   5   4   3   2   1

Contents

Acknowledgments

To start, I'd like to thank the many editing students I've taught at Brigham Young University. Their desire to learn more about freelancing led me to develop a course on the topic, and I eventually realized that I'd created enough content to fill an entire book. My students are the reason I love my job, and they provided a huge motivation to write this book.

I also want to thank the many freelance editors and other entrepreneurs who've provided me with insight on how to improve my freelance business. Though there are too many people in this category to name, I'm grateful for them and for others who generously provide guidance to freelancers who are trying to improve their businesses.

Additionally, I'd like to express appreciation to my parents, who supported my entrepreneurial endeavors as a kid and teen. Later, when I told them I was going to quit my in-house job so I could freelance full-time, they certainly had concerns but once again fully supported me. And they continue to do so in whatever I'm pursuing, even if they think it's a bit—or a lot—out of the norm.

I offer thanks to Aaron Ostler, who listened to me read every single word of this book and who provided feedback and additional ideas to consider. Along the way, he also prompted a lot of laughs, which I particularly appreciated when I craved a break from the writing or revising process. We'd both also like to thank Aaron's mom, Vickie Ostler, who is a skilled editor and gave Aaron informal but effective training in editing.

Finally, I want to thank the staff at the University of California Press. In particular, I express appreciation for acquisitions editor Eric Schmidt, who provided enthusiastic support for this book from the day I contacted him with my book proposal.

Introduction

What in the world was I doing? Why on earth would I quit my stable, good-paying editing job to become a full-time freelance editor? I liked stability and the comfort of a steady paycheck. But I'd also always had an entrepreneurial spirit. I'd been the kid who was constantly brainstorming ways to make money—whether by selling hair scrunchies (if you were alive in the '80s, you know what they are) or teaching piano lessons. So the idea of starting my own editing business was intriguing at the same time that it was frightening.

In addition to craving stability, I'm cautious and I like to think things through carefully before making big decisions. So I let the idea of starting my own business percolate. I began researching online what would be involved in making the jump. Where would I find clients? How would I market my services? What expenses would I have? How would my tax responsibilities change? Along with this research, I was also working on my MBA, so I paid special attention to course principles that were relevant to a one-person business.[1]

---

1. Though completing an MBA helped me start my business, freelancers *do not* need an MBA to establish a profitable gig. If you follow the principles I discuss in this book, you can make your business successful—without paying tens of thousands of dollars for a business degree.

After weeks and then months of researching and planning, I felt confident that I could become a full-time freelancer who earned as much as (or even more than) an in-house editor does and that I could also establish a lifestyle that I enjoyed—something that was definitely lacking while I was an employee for someone else. With this confidence, I set a date: the day I would quit my in-house job and become self-employed. The date was many months away, so I could ensure that when the day came, I'd be ready for the exciting but sometimes bumpy adventure as a business owner. But I also made the deadline somewhat aggressive; I wanted to ensure that I stayed focused on my goal and that I didn't lose motivation because the date seemed so far away. And the more I thought about the idea, the more excited I was about it, so it would have felt like torture to wait much longer than I did.

I learned a lot in the months leading up to my official start date, and I've learned even more in the years since. I've discovered strategies that are golden, as well as practices to skip. I've discovered aspects of freelancing that I love and aspects that I want to avoid whenever possible (and how to do just that). I've become passionate about learning how to improve my business, not only so that it operates the best it can but also so that I love owning it. Along the way, I've also become passionate about sharing my experiences with others who are interested in the freelance lifestyle. I want them to learn from my successes and failures so they can get on the fast track to operating high-achieving businesses themselves. Because of my desire to help others, I've developed and taught freelancing courses at Brigham Young University, presented at conferences and training meetings, and provided one-on-one mentoring to individuals interested in starting or expanding freelance businesses.

This passion is also the reason I've written this book. I've read a lot of articles, books, and other materials on freelancing, and some truly have been game changers for me and my business. But none of them included all the elements I consider to be vital for establishing a thriving freelance editing business. So I decided to write a book that included all those essentials, as well as other topics that freelance editors commonly wonder about. Now, I'm hoping this book will be a game changer for you.

In writing this book, I've collaborated with entrepreneur Aaron Ostler, who has business experience in a variety of industries, from publishing to real estate to internet marketing. Like me, he learned business best practices largely from trial and error. Through his expert networking skills, he's made connections that have led to business opportunities across the globe. Because of his strategic business mindset, he is often the lead partner in businesses he's helped develop and is frequently asked for business advice from other entrepreneurs. Thanks to his business background and acumen, he's helped refine the business strategies included in this book. Of course, Aaron and I haven't relied on our experiences alone. Over the years, I've read up on a lot of topics related to freelancing, and in this book I share the best information I've found.[2] I've also talked with and learned from many other freelance editors over the years, and their best practices are reflected in the ideas I include in the book. I also include some quotations from freelance editors so you can get a glimpse of their experiences and perspectives.

Why This Book Is for You

This book is for all editors, even those who never plan to complete a single freelance project. Why the latter group? Because I've found that a lot of editors don't set out to freelance but that they eventually

---

2. In citing ideas I include in the book, I cite popular sources when I haven't able to find scholarly sources. I hope that in the future, more research will be conducted on freelancing, freelance editors, and editing.

move into the freelance side of editing. They may freelance only sporadically, or they may take up freelancing as their main source of income. Some editors willingly jump the corporate ship, whereas others are escorted off because of budget cuts, a bad fit, or some other reason. This latter group of editors might not want to freelance long-term, but freelancing short-term can help pay the bills while these editors are searching for new in-house positions.

Whether you plan to freelance full-time, for only a short time, or only occasionally, you'll benefit from applying the concepts in this book—your business will likely be more successful, and you'll enjoy it more. For example, editors tend to love words but fear numbers, making budgets and taxes terrifying. This book will help you feel more confident in your ability to maintain personal and business budgets and to meet all your tax responsibilities (while decreasing the amount you have to pay). As another example, numerous editors are introverts and loathe the idea of networking and marketing themselves. In this book, I present a number of ways to market your business (including many that don't require face-to-face interaction), and I also provide ideas on how to become more comfortable talking with people about your business, often in low-key ways that don't feel salesy. As a final example, editors often struggle with perfectionism, so this book covers ways to turn this potentially destructive trait into an ally. By doing so, you'll have a better quality of life and you may even accept projects or pursue clients that you otherwise wouldn't because of fear of failure.

What We're Going to Cover

Now that I've mentioned a few of the book's concepts and how they can help you, let's go into more depth. My focus is on providing information that's relevant not only to editors new to freelancing but also to editors who've been freelancing for a while (even for decades) and who want to refine their processes to make their businesses more enjoyable, efficient, and financially rewarding. So, even if you've been freelancing for years, don't skip the chapters that seem directed to newbies (with the exception of chapter 1). You'll gain insight that can help you amp up your business—even if you think you know the topic of discussion inside and out.

With that being said, let's take a look at the topics in this book. We'll start with the pros and cons of editing, skills and traits that contribute to success, and how to know when you're ready to become a full-time freelancer. Then we'll move on to business considerations, including how to choose a business name, which type of business entity to select, how to create a business plan, and what business costs to budget for. We'll also talk about developing a strategic mindset through establishing a vision for your business, setting and (actually) achieving your goals, and getting involved in mentoring.

Next, we'll tackle the subject of marketing. Because this topic is critical to business success, we'll explore different aspects of marketing in different chapters. We'll start by discussing whether you need a niche and how to find clients. We'll then go into the details of how to implement the most effective and efficient strategies for securing business and keeping your schedule full. From there, we'll look at options for creating a website and what to include on your site. Finally, we'll discuss how to maximize the benefits of LinkedIn.

After covering marketing, we'll examine pricing, including how to decide what to charge, how to present your price quote, and how to overcome objections to your quote. Then we'll focus on the elements of contracts and invoices, which increase your likelihood of getting paid—and paid on time. Next, we'll discuss strategies to increase your productivity, followed by how to find work/life balance (and, I promise, it is possible—if you take the right approach). Then we'll shift our focus to taxes and other financial considerations, and we'll discuss the information in a way that won't make you want to run away screaming. In the appendices, we'll review the most important action items discussed in the book and we'll look at opportunities to continue developing editing skills.

By the time you finish reading this book, you'll have a full collection of tools you can use immediately to embark on your freelance journey or, if you've already begun, to elevate your business and lifestyle to the next level. Let's get started!

1   *Deciding Whether You Really Want to Be a Freelance Editor*

I love being a freelancer. In fact, the only gig I enjoy more is teaching in Brigham Young University's editing and publishing program, because I have the opportunity to help budding editors develop their skills and learn how to successfully navigate the freelance landscape. I firmly believe that all editors should learn the ropes of freelancing because almost all editors will freelance at some point in their careers—whether as occasional moonlighters who have full-time in-house positions or as part- or full-time freelancers with no other source of income. In the future, more and more editors are likely to freelance full-time because publishing companies are increasingly contracting with freelance editors rather than hiring in-house employees.[1] And the trend in hiring freelancers isn't limited to the publishing industry. As of 2019, 35 percent of US workers freelanced at least part-time, and the percentage is expected to increase.[2] Whether

---

1. See Reedsy, "The Lean Publisher: Evolving in the Freelance Economy," *Reedsy Blog*, May 1, 2020, https://reedsy.com/publishers/the-lean-publisher.

2. See Adam Ozimek, "Freelancing and the Economy in 2019," UpWork, press release, 2019, www.upwork.com/press/economics/freelancing-and-the-economy-in-2019; Shane McFeely and Ryan Pendell, "What Workplace Leaders Can Learn from the Real Gig Economy," Gallup, Workplace, August 16, 2018, www.gallup.com/workplace/240929/workplace-leaders-learn-real-gig-economy.aspx;

out of necessity or preference, editors need to know how to operate effectively as freelancers.

That being said, freelancing has its downsides, and not all people are cut out to be entrepreneurs. In this chapter, we'll explore the pros and cons of freelancing, as well as common skills and traits of successful freelancers. We'll also consider the question of whether to freelance part-time or full-time and the ideal timing for quitting a full-time position to focus on freelancing.

Benefits of Freelancing

I personally think freelancing comes with more benefits than downsides, so let's take a look at the benefits first.

Your Hours Are Flexible

As long as you complete your work by the deadline, you get to decide what days and times you'll work. You can start your workday early or late, take breaks when you want, and decide how many hours to work. You can also step away from your work if there's an emergency in the family or you learn about an event you really want to attend. For some freelancers, the flexibility of choosing when not to work is worth earning less money than they would if they put in more hours.

You Choose Where You Work

You can work from home, at a café, in an office space shared with other freelancers, or anywhere else you want. If you like to travel,

---

Nasdaq, "The Gig Economy: 2020 Freelance Workforce Predicted to Rise to 43%," June 14, 2017, www.nasdaq.com/article/the-gig-economy-2020-freelance-workforce-predicted-to-rise-to-43-cm803297.

"I love that I can work practically anywhere and at any time. If I wanted to go live in Europe for the summer, I would still be able to work."
—*Anonymous freelance editor*

you can take your work with you, earning money when not exploring your destination or visiting with friends and family.

You Can Choose What to Wear

If you'll be freelancing from home, you can wear whatever you want. Even if you occasionally have a videoconference with a client, you only need to worry about wearing a nice shirt—no one will know you're wearing sweatpants or your favorite but no-longer-suitable-to-wear-outside-of-the-house jeans. Sure, some freelancers prefer to put on something other than loungewear and to style their hair because doing so helps them get into work mode and be more productive. But I personally love to wear casual clothes when freelancing, and feeling comfortable helps me be more effective while working.

You Can Save Money

If you work from home, you can reduce the amount you spend on gas, since you won't be commuting to and from work. You can also save money on food, since you're less likely to eat out, as well as on other expenses, such as dry cleaning business clothes.

You Can Largely Avoid Office Politics

You're much less likely to get caught in office politics when you're not in the office and you're not a company's employee. Your contacts at a company are likely to be on their best behavior when interacting with you.

Your Earning Potential Isn't Limited

If you want to earn more money, it's easier to do so as a freelancer than as an employee. You get to set your rates (though, admittedly, average rates in some genres and types of editing are lower than in others). You also get to choose when you'll raise your fees. Plus, you largely choose how many hours to work and, therefore, how much you'll earn.

You Can Enter a New Genre of Editing

If you're an employee, you're likely limited in terms of the genres or topics you typically edit. For example, if you work for a software company, you're probably editing technical documents and marketing material. What if you get ridiculously tired of that type of content? You're pretty much stuck, unless you decide to find a new job somewhere else. Transitioning to a different genre is easier as a freelancer. You can continue taking on projects in your current genre while marketing yourself in the new genre, slowly taking on more and more projects in the new area. (I've done that several times, and currently I work on projects in a range of genres. I love the variety!)

You Can Specify What Type of Editing You Want to Provide

Do you love copy editing but despise substantive editing? Or do you want only developmental editing projects? As a freelancer, you get to choose the type of editing you do (and there's a plethora of work in each type, from developmental editing to proofreading). You can limit your services to one kind, or if you want to cast a wider net, you can offer several types of editing. And, as with the genres you focus on, you can transition from one type of editing to another as your interests change.

You Can Work with a Wide Range of Clients

As a freelancer, you can work with a variety of clients—companies and individuals. Establishing client relationships is often personally fulfilling and can also be beneficial professionally. I've been presented with awesome opportunities because I've developed relationships with clients and been introduced to members of their networks. These opportunities wouldn't have come if I were an in-house editor interacting mainly with other employees of the company.

Downsides of Freelancing

Most of the downsides of freelancing are related to financial matters. But if you approach your business the way I suggest in this book, you can minimize the impacts or even avoid them altogether. Still, it's important to be aware of the potential negatives of freelancing, so let's look at them now.

Your Health Insurance (Medical, Dental, Vision)
Won't Be Subsidized by an Employer

Even if the government doesn't require you to have health insurance, I think it's wise to have at least a basic policy. As a freelancer, you'll need to foot the bill without an employer subsidy. However, this downside may not be that significant, considering that individual health insurance plans can cost about the same as employer-sponsored plans.[3] Plus, when you're self-employed, health insurance premiums are tax deductible.

---

3. See, for example, Bradley T. Heim et al., "The Impact of the ACA on Premiums: Evidence from the Self-Employed," *Journal of Health Politics, Policy, and Law* 40, no. 5 (2015): 1061–1085; Kaiser Family Foundation, "Premiums and Worker Contributions among Workers Covered by Employer-Sponsored

You Don't Get Paid Time Off

Most employees wish they had more paid vacation days and holidays, but any paid time off is better than none. As a freelancer, if you're taking time off because you're sick, celebrating a holiday, or going on a vacation, you won't be making money.

You'll Be the Only Contributor to Your Retirement Fund

Many companies offer a 401K plan and make small contributions. As a freelancer, you'll need to take the initiative to set up a retirement account and contribute to it regularly. And please don't push off doing so—the sooner you start making contributions, the more money you'll have when you retire.

You'll Need to Pay More in Self-Employment Tax

Employees pay only half of the federal self-employment tax; employers pay the other half. As a freelancer, you'll pay the full amount. In 2021, you'll pay 15.3 percent on your first $142,800 of net income, plus 2.9 percent on net income of $142,801–$200,000, plus 3.8 percent on net income above $200,000.

You'll Need to Regularly Set Aside Money for Federal and State Income Taxes

Because your clients won't be withholding taxes for you, you'll need to set aside the money yourself. And in most cases, you'll need to pay federal taxes on a quarterly basis rather than just once a year.

Coverage, 1999–2019," September 25, 2019, www.kff.org/interactive/premiums -and-worker-contributions-among-workers-covered-by-employer-sponsored -coverage-1999-2019.

The Number of Hours You Work per Week May Vary

Even if you want to work a certain number of hours every week, you may need to make adjustments based on your project load. Every so often, you may experience a lull in your schedule. Or a client might request a rush job, requiring you to work extra hours (if you decide to accept the project).

Clients May Be Late in Sending You Their Work or May Never Send It to You

It's common for clients to not send work by the date they initially indicated. Sometimes, they'll put the project on hold (even for years). Other times, they'll go radio silent. These schedule changes can be frustrating and eat into your earnings.

Clients May Expect You to Be Available at All Times of the Day (and Night) via Phone, Text, and Email

Especially if clients don't consider you to be a traditional business, they might assume that you don't have traditional business hours or that you don't have other clients, responsibilities, or nonwork interests. As a result, clients might expect you to work in the evening and on the weekend—or at least expect you to be available to talk with them during those times.

You'll Likely Work for Hours without Talking to Other People

Freelance editing is typically a solitary gig. You'll occasionally talk with clients and leads via email or phone, and you might engage with other editors in online discussion forums, but the majority of the workday you'll go without speaking to anyone (particularly if you want to be as productive as possible). The isolation can be difficult for people who thrive on interacting with others.

Not Every Minute You Spend on Your Business Is Billable

Though you'll spend the majority of your time working on client projects—and, therefore, earning money—you'll also need to regularly devote time to networking and marketing efforts so that projects will continue to roll in. You'll also likely spend time discussing projects with potential clients and preparing price quotes, but you won't always get the job, meaning that you can't include the time spent in your project fee.

Don't Lose Hope

As I described the potential downsides, I was tempted to also explain why none of them should be deal breakers (they aren't for me, at least). But I resisted the urge because I provide these explanations in later chapters of this book. So, I just want to make a small note here: if the list of downsides has you doubting whether this freelance thing is a good idea for you, don't lose hope yet. As I mentioned in the introduction of the book, the idea of freelancing initially scared me silly. But as I researched and prepared—and then took the plunge— I realized that the downsides really aren't that bad. A smart freelancer not only understands the potential drawbacks but also knows how to avoid them. You'll learn the latter information in the following chapters.

With that being said, let's explore another aspect of the freelancing question: What skills and traits do freelance editors typically need in order to succeed?

Pros and Cons of Freelancing

Pros	Cons
• Your hours are flexible.	• Your health insurance isn't subsidized by an employer.
• You can choose where to work.	
• You can choose what to wear.	• You don't get paid time off.
• You can save money.	• You're the only contributor to your retirement fund.
• You can avoid office politics.	
• Your earning potential isn't limited	• You need to pay more in self-employment tax and to pay taxes quarterly.
• You can move into new genres.	• The number of hours you work per week may vary.
• You can decide what type of editing to provide	• Clients may send you projects late or may not send them at all.
• You can work with a wide range of clients.	• Clients may expect you to be available at all times of the day and night.
	• You'll likely be more isolated than if you worked in-house.
	• You won't earn money every minute you spend on your business.

Skills and Characteristics of Effective Freelance Editors

Obviously, to be an effective editor, you need to have solid editing skills. (See appendix B for a list of programs and other resources that can help you develop and refine these skills.) What I'll focus on here are skills and characteristics that can help you be a successful freelancer. Now, I'm not saying that you'll fail if you don't have each of the attributes. But they're helpful for a lot of freelancers, and you can develop most of these attributes over time and through practice. The sooner you start developing or refining them, the sooner you'll be able to leverage them to succeed. And now, without further ado, here are the skills and characteristics that can help you excel as a free-lancer.

Self-Direction and Discipline

As a freelancer, you won't have anyone standing over you to make sure you're working and earning money. (Well, if you do, it's time to have a talk with that spouse, parent, or other well-meaning but micro-managing person in your life.) You're responsible for keeping all aspects of your business moving, and doing so requires discipline. It's okay to every once in a while shut down your laptop early or put off your marketing to-do list. But you need to ensure you're consistently working toward your business goals, including through completing projects by the deadlines and providing high-quality editing. When you've blocked out time to work, make sure you're really focused on your work and not distracted by text messages, social media notifica-tions, children playing in the next room, the laundry that needs to be folded, or thoughts of your exciting plans for the weekend.

Self-Confidence

When engaging in marketing—from introducing yourself at confer-ences and networking events to talking about specific projects with potential clients—you need to be confident in your editing abilities. If your confidence doesn't come through, the people you talk with are less likely to feel confident in your skills. And who wants to hire someone who seems to be lacking in essential aptitudes? I've seen it happen: people will hire the editor who exudes the most self-confidence, and that's not necessarily the editor with the strongest editing skills. So practice being confident. Start by listing the editing training you've completed (courses you've taken, books you've read, etc.), the projects you've worked on, and feedback you've received. Also compare your edited versions of documents to the original versions to see how much you improved the documents. You might also get a confidence boost by taking and scoring well on editing quizzes, such as those offered online by *The Chicago Manual of Style*, the *New York Times*, ACES, and the Dow Jones News Fund.[4]

Ability to Work Alone

As I previously mentioned, freelance editing can be an isolating gig, so it helps if you tend to like alone time. If that's not you, don't worry; you have other options. Try working at a café for a few hours a day, or find a local coworking hub (an office that entrepreneurs share in terms of space, materials, and costs). Other strategies include talking to someone on the phone or in person during your lunch break, participating in online discussion forums for editors, and having music playing while you work. Though I typically like working alone, even I sometimes need a change, and I find that going for a run outside or completing errands midday is enough to prevent me from getting cabin fever.

Time Management Skills

As a freelancer, keeping tabs on your time is essential. How long does it typically take you to complete specific tasks? How much time do

---

4. For *Chicago Manual of Style* quizzes, see "Chicago Style Workouts" at https://cmosshoptalk.com/chicago-style-workouts. For *New York Times* quizzes, go to www.nytimes.com and search for "Copy Edit This!" For ACES quizzes, see "Grammar Guide Quizzes" at https://aceseditors.org/resources/quizzes. For Dow Jones News Fund quizzes, see www.dowjonesnewsfund.org/test.

you spend actually working versus gearing up to work (or procrastinating)? How long do you have until a project is due? With awareness of these and other factors, you can determine how many hours you need to work to complete all your projects and other tasks, and you can evaluate whether you'd benefit from managing your time more efficiently. For example, maybe you should check your email inbox only two times a day instead of every hour (or every fifteen minutes— I've been guilty of that on occasion). Limiting how many times you look at your email inbox increases productivity because you're better able to remain focused on your work and you'll feel less stress.[5] When you manage your time well, you'll complete your work faster, which will open up more opportunities: you can take on more projects and therefore earn more money, or you can work fewer hours and spend more time on other areas of your life. Whichever benefit you choose (and maybe it'll vary by the week), the freedom will come because you're managing your time effectively.

Project Management Skills

Unless you'll be working on very long, time-consuming projects, you'll likely be juggling more than one project at a time. For example, you might be in the early stages of copy editing an article for an academic journal, waiting for an author to respond to your final questions on a book manuscript, and setting up a contract before starting to work on a dissertation. Some editors love having a variety of projects on tap because the editors can move from one project to another when they need a break or are waiting for requested informa-

---

5. Kostadin Kushlev and Elizabeth W. Dunn, "Checking Email Less Frequently Reduces Stress," *Computers in Human Behavior* 43 (2014): 220–228. I don't think it's reasonable for freelancers to check their email only once daily, but you shouldn't be a slave to your inbox. Try checking it at the start and end of your workday. See chapter 10 for more details.

tion from a client. If that's not you, you can focus on securing longer projects or just accept that you'll likely have a gap in your schedule when you've finished one project and are waiting for another. Whether or not you like having multiple projects in hand, you'll want to rely on a project management system (it can be as low-tech as an Excel file) to keep track of all the projects on your plate.

Organizational Skills

As a business owner, you'll be responsible for keeping straight all the details of each project you're working on—and potential projects you're hoping to score. Even if your clients are on the ball and re-member everything that's been discussed (and from my experience, most don't), you won't appear very professional if you have to ask them to remind you of the scope of work, the style guide, due dates, payment details, and so forth. There are many ways to stay organized (we'll talk about them in chapter 10); the key is to find one that works for you and then to use it consistently. And don't forget to organize your project files, financial records, and any physical materials. By es-tablishing organizational systems—and actually using them—you'll feel less harried, and your clients will be impressed.

Oral and Written Communication Skills

Since you're an editor, the odds are good that you can communicate clearly in writing. What you might not be as good at in terms of writ-ten communication is responding promptly to emails, particularly when your schedule is packed with work and personal responsibili-ties. A good guideline is to respond to emails within twenty-four hours, Monday through Friday; emails that arrive on the weekend can be addressed the following Monday morning. If you won't be able to send a full response within twenty-four hours, send a brief message acknowledging you've received the email and noting when you'll respond in full.

Though most of your business communication will likely be written, it's also important to have strong oral communication skills—and to be willing use them. Although I much prefer communicating with clients via email, some of them prefer to talk with me on the phone. And so I comply (most of the time). During a call, I make sure to sound cheerful and to clearly answer the client's questions, while also moving the conversation forward so the call can be as efficient, effective, and short as possible.[6]

Customer Service Skills

One of the best ways to endear yourself to clients is to be a pleasure to work with. And achieving that goal really doesn't take a lot, considering that you probably won't have too much contact with your clients. So, take advantage of small opportunities. For example, in your emails to a client, always be positive, encouraging, and kind, such as by using phrases like "I hope you're having a great day," "Please let me know if you have any questions," and "I look forward to receiving your next chapter." Respond promptly to emails and calls, and return projects on time (and even a little early, if possible).

Particularly if you're working with individual authors (not companies), you'll want clients to see you as their most loyal cheerleader. Again, that comes across in the little things. For instance, be aware of how you phrase comments in the file you're editing. Instead of demanding a change (e.g., "You need to clarify the meaning"), make a

---

6. When you do talk to clients on the phone, it's a good idea to take notes and then to send an email recapping the discussion. That way, you can ensure that you and the client are on the same page. You'll also have documentation if (heaven forbid) you ever need to take legal action against a client.

suggestion (e.g., "Consider revising to clarify the meaning so readers aren't confused") or start your request with *please* (e.g., "Please cite a source to support this statement"). Add comments of encouragement in the file, as well as in the email you attach the edited file to. Authors might feel discouraged when they confront a lot of tracked changes and comments that request additional revisions, so authors need to know that you see value and positive points in their work. I've found that these strategies, which don't take much extra time, have helped me develop great relationships with clients and have led to repeat business and numerous referrals.

Understanding of Marketing Strategies

You don't need to have a degree in marketing to succeed as a freelancer, but you'll definitely benefit if you understand the basics, such as how to pitch your services persuasively (and, no, being persuasive doesn't require being slimy). You'll also benefit from understanding how to leverage social media and more traditional avenues of marketing, how to network effectively, and how to ask for repeat business and referrals.

Understanding of Financial Basics

As with marketing, you don't need to be a guru when it comes to finances. But your business will suffer if you don't understand—or

"I always say that being an editor means you need to be part English teacher, part therapist, part mediator, part friend, part cheerleader, part intuitive (actually a finely tuned radar). Editors need to be obsessive about details and highly curious (love to look everything up). Good editors also need experience and knowledge of how to communicate professionally and how to deal with difficult people and situations."
—*Lea Galanter, freelance editor*

aren't willing to pay attention to—principles such as cash flow. I don't blame you if you think the whole financial aspect is scary. I don't claim to be a math whiz (it's a miracle I passed calculus and statistics), and I'd much rather work with words than with numbers. But even I can understand and tolerate keeping track of the financial basics involved in a freelance business. And you'll want to as well, unless you like to live on the edge . . . the edge of financial security.

Final Thoughts

Hopefully you're feeling good because you already have several of the skills I've discussed above. Even if you're afraid that the number of traits you lack is greater than the number you can claim, don't doubt your ability to become a successful freelancer. I'll address these areas in later chapters so that you can develop the skills you currently don't have or you need to bolster. Knowledge truly is power; by recognizing areas you need to work on, you'll be able to develop a plan to turn your weaknesses into strengths (or, at the least, prevent weaknesses from becoming downfalls).

Now let's move on to the final topic I want to address in this chapter: freelancing part-time versus full-time.

The Decision of Whether to Freelance Part-Time or Full-Time

The Case for Starting Part-Time

Editors sometimes ask whether they should dive right into full-time freelancing mode or start off freelancing part-time, with the goal of slowly increasing to full-time freelancing. Each person's situation is different, so my advice might not fit your circumstances, but my general suggestion is to start by freelancing part-time while also working as an employee of a company. Now, let me explain. I'd much rather run my own editing business than work for someone else, but I realize that new editors can learn a lot from working in-house somewhere. By doing so, you're more likely to work in person with other members of the publishing team (writers, designers, etc.) and to get a better understanding of the entire publishing process than you are as a freelancer who's involved in only one or a few steps of the publishing process. The knowledge you gain from interacting with other members of a publishing team and from seeing other parts of the publishing process will help you be a more informed (read: better) freelancer. You'll be able to provide better advice to your clients when they have questions about publishing, and you may even choose to expand your business services to include more than just editing. For example, you may feel confident providing advice on book formatting and offering to convert traditionally formatted books into e-books.

As an employee, you'll also have opportunities to expand your network, potentially leading to freelance projects. If your employer pays for you to attend conferences or external training, you might meet individuals who are looking for a freelance editor to help with personal or company projects. Through your work projects, you might interact with employees at printing presses, who likely are asked by other clients to recommend freelance editors. Your coworkers might even ask you to edit documents for them (I had that experience multiple times, and it was a huge help in getting my business thriving). And if you eventually do leave your job to freelance full-time, your former employer might hire you as a contractor, either short-term while looking for your replacement or long-term because you've proven yourself to be invaluable to the company.

Of course, there are other benefits of initially freelancing part-time while working as an employee. For one, you'll feel less pressure to make your freelance business a success from day one. If you experience a few dry spells, you'll still be receiving a steady income from your full-time job. You'll have the time to refine your business model, niche, marketing strategy, and client base. Likewise, you'll have time to build your portfolio, which might be limited if you want to transition to a new genre or you can't include your in-house editing work in your portfolio for confidentiality reasons. Another benefit is that you can be more discriminating in terms of which freelance projects you agree to work on. (It's much easier to say no to a project when the project fee won't be paying your rent next month!) Additionally, you can put all your part-time freelance earnings in your savings account, to build a safety net for when you do become a full-time freelancer. The more you have in savings, the more confident you'll be to make the jump.

Finally, starting out part-time will help you figure out whether working from home and being your own boss are good fits for you. After all, some editors prefer working in a business office with co-workers and don't want the responsibilities required of a boss. Perhaps you'll decide that you do want to go full-time but that you need to strengthen your business skills or ability to remain focused without a manager keeping tabs on you. In that case, freelancing part-time will give you the opportunity to work on those areas before expanding to full-time freelancing.

Drawbacks to Starting Part-Time

To be fair, there are also downsides of juggling a full-time job and part-time freelancing. The biggest challenge is finding the time to fit in the freelance work. You'll likely be putting in hours in the evening and on the weekend, meaning you'll have to cut back the time you spend on other parts of your life. Missing out on being with your family and friends, working on hobbies, or just relaxing can get old—and exhausting. So, make sure you set boundaries: How much time will you allot for freelancing each week? What about on holidays? What personal obligations take precedence over freelancing? How long will you freelance part-time before quitting your full-time job? If you live with family members, make sure to include them in these decisions, or you'll likely have even more issues to deal with in the long term.

Another drawback is that you likely won't be able to communicate with clients during regular business hours. That being said, most clients won't mind as long as you let them know how soon you'll respond (e.g., within twenty-four hours). Other ways to address this issue are to check your freelance-business email during lunchtime and to allow clients to call your cell phone if pressing matters come up (but do emphasize that the matters must be urgent; otherwise, you might get a lot of calls about nonemergency issues).

A final drawback is that you might have to turn down freelance projects because you won't have time to complete them by the requested deadline. But before you decline a project—particularly one you're really interested in—see whether you can negotiate a new due date. Perhaps the client will be okay with you completing the first half by the original deadline if you can finish the second half by the following week. And explaining to clients that your schedule is full for the next month or beyond might make you even more desirable to clients. The thinking is that if you're in high demand, then you must be good at what you do. As a result, clients may be willing to wait so they can benefit from your skills.

Signs You're Ready to Transition to Full-Time Freelancing

Now, how do you know when it's time to give your employer your two weeks' notice and start freelancing full-time? The answer depends on multiple factors, so it'll differ from editor to editor. But here are some signs that will help you gauge when you're ready.

SUFFICIENT PROJECT REQUESTS

One sign is that you receive a steady stream of project requests and you have to turn down some of them because you don't have time to fit them into your schedule. It might help if I define what I mean by *steady stream*. I'm talking about regularly receiving project requests for a few months, not just for a few weeks. And within that longer time frame, you're ideally receiving at least one request per week. That frequency might sound like a lot, but when you're freelancing full-time you'll have a lot of hours to fill per week, so you'll need a lot of projects coming in. (The exception is if you tend to work on long-term projects, such textbooks, which can take a couple of months or more to edit. In that case, you're probably in an okay spot if you receive a project request every three weeks.)

The bottom line is that you should be receiving enough requests to make you confident that when you freelance full-time, you'll have enough work to fill most of your allotted hours. Before you make the switch, you don't need to be receiving enough requests to cover forty hours a week; when you make the switch to full-time freelancing, you'll also ramp up your marketing, which will help you bring in extra projects. But, ideally, before you make the jump, you should be receiving enough requests that you'd be freelancing more than twenty hours per week in order to complete the projects.

ADEQUATE IN-HOUSE EXPERIENCE

Another sign that you might be ready to freelance full-time is that you've worked in-house somewhere long enough to receive adequate on-the-job training and mentoring to refine your editing skills. That statement might be one of the more controversial assertions I make in this book, since many editors (particularly freelance editors, it seems) are self-taught. I'm not saying that you have to be employed at a company to become a high-quality editor, but I do think it helps if you receive feedback on your editing from more-experienced editors (or, perhaps, writers who know the real grammar rules from the myths, such as not ending a sentence with a preposition). Without receiving feedback from knowledgeable peers, it's hard for editors to know whether they're actually providing high-quality editing. (After all, people typically don't know what they don't know.) And it's much easier to receive knowledgeable feedback when you work in-house than when you're a full-time freelancer. Some freelancers do find mentors, but you're not likely to receive as much training and feedback as you would working in-house.

How do you know if you've received enough training and mentoring to strike out on your own? Again, there's not a definitive answer, but one indicator is that the people reviewing your work are noting that fewer and fewer changes are needed. Another sign is that you no longer need to open up *The Chicago Manual of Style* (or whatever style guide you're using) every thirty minutes to figure out how to address a style or grammar issue—you have the basic rules memorized (and might even be able to cite the section numbers!). Similarly, you don't feel the need to regularly ask coworkers how they would fix a problematic sentence; you feel confident in your abilities to independently improve an author's writing and can clearly explain the rationales for your edits.

Different editors will need different amounts of time working in-house to gain adequate experience, mentoring, and training. As a general rule, I'd recommend working in-house for at least a year. As antsy as you might be to run your own business full-time, it's essential to ensure that you have the editing skills needed to provide excellent service. Patiently developing those skills under the tutelage of other editors will pay off for the rest of your career. In fact, with in-house experience you'll probably be more desirable to potential clients because a full-time editing job is typically considered proof that you have strong editing skills. The thinking goes that if you didn't have the skills, you wouldn't have been able to get the job or to keep it. And the longer you had the job before becoming a full-time freelancer, the more impressive your experience might seem.

SUFFICIENT SAVINGS

Unless you're not the main financial provider in your household, you need to build up your savings account before freelancing full-time. Otherwise, you're likely to feel extremely stressed, particularly in the first months of your venture, wondering whether you'll earn enough to cover your personal expenses. The stress will greatly dampen your enjoyment of the perks that come from running your own business. And you'll also be more likely to accept projects that are low paying or that you otherwise dread (e.g., a manuscript on a subject you despise or with content that conflicts with your morals).

Various freelance experts have recommended different amounts of money to save before freelancing full-time; typical suggestions are to have enough money to cover three, six, or twelve months of living costs. My personal recommendation is to save six months' worth—an unexpected emergency could quickly wipe out three months of savings, and it's unrealistic to assume that most people will be able to save a whole year's worth of living costs before freelancing full-time. Six months' worth will give you peace of mind during any times that you're twiddling your thumbs, waiting for your next project to arrive.

You might be thinking that saving even six months of living costs is unrealistic, but keep two things in mind: First, if you freelance part-time while working full-time, you'll be speeding up the savings process (and from my experience, the money can add up quickly). Second, I'm talking about *living expenses*, not the vacation fund, costs for entertainment, and other things you spend money on that aren't essential. As a full-time freelancer, if you do need to dip into your

---

Signs You're Ready to Freelance Full-Time

- You're receiving a steady stream of project requests—enough to fill about half of the hours you plan to work per week after quitting your in-house position.
- You've worked in-house long enough to receive sufficient on-the-job training and mentoring to refine your editing skills.
- You've saved six months of living costs.
- You understand the basics of operating a business.

---

emergency fund, you may decide that rather than heading to the movie theater to watch that new *Star Wars* movie, you can wait until it comes out on DVD.

ADEQUATE KNOWLEDGE OF WHAT FREELANCING WILL ENTAIL

It might seem obvious that you should understand the basics of operating a business before starting one full-time, but I know of many editors who seem to skip this step. They dive into freelancing as their only source of income and then realize that they don't understand what it takes to run a business successfully. Sure, you might be a company of one, but you still need to understand business concepts such as marketing and taxes. This book will provide the basic information you'll need, but don't stop here. The more you research, learn, and prepare, the more likely you'll be to succeed—and to enjoy the process.

Key Takeaways

- Becoming a freelancer offers numerous benefits, particularly in terms of flexibility and control. You can choose when you'll work and where you'll work from, you can save money by eliminating your work commute, and you can avoid office politics. You'll also have more control over your income, what types of content you work on, the services you provide, and whom you work with.

· The potential downsides of freelancing are mainly financial: Your health insurance premium won't be subsidized, you won't receive paid time off, you'll be the only contributor to your retirement plan, and you'll need to pay more in self-employment taxes. Additionally, your project load might vary, clients might expect you to be available during nonstandard hours, you'll often work alone, and you won't earn money every minute you spend on your business.

· Successful freelancers typically possess several skills and characteristics, including discipline; self-confidence; and the ability to work alone, to manage time and projects efficiently, and to communicate well. Effective freelancers also have a basic understanding of marketing strategies and financial principles.

· You'll likely benefit from initially working in-house and slowly taking on freelancing projects part-time.

· You're probably ready to freelance full-time if you're regularly receiving freelance requests, you've worked at least one year as an in-house editor, you've saved six months' worth of living expenses, and you've learned the basics of what freelancing will involve.

2 *Setting Up Your Business*

Whether you've decided to freelance part-time or full-time, it's important to think of yourself as a business owner—because you are! So, even before you start accepting projects, you should set up the business aspects of your company, including writing a business plan, choosing a business name, selecting a business entity, and opening a business bank account. Completing these and other steps will take some thought and time, but the outlay will pay off in the long term (and in the short term too). Here are just two of the reasons: When you spend the time needed to set up the business aspects, you'll be more likely to take your business seriously and to think like a strategic business owner. As a result, other people and companies will also be more likely to take your business seriously, meaning you'll have a better chance of commanding high wages and avoiding clients who try to take advantage of you. This chapter will walk you through the steps of setting up your business for success.

Business Name

One of the first decisions to make is what to call your business. The name can be as simple and straightforward or as creative and catchy as you want. The two main approaches are to use your personal name and a description of your services (e.g., Editing by Jane) or to use a fictional name that, ideally, is relevant to your services (e.g., Red Pen Editing Services). Which approach is better? Each has benefits.

Using your personal name is more straightforward in terms of connecting yourself with your business. You can use the name to capitalize on the reputation you've established for yourself as an editor, and your business can be easy to remember and to find through an internet search. Using your personal name can also simplify matters related to setting up financial accounts, getting paid by clients, and paying taxes. On the other hand, using a creative fictional name can evoke an image or message you want to convey about your business. A creative name might be more memorable than your personal name and might be easier for people to find on the internet if your personal name is hard to spell or pronounce. Additionally, a creative name might be best if your personal name is quite common or is the same as that of someone you don't want to be connected with.[1]

Whichever approach you prefer, you'll want to complete a few steps in choosing a business name. The first step is to brainstorm. Write down every idea that comes to mind, regardless of how silly or bad it might seem. The simple process of listing ideas will spur more, some of which may be great. Don't stop after you've written down just ten. Challenge yourself to list at least twenty—and fifty is even better. Each idea doesn't have to be unique; play around with the order of words, and think of synonyms. Think of messages you want to convey with your name, such as regarding the quality of your editing or how you provide value to clients. I wouldn't recommend getting

---

1. Many years ago, I and others wrote health and fitness articles for a company's blog. After a post from one of the other writers performed very well, everyone wanted to identify exactly why the article received so many hits. It turns out that the author has the same name as a well-known porn star, and a lot of people viewing the article were *not* seeking information on wellness, as indicated by their quick exit from the article's webpage.

too specific in terms of the genre or type of editing you specialize in or where you're located, because you don't want to box yourself in. True, you can always rename your business (including through using a "doing business as" title), but you'll dilute the branding you've already established and you'll need to update your website, business cards, other marketing materials, and so forth. I'd rather spend my business hours making money.

The second step is to narrow the brainstormed list to your top five and then to get feedback from family and friends. Ask them which names they prefer and why. Also ask what the names seem to suggest. The answers may identify a clear winner, stimulate additional options, or signal that you need to brainstorm some more. Repeat steps one and two until you've landed on a couple of great names.

The third step is to check whether the names you've selected are already being used. You'll want to check a few places. Start by searching the US Patent and Trademark Office's database (http://tmsearch .uspto.gov) for each name. If a name appears in the database, the name's a no-go. If a name passes that test, then google the name to see what comes up. If another company is using that exact name (or perhaps something quite close), cross it off your list. Even if the company is located far away from you, you don't want to risk being sued for copying the name or risk being confused with the other business. Finally, see if the URL for your company name is available. True, your website URL doesn't have to exactly match your business's name, but you don't want to create confusion for potential clients (and potentially lose projects because people went to what they assumed, because of the URL, was your site).

Hopefully at least one of your top names will have passed these tests. If not, go back to your list and select the next-best choices. If at least two of your names are viable, it's time for a tiebreaker. Again get input from family, friends, and perhaps colleagues. Also consider whether one name will lend itself to a logo design for your business.

If you're still having a hard time deciding, try not to stress too much. Though your business name is important, what's more important is that you've selected one and can start building awareness of your business.

With your business name selected, you're ready to move on to formalizing your business, such as by deciding on a business entity. And that's exactly where we're headed next.

Business Entities

You've probably seen the terms *sole proprietor*, *LLC* (limited liability company), and *S corporation*, but you might not have paid much attention to them and might not know which of these business structures is the best choice for your freelance business.[2] Let's take a look at each.

Sole Proprietorship

Most freelance editors start out as sole proprietors because a sole proprietorship is the default business structure—you don't have to file any forms or complete any other steps (though, as I discuss in a later section, you do typically need to get a business license). Simply by freelancing, you're a sole proprietor, and for that reason many freelancers remain sole proprietors. Filing your tax return is relatively simple because you file as an individual, the same way you would as an employee of a company, and you don't need to fill out as many forms as you would if you chose a different business structure.

However, being a sole proprietor has some disadvantages. For one, it's more difficult to build business credit as a sole proprietor

---

2. While these business entities aren't the only types, they're the ones that are most relevant for a one-person business.

than if you register your business as another entity type. This difficulty might not be a big deal in the short term, but it could be frustrating if later on you want to expand your business to include employees, which would result in higher overhead costs and possibly necessitate getting a business loan (e.g., for office space or equipment). Another downside is that you're personally responsible for all of your business's liabilities. So, if your business incurs debts that it can't pay, creditors can sue you as an individual. And if you don't have the personal funds to pay, your car could be repossessed and you could even lose your home. That being said, freelance editing businesses typically don't have huge expenses, so this risk probably won't be too great. In addition to being liable for business costs, you'll be liable for any harm that your business causes. For example, if a client sues your business for errors you didn't correct or (even worse) errors you introduced, you'll be personally responsible if the court rules against you. Again, there's not much risk you'll actually be sued, but if it does happen, you won't be protected if you're a sole proprietor.

A further disadvantage relates to taxes. Though the filing process isn't too bad, you'll probably have to pay more in taxes than if you choose a different business structure. That's because sole proprietors are required to pay the full self-employment tax (typically 15.3 percent), whereas other business entities need to pay only part of the percentage. If you're editing on a very part-time basis and therefore not earning that much per year, then you might not see much difference in the tax liability resulting from a sole proprietorship verses other business types. But if you're consistently earning money through your business, you'll likely benefit at tax time if you've selected a different business structure.

Unfortunately, there's not a specific income amount at which everyone will benefit from switching to a different structure. Factors that come into play include whether you file jointly with a spouse, whether you have dependents, and what deductions and credits you qualify for. To figure out what the best choice is for you, talk with a certified public accountant who has experience working with freelancers.

LLC

An LLC removes the main risks associated with being a sole proprietor: your personal liability is limited if your business incurs expenses it can't pay or is sued. With an LLC, you also get to choose how your business will be classified when it comes to taxes. You can file as a sole proprietor, a C corporation, or an S corporation. By choosing to file as an S corporation, you'll reduce your tax liability.

Unfortunately, the benefits of an LLC do come at a price—in both money and time. To become an LLC, you'll need to file paperwork with your state and pay an initial fee, and you'll likely need to complete a renewal form every year and pay a renewal fee. (Different states have different rules and fees, so make sure to get the details about the state you're creating your LLC in. You'll find a lot of state-specific information at www.nolo.com.) I've also read various articles that an LLC requires more record keeping than a sole proprietorship does, but I don't agree. Regardless of the type of business structure you select, you should be keeping records of all your business income and expenses, tax returns, contracts, and other business-related documents. So having an LLC shouldn't significantly add to your administrative tasks.

You can pay a company to set up an LLC for you, but I don't think the price tag of $200–$500 is worth it. For example, I set up an LLC in Utah in less than thirty minutes, and I only had to pay the filing fee of $70. Though states may have different online systems for creating an LLC, most systems are pretty straightforward; the filing process isn't something that requires the expertise of a lawyer. And if you do have any questions, a quick Google search should turn up more than enough answers to help you feel confident when it comes time to hit the Submit button.[3]

S Corporation

Technically, an S corporation isn't a type of business entity. Rather, it's a tax designation that you can elect to have if you've created an LLC (or a corporation, though that business entity isn't relevant for most freelance editors). To be designated as an S corp for tax purposes, you need to complete Form 2553: Election by a Small Business Corporation and submit it to the IRS. With this filing status, you'll be able to reduce your tax bill because you won't be paying as much in self-employment taxes. From personal experience, I know that the reduction can be large—as in thousands of dollars. Of course, to get the reduction, you'll have to deal with additional paperwork and administrative tasks, but with the money you'll likely save, you'll be able to pay an expert to complete the paperwork for you. (For more details on filing as an S corp for tax purposes, see chapter 12.)

Business License

Whether your business is a sole proprietorship or an LLC, you'll likely need to get a business license from the state you live in. In some locations, you'll also need a permit from your county and/or city. The best way to find out whether your state and local governments require your business to have a license is to search on the internet

---

3. However, if you ever decide to hire employees, it's a good idea to ask a lawyer to help in drafting an operating agreement for your LLC.

(googling "Do I need a business license in [state/city]" will do the trick). One of the top results will probably be the relevant government's website for business licensing, and the site will provide the information you'll need. The registration process is typically pretty simple, and the fee isn't too bad (e.g., around $30 in Utah). You'll probably need to renew your license (and pay a renewal fee) annually.

Employer Identification Number

An employer identification number (EIN) is a federal tax ID; think of it as a Social Security number (SSN) for a business. Instead of providing your SSN on business and tax forms (e.g., a W-9), you'll provide your EIN. If you choose to be a sole proprietor, you typically won't need to get an EIN. In some states, you'll need one before you can become an LLC. Even if you don't need an EIN, you might want one. Using an EIN keeps your SSN safer, making you less likely to be the victim of identity theft. Additionally, some banks require that you have an EIN before you can open a business checking account or apply for a business credit card. Using an EIN instead of your SSN can also make your business appear more professional to clients.

Applying for an EIN is easy and free (now *that's* a refreshing change). Simply fill out the form at https://sa.www4.irs.gov/modiein /individual/index.jsp. Completing the form takes only a few minutes, and then you'll immediately receive your EIN via email. (You can also apply for an EIN via phone, fax, or mail, but the process will take longer.) Because the application process is so quick and easy, don't waste your money paying a company to complete the process for you. You don't ever need to renew your EIN, but if you apply for an EIN as a sole proprietor, you will need to apply for a new EIN if you change your business to an LLC and want to file taxes as a corporation or want to hire employees.

Bank Account and Credit Card

If your business is an LLC, it's essential to set up a business-only bank account—doing so is a way to demonstrate that you and your company are separate entities (an important element in limiting your personal liability if your business is ever sued or in debt). Even if you're a sole proprietor, opening a business bank account is a good idea. For one, having a business bank account looks more professional to clients—they'll be writing checks to your business, not to you personally. Also, maintaining separate business and personal bank accounts makes it easy to see which financial transactions are related to your business and which are personal. That distinction is helpful when tax time rolls around—and even more so if you're ever audited by the IRS or a state or local taxing authority. Additionally, having a business bank account can help you be more financially responsible. Decide how much you'll pay yourself each month, and transfer that amount from your business account to your personal account. That way, you'll be less tempted to spend all the money you earn.

For many of the same reasons that you should get a business bank account, you should get a business credit card if you plan to use a credit card for business expenses. Whether you do use a credit card is a personal decision. I prefer to because the one I use doesn't have an annual fee and I pay the full balance every month, so I'm not charged interest. I also earn cash back on purchases, meaning I'm actually earning some money. If your business is an LLC, using a credit card can also help build your business's credit history. And that's critical if at some point you want to get a business loan; without a business credit history, your loan request is almost guaranteed to be rejected. Regardless of the benefits, if you're likely to make unnecessary purchases that you can't pay off before incurring interest, then you're probably better off not using a credit card for your business.

When you're ready to open a bank account, shop around before choosing a bank and type of business account. Different account types have different monthly fees, required account balances, and permitted numbers of transactions per month. Usually, monthly fees will be waived if you meet certain conditions, such as maintaining a high-enough balance or linking your business account with other accounts at the same bank. Try to find an account option that meets your needs well enough that any fees will be waived each month. I prefer having my business account at the same bank as my personal accounts; that way, I can see and manage all my accounts in one place (whether on the bank's website or at one of the bank's physical locations). If you plan to open a credit card account, look at various cards' interest rates and features, such as the ability to earn points or cash when you make purchases.

Business Plan

Another important element in setting up your business is developing a business plan. I'm pretty sure that merely reading the words *business plan* made some of you shudder. Maybe you're afraid that preparing a business plan requires a degree in business or that a business plan has to include so much content that it'll take a lot of time to complete. Or maybe you think that a business plan is needed only if you want to obtain external funding or you intend to eventually expand your business to include multiple employees. In fact, none of these assumptions are correct. Every business—including a part-time freelance editing enterprise—can benefit from having a business plan. It doesn't need to fill thirty pages, though you do need to spend enough time to really consider your business. And you don't need to share it with anyone, though I do recommend having your significant other (if applicable) read it, and it would be a good idea to get feedback on it from another entrepreneur.

One of the main purposes of creating a business plan is that it helps you think about what you want your business to be—now and in the future. A business plan helps you establish goals and provides a road map for how to achieve the goals. That being said, a business plan doesn't need to box you in; you can change it as your circumstances and interests change. Your business plan can be as informal as you want—as long as it includes the essential elements. So, state things in the way that works for you. And make it easy to skim, such as by including headings and using bulleted lists.

Now that I've hopefully convinced you to create a business plan, let's talk about the essential elements. You might already have a clear idea of what you want to include in some of the sections. Other sections will require more thought—and research. Give yourself some time. Don't try to complete your plan in one sitting. Rather, start by writing down what you already know and what aspects you need to think about. Identify what you need to research. Talk with other freelance editors. Consider various options before making decisions. Then add to each section of your plan. Keep in mind that you can revise your plan later as you gain more experience operating your business. In fact, I hope you do continue refining your plan. Review it every few months, especially for the first year or so, and decide how you can tweak your plan in order to improve your company. Have fun with the process of creating and revising your plan—consider it the blueprint for your dream business.

"Even if the plan is simply broad strokes, it can still give you a general direction to go in and a target to reach for."
—*Virginia St-Denis, freelance editor*

Executive Summary

The executive summary should highlight the main ideas you describe in the rest of your business plan. Therefore, you should write the summary after you've completed the other sections. Keep the summary short, and see if you can present some of the information in an easy-to-scan list.

Description of Your Business

In the second section, describe your business in detail. Which types of editing will you offer? Will you also provide writing, design, or other types of services? Will you focus on specific genres or industries? Describing your business will help you develop the rest of your business plan.

Mission and Vision Statements

In preparing your mission statement, think about the value you want your business to provide to clients. Maybe you want to help indie authors refine their books before self-publishing. Or perhaps you want to ensure that companies' website copy is as engaging, clear, and helpful as possible. If you're having a hard time crafting your mission statement, it might help to think about the aspect of editing that brings you the most fulfillment.

The vision statement is your opportunity to dream really big. What are your long-term goals for your business? What do you want it to become? For instance, do you eventually want to transition from mainly editing dissertations to editing fitness books? Do you want to raise your rates enough over time that you'll need to work only twenty-five hours a week instead of forty? (For more ideas on your business vision, see chapter 3.)

Market Analysis

The market analysis section should discuss the main market you'll be working in (e.g., YA fantasy). Describe your market, trends in the market, your competitors (companies and individuals), and how you'll fit in the market. You'll likely need to conduct some research to complete this section. As part of the research process, try to determine how big the market is and verify that there's room for you to join the fray.

After getting a general idea of your competitors, go a little deeper by comparing them to each other and to your business. What specific services do they offer? At what prices? How does your company differ—what sets you apart and could be leveraged to create a competitive advantage? How are your competitors marketing themselves? What are they doing that you might want to incorporate into your business—or that you might want to avoid? Use this analysis to develop your marketing strategies.

Strengths, Weaknesses, Opportunities, and Threats Analysis

Take some time to thoughtfully assess your company's strengths and weaknesses. For this analysis, strengths and weaknesses are things that you have control over. Perhaps a strength is that through your ten years as an editor, you've mastered grammar and style rules. A weakness might be that you want to move into a new genre, perhaps from academic to technical documents. Though it's not fun to identify your weaknesses, doing so will help you develop strategies to overcome your weaknesses—or at least to be successful despite them. Listing your strengths can give you confidence in what you currently have to offer. You'll likely want to mention at least some of your strengths in your marketing efforts.

Next, list opportunities and threats that your business faces. Opportunities and threats are external factors, meaning you don't have control over them. An example of an opportunity is the increasing number of authors who need help preparing their manuscripts for self-publishing; you can market your services to this group. A threat could be freelance job-bidding sites, on which projects are often awarded to the lowest bidders, thereby driving down market prices.

Once you've listed your business's strengths, weaknesses, opportunities, and threats, look for how you can pair them to maximize strengths and opportunities while reducing weaknesses and threats. For instance, can you use a strength to take advantage of an opportunity or to avoid a threat? What opportunities can you take action on to minimize a weakness? Using the example strength of strong editing skills and the threat of low market prices, you could justify your higher fees by referring to your years of experience and expert-level editing skills. After you've identified pairs, create steps to implement your action item related to each pair.

Marketing and Sales Strategies

Now it's time to describe how you'll market your business. In developing this section, pull information from the previous sections of your business plan and also refer to chapters 4 and 5 of this book, which cover marketing in depth. After you've described all the marketing strategies you'll use, rank them according to how effective you think they'll be. Then make sure to prioritize implementing the strategies at the top of your list.

Description of Your Operations

Next, describe the day-to-day operations of your business. Where will you work (a home office, a designated space in your family room, or a coworking space)? What will your standard working days and hours be each week? The more operational aspects you identify in this section, the easier it will be to get your business running smoothly. You'll be more likely to work efficiently and to make progress on achieving your goals. Here are additional operational elements to consider:

- When will you regularly work on your marketing efforts?
- How often will you respond to emails?
- How much time will you set aside for ongoing professional development (e.g., reading editing or writing books, engaging in editing discussion forums, and completing editing quizzes)?
- How will you keep track of projects and payments?
- How will you name project files, where will you save them, and how will you back them up?

Financial Overview

The final section of your business plan should address the financial aspects of your business. Make sure to discuss your pricing method (e.g., hourly rates versus project fees; see chapter 8 for an extensive discussion of all things related to pricing). Also estimate what you'll earn per week and per month. In making these estimates, it's important to consider holidays and vacation time. By factoring in those no-work days, you're less likely to feel pressure to put in hours when those days arrive. This section should also list all your expected business costs, both those that are recurring and those that come up every once in a while. Ensure that your income will cover your business expenses as well as your living expenses, either the full amount or the part that your business needs to contribute to the household income.

Sample Business Plan

This sample contains excerpts from a business plan. In your own business plan, you'll likely want to include more content and details in each section.

EXECUTIVE SUMMARY

Jane Grammar Edits is a business that focuses on editing YA fantasy novels and doctoral dissertations. In the long term, the company wants to become well-known for providing exceptional editing, noteworthy customer service, and insightful one-on-one coaching and group training. Jane Grammar Edits has two niches—in quite different areas—providing the company with more opportunities than would be available with only one niche while also keeping the focus limited enough that the company can become well-known as an expert in each niche. For each target group, marketing strategies will be tailored to the needs and expectations of the group's members, and marketing activities will be part of the business's weekly schedule . . .

BUSINESS DESCRIPTION

Jane Grammar Edits provides developmental, substantive, and copy editing services, mainly for YA fantasy novels and doctoral dissertations, but other genres will be considered. Regarding fantasy novels, Jane Grammar Edits targets publishing companies, individuals preparing to submit their manuscripts to agents or publishers, and individuals planning to self-publish. Regarding doctoral dissertations, Jane Grammar Edits targets doctoral students at universities offering online programs largely for nontraditional students because such students are more likely to have funds to pay for editing.

In addition to providing editing services, the business offers typesetting services for documents in all genres. Target clients include companies and individuals. At this time, Jane Grammar Edits isn't interested in converting typeset books into e-books . . .

MISSION STATEMENT

The mission of Jane Grammar Edits is to provide a range of high-quality publishing services for clients, particularly individual authors. In work-

Sample Business Plan *(continued)*

ing with clients, Jane Grammar Edits will provide excellent customer service, fostering trusting, long-term relationships and helping clients achieve their ultimate publishing goals . . .

VISION STATEMENT

Jane Grammar Edits will ultimately become well-known in the YA fantasy market for having expertise in all levels of editing as well as in coaching authors. In addition to providing editing and one-on-one coaching, Jane will provide group training through relevant organizations and will present at relevant conferences . . .

MARKET ANALYSIS

Jane Grammar Edits will initially focus on the following markets: companies that publish YA fantasy novels, authors who've written YA fantasy novels, and doctoral students who've written dissertations. Each of these markets will be analyzed in detail below.

YA Fantasy Publishers

The majority of publishers contract with freelance editors, and many large and small publishers have YA fantasy lists. Examples include DAW Books (an imprint of Penguin Random House), Tor Teen (an imprint of Macmillan), Harlequin Teen (an imprint of Harlequin), Equinox Books, and Curiosity Quills.

Though many YA fantasy books are published every year, a large number of editors are interested in working on YA books, so Jane Grammar Edits has strong competition in obtaining work from traditional publishers. Nevertheless, Jane Grammar Edits can be competitive because Jane is widely read in YA fantasy and has worked with authors who have self-published YA fantasy novels that have sold well on Amazon.

It's unclear how many editors specialize in YA fantasy, but a sampling was identified through searching profiles on LinkedIn. Through reviewing the profiles and the editors' personal websites, various trends were identified . . .

Sample Business Plan *(continued)*

STRENGTHS, WEAKNESSES, OPPORTUNITIES, AND
THREATS ANALYSIS

Strengths

Jane Grammar Edits has a variety of strengths that can help it be successful. For example, Jane is an avid reader of YA fantasy, so she's familiar with the norms in that genre and can provide YA fantasy authors with
fine-tuned guidance on how to ensure that their manuscripts will engage
readers and meet their expectations. Another strength is that Jane
Grammar Edits has selected a second niche—dissertation editing—
which will bring a more diverse clientele and greater opportunities for
business . . .

Weaknesses

Just as Jane Grammar Edits has strengths, it also has weaknesses. Two
related weaknesses are that Jane Grammar Edits hasn't previously edited YA fantasy novels for traditional publishers and hasn't established
relationships with these publishers. Therefore, getting business from
traditional publishers could take time and significant effort. An additional weakness is . . .

Opportunities

Given that fantasy is a popular genre and that a large number of authors
are self-publishing (1.6 million books were self-published in the United
States in 2018), there's a large potential market for Jane Grammar Edits'
services—in terms of traditional publishers and indie authors. Further,
many self-publishing authors are interested in more than just one service, from manuscript evaluation to developmental editing, copy editing,
and proofreading, so there are opportunities to provide multiple services to the same authors . . .

Threats

One threat is that many YA fantasy authors have small budgets for editing, so Jane Grammar Edits may experience price resistance and may

Sample Business Plan *(continued)*

not be able to charge the desired rates when working with independent authors. Another threat is . . .

Strategies to Leverage Strengths and Opportunities and to Mitigate Weaknesses and Threats

The strengths and opportunities identified above can be leveraged to minimize the weaknesses and threats and to increase the business's success. First, Jane Grammar Edits has already worked with self-publishing YA fantasy authors and has started to develop a positive reputation and to receive referrals from previous clients. As Jane Grammar Edits becomes more in demand, the business can experiment with increasing its rates. Additionally, working on more YA fantasy novels from indie authors may give the company more credibility when approaching traditional publishers about the possibility of receiving projects. Second, the strength of editing doctoral dissertations and the opportunity to charge higher rates for dissertation editing than for fiction editing can help mitigate the threat of low wages that might result from editing fiction only . . .

MARKETING AND SALES STRATEGIES

Jane Grammar Edits will direct its marketing efforts toward traditional publishers with YA fantasy lists, authors of YA fantasy novels, and dissertation authors. A different marketing approach will be used for each target market so that the marketing efforts are as effective as possible.

Traditional Publishers

The main strategy for marketing to traditional publishers will consist of contacting these publishers and asking to be added to their lists of freelance editors. This approach will involve the following steps:

- Identify which publishers have YA fantasy imprints or lists.
- Identify which employee in the company to contact; this information may be available on LinkedIn, the publishers' websites, or other sites.
- Send each contact a compelling email.
- Follow up if needed.

Sample Business Plan *(continued)*

A secondary strategy that will likely take longer to produce results will involve establishing relationships with managing editors at publishing companies by connecting with these individuals at conferences and by engaging in discussions with these individuals on social media . . .

OPERATIONS DESCRIPTION

Jane Grammar Edits will operate in a small home office; working from this space will reduce distractions from other members of the household. The normal hours of operation will be 9:00 a.m. to 5:30 p.m., Monday through Friday. If needed, the business will occasionally operate on Saturdays; Jane Grammar Edits will never operate on Sundays. The business will strive to put in thirty-five billable hours per week, with two additional hours set aside for marketing efforts, two hours for professional development, and one hour for administrative tasks.

Jane will check the business's email inbox at the start of the workday and toward the end of the workday; she'll respond to emails within twenty-four hours during the workweek. She'll track all projects, income, and expenses in an Excel file. Project files will be stored in subfolders in a main folder on her laptop, and that folder will be linked to a cloud storage service so that the files are available even when her laptop can't be accessed. For version control, files will be named using the following format: AuthorName_ProjectName_JGE_MM-DD_YY. Within a project folder, old versions of a file will be stored in a subfolder titled . . .

FINANCIAL OVERVIEW

In most situations, Jane Grammar Edits will charge project fees rather than hourly or per-word fees. The main exception will be publishers that pay freelancers by the hour. The business needs to earn an average of $45 per hour to cover personal and business expenses. To achieve this hourly goal, Jane Grammar Edits will need to receive a steady stream of dissertations to edit in addition to YA fantasy novels because rates for editing dissertations are typically higher than for editing novels . . .

Business Costs

Luckily, a freelance editing business typically has low operating costs. And most of these costs are tax deductible. The following list might not exactly match what you'll purchase for your business, but the list will help you start thinking about relevant expenses. Keep in mind that you don't have to use items such as a cell phone exclusively for business purposes in order to claim the items as business deductions. (For more information, see chapter 12, which provides a primer on taxes.) Some of the costs are monthly, whereas others come up less often. Don't forget to regularly set aside money for the latter expenses, so you won't be in a tight spot when payment time arrives.

- Business license and renewal
- LLC setup and renewal
- Computer/laptop
- Printer and ink
- Paper
- Office furniture
- Internet access
- Website domain and hosting
- Microsoft Office (at least Word and Excel)
- Adobe Acrobat, InDesign, and Photoshop
- Business cards
- Marketing collateral (e.g., postcards to send to potential clients)
- Phone and phone line
- Style manuals and other reference materials
- Subscriptions (to professional associations, editing tools, etc.)
- Accountant fees
- Conference registration fees

Make sure to keep track of all receipts. Doing so will ease the tax-preparation process and will be very helpful if you're ever audited. I like to keep an electronic copy of each receipt, and I also enter the expense in an Excel spreadsheet. At tax time, I simply refer to the spreadsheet, but if I, my accountant, or the IRS ever has any questions, I can easily access the receipts.

Key Takeaways

- Choose a business name that will be easy to remember and that indicates what type of services you provide.
- A sole proprietorship is the default business model for freelance editors. Creating an LLC requires more effort but can provide personal protection, as well as tax benefits if you file as an S corporation with the IRS.
- Regardless of your business structure, you'll likely need to obtain a business license at the state level and maybe also at the local level.
- If you're an LLC, you'll need an EIN and a business-only bank account. They're optional but good ideas for sole proprietorships.
- Create a business plan, and then regularly review it—particularly in the first few years of your business—to ensure that your business is working toward the goals you've established. Revise the plan as needed to meet your changing needs and interests.
- Business costs are typically low for freelance editing businesses. Make sure to document your costs so you can use them as tax deductions.

3   *Establishing a Strategic Mindset*

Almost anyone can be a successful freelance business owner—*if* they have the right mindset. Without a strategic mindset, your business won't necessarily fail, but one or more aspects of the business or your life will be out of balance. And you'll feel it. You'll know that something is off, and you'll experience some (or a lot of) discontent. So, that's why I'm focusing this chapter on the critical aspects of a strategic business mindset. This chapter might turn out to be your favorite in the book because you'll be envisioning the elements of your ideal business and life overall. You'll create your ultimate wish list and then learn how to work toward achieving each item. Let's get started!

Creating a Vision

To have the right mindset, you need to have a vision of what you want your life to be like, both professionally and personally. It's important to consider the two together, because each affects the other. So, what's your vision of an ideal life? How can your freelance business contribute to achieving that ideal? To help you start brainstorming, I'd like you to complete an exercise. Pull out a piece of paper or open a Word document, and then describe your ideal (1) projects and clients, (2) business standards, (3) income, and (4) lifestyle.[1] You really do need to write down or type out your descriptions; simply listing your ideas in your head won't be as effective.[2] For each of the four categories, be as specific as possible. Below are some ideas regarding each category.

Projects and Clients

Your projects and clients will have a huge effect on whether you enjoy your work, so it's essential to define what you do and don't want in this category. For example, what genre(s) do you want to edit? What type of editing do you want to provide? What's your ideal word length—five hundred words, five thousand words, fifty thousand words? Do you want to work with independent authors or companies? If companies, do you prefer small, medium, or large ones? Do you want to work with writers whose manuscripts need a lot of TLC or just a little polish? How would you prefer to communicate—and how often?

Business Standards

Establishing your business standards will likely bring you a lot of satisfaction. Yes, as a business owner you get to set a lot of the rules—quite a liberating feeling! The following are some of the areas you'll want to set standards in: What boundaries do you want to establish for yourself and clients? For example, what days and times are you unwilling to work or to respond to client calls and emails? Will you

---

1. These categories are based on ideas in *The Wealthy Freelancer*, a fantastic book by Steve Slaunwhite, Pete Savage, and Ed Gandia (New York: Penguin /Alpha, 2010).

2. Cheryl J. Travers, Dominique Morisano, and Edwin A. Locke, "Self-Reflection, Growth Goals, and Academic Outcomes: A Qualitative Study," *British Journal of Educational Psychology* 85, no. 2 (2014): 224–241.

accept rush requests? Will you provide sample edits? What percentage of the project fee must a client pay before you'll start on a project? What's the lowest hourly rate you'll accept? Will you offer or agree to give discounts? If so, under what circumstances? What type of content are you unwilling to work on? What software are you willing or unwilling to use?

Income

Your ideal income might change over the years, so instead of deciding on a hard number, consider thinking in terms of what your ideal income will allow you to do. For instance, do you want to earn enough that you can pay off your student loans quickly or have enough for a down payment on a home? Or maybe go on a two-week vacation every year without having to scrimp and save the rest of the time? How about make donations to charitable organizations you believe in? Do you want to earn enough that you need to work only part-time? Or do you want to work forty hours a week so you can save more of your income and then retire early?

Lifestyle

Now, think about your overall lifestyle. What do you want it to be like, and how can your business help you achieve that lifestyle? For instance, do you want to volunteer at your child's school and take guitar lessons? You can by scheduling your work hours around those commitments. Do you want to live abroad for a year? That's totally doable as a freelance editor. You might even expand your project opportunities by networking with people in the host country.

After describing your ideal lifestyle, get more specific by describing your ideal day—or maybe an entire week, since you'll likely have different activities planned for different days. I really want you to think about this one, even if it feels more like a daydream than a possibility. The more detailed you are, the better. Here's an example:

7:00 a.m.	Wake up and eat breakfast
7:30 a.m.	Check emails and browse an editing-related discussion forum or blog post
8:00 a.m.	Go for a walk or run
9:00 a.m.	Return home and get ready for the day
9:30 a.m.	Work on an editing project
12:30 p.m.	Eat lunch while watching a show on Netflix
1:00 p.m.	Respond to client emails, check social media, and work on a marketing initiative
1:30 p.m.	Chat with a prospective client
2:00 p.m.	Work on a second editing project
6:00 p.m.	Respond to emails and finalize tomorrow's to-do list
6:30 p.m.	Make and eat dinner
7:30 p.m.	Work on a hobby
8:30 p.m.	Chat with a family member on the phone
9:30 p.m.	Finalize plans to help at a community service project tomorrow evening, and browse the internet for a new pair of running shoes
10:00 p.m.	Get ready for bed
10:30 p.m.	Read a book or watch a TV show
11:00 p.m.	Turn out the lights

Okay, your ideal day might not look anything like the one above (though it looks pretty great to me). Your day might include helping kids or elderly family members get ready in the morning, taking kids to extracurricular activities in the afternoon, and completing various household chores in the evening. Or maybe your norm is yet something else. The point of the sample schedule above is to give you an

Sample Business Vision

Projects and Clients	Business Standards
• Provide manuscript evaluation and developmental, substantive, and copy editing.	• Work between 9:00 a.m. and 5:30 p.m. on weekdays; no work on weekends.
• Focus on YA fantasy.	• Charge at least $60 per hour.
• Work with self-publishing authors who recognize the value of editing and are polite, patient, and serious about their writing.	• Charge 50 percent of payment in advance.
	• Charge a fee for rush requests.
	• Edit in Word only.

Income	Lifestyle
• Work thirty hours a week.	• Walk younger children to school every day.
• Pay off debt.	• Exercise every morning.
• Maintain six-month emergency fund.	• Take classes to expand hobbies and develop new ones.
• Take four weeks of vacation every year.	• Achieve feeling of work/life balance.
• Retire at sixty.	

idea of what's possible. As a freelancer, you have a lot more control over your daily schedule than you would as an employee.

You likely had a lot of fun imagining your ideal day or week, but you might also be feeling a bit discontent if it drastically differs from your current reality. Maybe you wonder whether your ideal is really obtainable. You'll have to be the judge, since I don't know how you described your ideal day, but my guess is that it's more possible than you might suspect. Achieving the ideal is largely about whether you think it's possible and whether you're willing to take the steps to make it happen. And even if your ideal isn't 100 percent achievable,

I bet you can get close if you focus on applying the strategies I discuss in the rest of this chapter.

Setting and Achieving Goals

If you're like most people, you've heard a lot about how to create and achieve goals—but you still struggle with the process. In fact, research shows that only 8 percent of individuals attain their New Year's resolutions.[3] Yikes! Why can't people stick with and achieve their goals? You can probably identify with some of the following reasons:

- We set too many goals, which means we can't focus on them all and we don't have enough energy or willpower to make progress on each goal.[4]
- Pursuing goals requires us to get out of our comfort zone and change our habits, and both create stress.
- Our goals aren't clear or specific enough.
- We get discouraged when our goals take too long to achieve.
- We're not sure what steps we need to take.
- We're uncertain whether our efforts will have the desired results.
- We frame our goals negatively instead of positively (e.g., "Don't do ABC" instead of "Do XYZ").[5]

---

3. John C. Norcross, Marci S. Mrykalo, and Matthew D. Blagys, "Auld Lang Syne: Success Predictors, Change Processes, and Self-Reported Outcomes of New Year's Resolvers and Nonresolvers," *Journal of Clinical Psychology* 58, no. 4 (2002): 397–405.

4. Amy N. Dalton and Stephen A. Spiller, "Too Much of a Good Thing: The Benefits of Implementation Intentions Depend on the Number of Goals," *Journal of Consumer Research* 39, no. 3 (2012): 600–614.

5. Laura Hills, "The Medical Practice Employee's Guide to Establishing Worthwhile Professional and Personal Goals," *Journal of Medical Practice Management* 27, no. 3 (2011): 159–163.

• We set goals that other people think we should achieve or that will impress other people but that don't personally motivate us.[6]

When we consider these and other reasons, it's easy to see that even when we have good intentions and are motivated to achieve our goals, we face a lot of barriers in the process. So let's now take a look at how to overcome the barriers and ease the process of accomplishing our goals.

The SMART Model

Many experts have recommended the SMART model for achieving goals. *SMART* is an acronym for *specific, measurable, attainable, relevant,* and *time bound,* and keeping these categories in mind while crafting goals can increase your chances of being successful.

SPECIFIC

Each goal needs to be specific. What exactly do you want to accomplish? Why? What resources are available? Let's look at a few examples. The goal "marketing my business" is definitely too vague. The wording doesn't provide any direction on how to achieve the goal. Also, though that goal might lead you to do some marketing, your steps won't be as targeted, meaning they probably won't be as effective as they could be. What about "market myself on Facebook, Twitter, and LinkedIn"? That goal is better than the first one but could still be improved. What exactly will that marketing look like? What do you want to accomplish—to create brand awareness, bring in new clients, or do something else? Keep getting more specific until you have something like the following: "Once a week, market myself

---

6. Hills, "Medical Practice Employee's Guide."

on LinkedIn by reaching out to a potential client or posting a writing tip." That goal is clear enough that you'll know what you need to do to achieve it. And because it's specific and straightforward, you'll likely feel more motivated to take action on it.

MEASURABLE

That last goal is not only specific but also measurable. It's easy to determine whether you logged on to LinkedIn during the week and contacted a potential client or posted a writing tip. Another example of a measurable goal is "Earn $4,000 per month during each of the first six months I operate my business." As each month progresses, you can gauge your progress on reaching your goal earnings. You'll be able to determine whether you need to put in more hours or secure additional projects so that you can hit $4,000 by the end of the month. Even if you don't achieve the goal one month, you'll know how close you were and can try new strategies, if needed, the next month to get closer to your goal amount.

ACHIEVABLE

It's also important to make sure you can realistically achieve your goal. If you can't, you'll probably end up feeling demotivated and you might completely give up on the goal. That's not to say your goal should be easy. In fact, multiple studies show that when goals are challenging and specific, people achieve higher performance than when the goals are easy.[7] So, take the time needed to figure out what a challenging but feasible goal will be for you. If you're freelancing only part-time, then earning $4,000 per month is probably

---

7. E.A. Locke, K.N. Shaw, L.M. Saari, and G.P. Latham, "Goal Setting and Task Performance: 1969–1980," *Psychological Bulletin* 90, no. 1 (1981): 125–152.

unrealistic. On the other hand, if you're a technical editor with steady work, making $4,000 might not stretch you enough, so increase your goal amount.

What if you really don't know what will be challenging but still realistic? Consider what you're currently doing in the area related to your goal, think about time and financial constraints, talk to other freelance editors, and look for information online. Make your best guess, and then monitor your progress. You can always modify your goal later when you have a better idea of what the sweet spot is.

RELEVANT

Your goal also needs to be relevant in terms of mattering to you and aligning with your current situation, your other goals, and your vision statement. As an example, maybe you've read an article stating that you should start a blog as a marketing tool but you have no desire to regularly write blog posts. If you lack the interest, don't create a goal about blogging. You probably won't enjoy the experience, which means you probably won't follow through. As another example, maybe you want to speak at editing conferences but you're a single parent of young children and know that traveling to conferences will create more stress than enjoyment. Decide to wait a few years before putting that goal into action; maybe once your kids have started school, you'll feel comfortable having them stay with extended family while you're at a conference.

TIME BOUND

Additionally, include the time frame for achieving your goal. It's okay to have some three-, five-, and ten-year goals, but those should be broken down into smaller goals that you can be working on this year. The shorter time line will help you remain motivated to work toward the goal and will make measuring your progress easier. One of your goals might be to secure three new clients in three months. Or maybe you want to edit twelve YA novels within six months. In deciding on a time frame, remember to make it achievable but challenging.

Visualization

Another powerful tool in achieving goals and maintaining a strategic mindset is visualization. It's important to visualize yourself completing each task required to achieve your desired outcomes as well as to visualize yourself actually achieving the outcomes.[8] Imagine yourself working on each task. What time of the day is it? What's the first step you'll take? What about the second one? How long will you spend working on a task? What specific challenges will you face? Will you feel any discomfort? What will you do to overcome the challenges and discomfort so you can move forward? Similarly, when envisioning achieving the desired outcome, get into the details. Where will you be physically? How will you feel? Whom will you share the exciting news with? Will you do anything special to celebrate?

I realize that some people might think visualization is a bit woo-woo. But its effectiveness is backed by research. Studies have found that athletes who practice visualization improve their concentration, motivation, and coordination, resulting in better performance.[9] Just a few of the well-known athletes who've recognized the benefits of

---

8. Adam Mickiewicz, "Facets of Imagery in Academic and Professional Achievements: A Study of Three Doctoral Students," *Studies in Second Language Learning and Teaching* 3, no. 3 (2013): 397–418.

9. See, for example, Vanessa R. Shannon et al., "Striking Gold: Mental Techniques and Preparation Strategies Used by Olympic Gold Medalists," *Athletic Insight* 4, no. 1 (2012): 1–11; Melanie J. Gregg, Jenny O, and Craig R. Hall, "Examining the Relationship between Athletes' Achievement Goal Orientation and Ability to Employ Imagery," *Psychology of Sport and Exercise* 24 (2016): 140–146.

visualization are Michael Jordan, Tiger Woods, and Michael Phelps.[10] Of course, athletes aren't the only ones who use visualization to achieve their goals. Other hugely successful individuals who use visualization include Sarah Blakely and Oprah Winfrey.[11]

Why exactly does visualization work? The simplified answer is that visualization activates the same neural networks as does the real action, and whether the action is visualized or actually performed, your brain stores the performance in memory. You draw on these memories the next time you perform the activity and are better able to complete it. So, the visualization helps you develop behaviors and improve performance even when you're not performing the action.[12]

I've used visualization since I was a teenager and can personally vouch for the benefits. I learned of this strategy from my high school band teacher my freshman year, and I applied the strategy to eventually earn my school's highest award for seniors. I imagined what it would feel like to receive the award. I visualized what I would need to do in order to be the student most qualified for it. At times that I was tempted to slack off, I'd remember my goal and my visualization of winning the award, and I'd be motivated to keep applying the strategies I'd envisioned completing so I could achieve my objective.

Toward the end of my senior year, it was time for the award winner to be announced. I hoped that my hard work meant that my

---

10. Frank Niles, "How to Use Visualization to Achieve Your Goals," *HuffPost*, June 17, 2011, www.huffpost.com/entry/visualization-goals_b_878424; Jessica Rovello, "5 Ways Katie Ledecky, Michael Phelps, and Other Olympians Visualize Success," *Inc.*, August 23, 2016, www.inc.com/jessica-rovello/five-steps-to -visualize-success-like-an-olympian.html.

11. Rovello, "5 Ways."

12. Paul S. Holmes and David J. Collins, "The PETTLEP Approach to Motor Imagery: A Functional Equivalence Model for Sport Psychologists," *Journal of Applied Sport Psychology* 13, no. 1 (2001): 60–83: David J. Wright, Caroline J. Wakefield, and Dave Smith, "Using PETTLEP Imagery to Improve Music Performance," *Musicae Scientiae* 18, no. 4 (2014): 448–463.

name would be on the award plaque, but I had no idea what the outcome would be. Well, since I already gave away the ending, you know that I received the award. I was thrilled when my name was announced, and I knew that visualization had helped my goal become a reality. Since then, I've used visualization in my efforts to achieve academic, career, and running goals.

Visualization isn't enough on its own, but it certainly can increase your likelihood of succeeding. So, make this tool a regular part of your schedule. You could devote the first ten minutes of your workday to visualization, or maybe you'd prefer to use this strategy after you've gotten into bed for the night. And, really, you don't need to visualize every day. But do make visualization at least a weekly habit so that you can benefit from this powerful tool.

Affirmations

As with visualization, affirmations can help you achieve your goals. What exactly are affirmations? They're statements you repeat every day to help establish a positive, proactive state of mind. They inspire and remind you to work, sometimes unconsciously, toward achieving your desired life.[13] For example, one of your affirmations might be "I work with clients who recognize my expertise and pay me well for the services I provide." When you frequently repeat these statements, over time you start to believe them, and you consequently act in ways that are consistent with the statements.

Study results support the effectiveness of affirmations. For instance, researchers have found that affirmations help individuals improve their education-related intentions and behaviors, leading to

---

13. Judith M. Harackiewicz et al., "Closing the Social Class Achievement Gap for First-Generation Students in Undergraduate Biology," *Journal of Educational Psychology* 106, no. 2 (2014): 375–389.

higher achievement.[14] Other research indicates that using affirmations improves problem-solving in people who are chronically stressed.[15]

To get maximum benefit from using affirmations, you need to craft them carefully. Here are some keys to success:

- Use first-person pronouns.
- Use the present tense. If you use the future tense instead, you'll be signaling to yourself that you don't need to immediately implement the actions necessary to fulfill your statement. By using the present tense, your brain will (often subconsciously) start figuring out what steps you need to take so that your statement is true. For instance, using the example earlier in this section, you'll start thinking about what you need to do to ensure that you have expertise, that you demonstrate it to clients, and that you don't work for clients who aren't willing to pay your established rates.
- Word your statements using positive, not negative, words. Instead of stating, "I won't . . .," state, "I will . . ." Perhaps you're wondering whether the phrasing really makes a difference. Framing ideas positively leads to a more positive outlook and to better performance physically and mentally.[16] It's important to

---

14. Harackiewicz et al., "Closing the Social Class Achievement Gap."

15. J. David Creswell et al., "Self-Affirmation Improves Problem-Solving under Stress," *PLOS ONE* 8, no. 5 (2013): e62593.

16. See, for example, Thi Thao Duyen T. Nguyen et al., "Fruitful Feedback: Positive Affective Language and Source Anonymity Improve Critique Reception and Work Outcomes," in *Proceedings of the 2017 ACM Conference on Computer Supported Cooperative Work and Social Computing* (New York: ACM, 2017), 1024–1034; Javier Horcajo et al., "The Effects of Overt Head Movements on Physical Performance after Positive versus Negative Self-Talk," *Journal of Sport Exercise Psychology* 41, no. 1 (2019): 36–45.

focus on what you want rather than on what you don't want, because if you focus on the latter, you're likely to feel stuck in the undesirable state and to not brainstorm ways to achieve the positive state you're aiming for.

· Include words that convey emotion. Your affirmations will be more inspiring and motivating if you specify how your desired state makes you feel. For example, "I feel empowered when I maintain the boundaries I've set for my clients."

Once you've written down your affirmations, it's time to decide when you'll review them each day—and you do need to make the review a daily habit. You might want to start your day by saying each affirmation a few times, to set a positive perspective for your entire day. You could also end the day by repeating them again, to reinforce your desired state and to encourage your mind to think about them while you sleep. In addition to saying them verbally, you can benefit from writing them out multiple times. Also consider placing them on note cards that you then tape to your computer screen, fridge, or bathroom mirror; you might also want to put them in a note app on your phone. Before you've made a habit of reciting your affirmations each day, consider adding an alarm on your phone or online calendar to remind yourself when it's time to review your affirmations.

Though at first you might feel silly saying your affirmations, give this strategy a chance. After a month, you'll probably find that using affirmations is having a positive effect on your outlook and behaviors and is helping you progress toward achieving your goals.

Additional Strategies for Achieving Your Goals

Beyond using the SMART method, visualization, and affirmations, consider applying the following suggestions to increase your ability to accomplish your goals.

IDENTIFY POTENTIAL OBSTACLES TO ACHIEVING
YOUR GOALS, AND CREATE A PLAN TO OVERCOME
THE OBSTACLES

It would be nice if using the SMART method removed all obstacles to achieving goals, but it doesn't. So, it's important to brainstorm what factors might prevent you from accomplishing what you've set out to do. Maybe one obstacle will be a lack of experience, such as using a specific online platform to market yourself. In that case, read a few relevant articles (you'll find tons on the internet), talk with other free-lancers to see what they do, and accept the fact that you'll have a learning curve. Instead of expecting to market yourself perfectly from the start, acknowledge that you will make mistakes at first and will probably be less effective than you'd like. But the more you prac-tice, read about effective strategies, and pay attention to what works for others, the sooner you'll become skilled at marketing yourself. The best thing to do is to get started.

Another obstacle you'll likely face is limited time. How can you overcome that challenge? Start by keeping track of everything you do for two days. You'll probably discover that you're spending some of your time on unnecessary, ineffective activities, such as checking social media every thirty minutes, responding to text messages whenever they arrive, or watching several hours of Netflix in the evening. (I promise I'm not judging—I've done the same!) Of course, everyone needs downtime in order to recharge, but engaging in these types of activities too often can actually drain you and make you less productive. So, set boundaries regarding how often you'll do something, such as check your social media accounts. I bet you'll be pleasantly surprised at the time you free up to make progress on your goals. Another way to find more time is to out-source some of your tasks. For instance, pay a teen in the neighbor-hood to mow your lawn. If you have kids, set up a carpool so that

"With every challenge I've come across, I've used it as a stepping-stone in my navigation of where I want to go with it."
—*Melanie Bright, freelance editor*

you and other parents take turns driving everyone's kids to school and activities.

Another way to overcome barriers is to create "If . . . then . . ." plans. Basically, you state that if ABC obstacle occurs, then you'll do XYZ. For example, if your goal is to start editing every morning at eight o'clock but sometimes you feel like procrastinating (cat videos, anyone?), then you might create the following "If . . . then . . ." plan: "If I don't feel like starting to edit at eight, then I'll work for just thirty minutes and then take a break by reading something editing related." The low time commitment will make the task seem easier, and you'll likely find that when the thirty minutes have lapsed, you're in full editing mode and don't need a break after all. Researchers have found that people increase their likelihood of achieving goals by two to three times when using "If . . . then . . . " plans.[17] One reason is that after you've created your plans, you won't have to exercise mental effort to make the right choice—you'll already know what you're going to do. You may not be able to overcome obstacles in all cases, especially if the obstacles are largely out of your control, but having an action plan will help you continue working toward your goal and do the best you can within the constraints you're facing.

START WITH SMALL GOALS

It can help to start with small goals that you can complete in a short period and that are less challenging. Succeeding with those goals can

17. Marc D. Hauser, "The Mind of a Goal Achiever: Using Mental Contrasting and Implementation Intentions to Achieve Better Outcomes in General and Special Education," *Mind, Brain, and Education* 12, no. 3 (2018): 102–109.

give you confidence and motivation to work on bigger goals. Also, working on small goals will help you build willpower,[18] which will help you stick with more-challenging goals in the future.

LOOK AT YOUR OVERALL PROGRESS

As everyone knows, some days—and weeks—go better than others. On the less-than-ideal days, you might not make progress on your goals. That's okay. What matters is whether you're making progress overall, such as during an entire month. On the days that you don't follow through on working toward your goals, instead of being discouraged, think about what you can do in the future to overcome the obstacles you faced and to get back on track.

CHANGE YOUR MINDSET

If you think it'll be too uncomfortable to complete the tasks related to achieving a goal, you probably won't work on those tasks. The problem usually isn't that the tasks are that bad but that you *think* they are. So, you need to change your perspective. Sure, that may not be easy at first, but it is doable and can make a huge difference.

Let's consider an example from my personal life. I'm a rather competitive long-distance runner. Though I'm not Olympic caliber, I like to place in local races, and so I have to train hard. Every Thursday morning, I run fifteen or so miles at slightly faster than race pace. By that time of the week, I have already put in about forty-five miles, have done strength-training, and am a bit sleep deprived. So, when Thursday comes, I know my run will be challenging. For a long time, I dreaded starting the run. I'd procrastinate as long as I could

---

18. Jennifer M. Morton and Sarah K. Paul, "Grit," *Ethics* 129, no. 2 (2019): 175–203.

because I was afraid of the discomfort and the possibility that I wouldn't finish at the targeted pace. Eventually I realized that I was letting my mind exaggerate how unenjoyable the run would be. I decided to focus on the sense of accomplishment I always felt after finishing. I reminded myself that I'd successfully completed the run almost every week, so I knew I could do it. I also told myself that if I really did need to scale back the pace, I could. Because I changed my perspective, I no longer dread that Thursday run, and I've been able to achieve many running-related goals.

UNDERSTAND WHY YOU'RE PROCRASTINATING

In my example about running, I mentioned that I procrastinated starting the hard Thursday-morning run. After I defined the reasons for procrastinating, I was able to implement a strategy to stop delaying my run. So, when you find yourself procrastinating, identify the underlying issue. Fear of failure? Unfamiliarity with the topic of an article you need to edit? After you've identified the issue, figure out what you can do to address it and move forward. Sometimes it's a simple matter of telling yourself to just get started. You'll likely find that once you've started, the task doesn't seem too hard after all.

You might also procrastinate because you're not organized. If that's the case, create daily, weekly, and monthly to-do lists. Create a daily and weekly schedule (for work and personal time). Set deadlines, and focus on a single goal-related task at a time.

USE DECISION-FOCUSED WORDS

Avoid noncommittal words; instead, use decision-focused words. When you say that you *should* do something, you're giving yourself a

> **Steps for Setting and Achieving Goals**
>
> - Make goals specific, measurable, achievable, relevant, and time bound.
> - Visualize yourself working on each task required to achieve the goal, and visualize yourself achieving the goal. Be specific: Where will you be? How will you feel? How will you celebrate?
> - Create and repeat affirmations that align with your goals.
> - Create a plan for how to overcome obstacles to achieving your goals.
> - Change your perspective of how hard it will be to accomplish the goal. If needed, break the goal into smaller tasks to make the goal less intimidating.
> - Understand why you're procrastinating, and then implement strategies to stop procrastinating.
> - Use present-tense, decision-focused words, such as "I'm engaging in three professional development opportunities each year."

way to avoid working toward your goal.[19] Maybe you *should* engage in professional development opportunities, but if you don't, it's not a big deal because *should* indicates a possibility but not a requirement or reality. Instead, use strong, decision-based words such as *will* or—even better—*am*. For example: "I am engaging in three professional development opportunities each year." By using that phrasing, you're committing yourself to follow through. You're also subconsciously telling yourself that the goal is achievable.

---

19. Lindsay Dodgson, "The Psychology behind Why We're So Bad at Keeping New Year's Resolutions," *Business Insider*, January 7, 2018, www.businessinsider .com/the-psychology-behind-why-we-cant-keep-new-years-resolutions-2018-1.

Finding a Mentor

Having a mentor can be beneficial at any point in a person's career but particularly when starting a business. According to various studies, 50 percent of small businesses don't make it past five years, but having a business mentor increases your chances of succeeding long-term.[20] In one study, 70 percent of small-business owners reported that having a mentor helped them remain sustainable past the first five years.[21] In another study, 79 percent of business owners said that receiving mentoring was critical to their success.[22]

A business mentor can assist you in numerous ways, from helping you brainstorm potential markets and clients to helping you expand your network, answering business-operations questions, providing advice on how to address sticky situations, and ensuring that you're on track to achieve your goals. Mentors can also help you identify areas you need to improve in and can help you avoid beginner mistakes. Overall, a mentor will help you maintain the entrepreneurial mindset that's needed to operate your business successfully.

Though having a mentor is important, it's not necessarily easy to find one who'll be a good fit. When looking for a mentor, start by considering people who are already in your network. Maybe you met an experienced freelance editor at a conference last year or have interacted with a thriving small-business owner in an online discussion forum. Add these people to your list of potential mentors. The indi-

---

20. See, for example, Susan Turner and Al Endres, "Strategies for Enhancing Small-Business Owners' Success Rates," *International Journal of Applied Management and Technology* 16, no. 1 (2017): 34–49; Daniel Holloway and Thomas Schaefer, "Practitioner Perspectives on Leadership in Small Business," *International Journal of the Academic Business World* 8, no. 2 (2014): 27–36.

21. Holloway and Schaefer, "Practitioner Perspectives on Leadership."

22. Jeffrey Overall and Sean Wise, "The Antecedents of Entrepreneurial Success: A Mixed Methods Approach," *Journal of Enterprising Culture* 24, no. 3 (2016): 209–241.

viduals don't need to be editors (though that would be ideal), but they do need to have experience operating a small business they started from scratch. And, preferably, they've been running the business for several years, enabling them to give you guidance based on a long-term perspective. It's not necessary for you and your mentor to have the same outlook on everything business related; in fact, you'll grow more if you and your mentor differ in some ways. However, it's helpful if you and your mentor share some core values, whatever you decide those are.

If you don't think that anyone in your network would be a good fit (or if they're unavailable), then it's time to branch out. Join groups on LinkedIn and Facebook that are for small-business owners. Attend local networking meetings. Go to www.score.org/find-mentor, and search for mentors in your geographic area.[23] Ask family and friends whether they know of anyone who might be a good fit. With some effort, you'll be able to identify several people you'd like to be mentored by.

After you've created a list of potential mentors, it's time to see whether any of them are interested and available. Don't immediately jump to the mentorship question. First, spend some time establishing rapport with the individuals, if you haven't already. Completing this step will give you a better idea of which individuals might be the best choice for you, as well as how you might provide value to them (and it's important for the mentor to benefit from the relationship too). During this stage, ask the individuals what they've done to reach their current business situation. Also find out what resources and strategies have been most effective for these individuals. Gauge whether they'll likely help push you to excel.

---

23. SCORE is a great resource not only for finding business mentors but also for accessing webinars, templates, marketing tools, and other resources for small businesses.

When the time comes to ask someone to be your mentor, make sure to be clear about your vision and expectations for the mentoring relationship. For example, do you want to meet in person, on the phone, or via some other means? How frequently do you want to touch base? How long do you foresee the mentorship lasting? What areas do you want the most mentoring in? Providing detailed information will help the individual determine whether he or she has the time and abilities needed. Keep in mind that the individual is likely very busy and might want to modify aspects of your proposal to better fit his or her situation. Be as flexible as possible while also ensuring that what you and the individual agree on will indeed help you.

After you've established a mentorship, periodically talk to your mentor about how the mentorship is going. Are both of you benefiting? Does anything need to change so that you can better achieve your goals and move your business forward? Additionally, always express gratitude for your mentor's assistance. Make sure that you're humble enough to consider your mentor's advice, even if at first it doesn't seem to make sense or fit your situation. You don't need to implement every suggestion your mentor gives, but considering the information will help you make the best, most informed decisions you can. Then, after you've established yourself as an experienced, thriving entrepreneur, give back by agreeing to be someone else's mentor.

Key Takeaways

- Establishing a strategic mindset is essential to becoming a successful freelance editor.
- Create a vision of your ideal projects and clients, business standards, income, and lifestyle. Then, set goals to make this vision a reality.

- Use the SMART (specific, measurable, attainable, relevant, and time bound) model to increase your likelihood of achieving your goals.
- Identify potential obstacles to achieving your goals, and create strategies to overcome the obstacles.
- Visualize working on your goals and achieving them.
- Repeat self-affirmations daily to get in a positive mindset and establish the behaviors that will lead to goal achievement.
- Find a business mentor to help you navigate the challenges of starting a business and identifying opportunities and to help motivate you to achieve greater success.

4   *Looking for Clients*

Now that you've formally set up your business and started working on your strategic mindset, it's time to focus on finding clients. (I know what you're thinking: *finally!*) Finding clients is obviously an essential aspect of building a business, but a lot of freelance editors find the prospect intimidating. How do you identify potential clients? How do you reach out to them? How do you make the whole process less time intensive? I'll answer these and other questions in this chapter. We'll start by exploring whether you need a niche, since the decision will affect where you look for clients. Then we'll dive into specific strategies for finding and, even more important, connecting with ideal clients. Once you've read through this chapter, you'll be ready for the additional marketing advice that's featured in chapter 5.

Deciding Whether to Specialize

Many editors have asked me whether they need a niche in order to effectively market themselves and bring in new projects. I don't think there's a definitive yes-or-no answer, so instead I'll explain the pros and cons of starting out with a niche, as well as other factors to keep in mind when deciding whether to specialize and how to choose a niche. Let's start with why you might or might not want to choose a niche when opening your freelance biz.

Having a niche can make marketing easier because you'll know who your target market is and you can tailor your marketing message to the target market's needs and interests. Having a niche also helps you to become known as an expert in an area. That reputation can lead to more referrals and work, as well as the opportunity to command higher fees. You'll also likely increase your editing efficiency and quality because you're familiar with the content. For example, you won't need to look up as many words and phrases, because you'll know the jargon and terms of art. You'll be more likely to notice when wording or statements are a little off (and clients will greatly appreciate editing that helps them avoid looking foolish). You'll also be familiar with the style guide used in your area of specialty.

On the other hand, establishing a niche and becoming well-known in it can take time. So, in the beginning you might be limiting the number of project requests you receive. Generalizing can help you fill up your work schedule. By bringing in a variety of projects, you'll have the opportunity to explore which genres and topics you enjoy working on the most, and this exploration can help you establish a niche later on. In fact, many freelancers have said that their niche *eventually found them*—it was an organic process that occurred over time. Additionally, some people may never want to establish a niche, because they get bored working on the same type of content all the time. Though establishing a niche can be beneficial, don't do it if it doesn't fit your ideal work situation.

Whether you choose to be a specialist or a generalist, it's helpful to know the markets that editors direct their services to. Here's a list of some of the most common and largest target markets:

- *Traditional fiction and nonfiction book publishers*: Most publishers contract with freelancers to complete substantive editing, copy editing, and proofreading. Book publishers typically don't pay freelancers high-dollar rates. Some editors get steady work from publishers and consider it a good trade-off for the relatively low pay they receive.

- *Academic and trade journal publishers*: These days, you can find a periodical on almost any topic, and most journal publishers farm out copy editing to freelancers, either directly or through packagers. As with book publishers, journal publishers typically don't pay freelancers high rates.

- *Packagers*: Packagers are companies that take on the production tasks (editing, design, etc.) for manuscripts that will ultimately be published under a traditional publisher's name. The types of publications include encyclopedias and other reference works, academic journals, textbooks, and cookbooks, among others. Packagers often contract the production tasks to freelancers. As with traditional publishers, packagers typically do not pay freelancers well; in fact, freelancers often earn less when working for packagers than for publishing companies.

- *Businesses*: Companies of all sizes and in all industries need help writing and editing content, such as website materials, advertisements, customer emails, product manuals, annual reports, and internal documents. Start-ups in particular often need a lot of assistance because they're developing a considerable amount of content in a short amount of time. And don't assume that start-ups aren't willing to pay editors to develop and refine the content. Many new business owners recognize that having clear, engaging content is important in achieving success. Often, editors earn more when freelancing for nonpublishing companies than when freelancing for publishing companies.

- *Nonprofits*: As with companies, nonprofits publish a variety of content, from website materials to brochures, grant proposals, and letters asking for donations and volunteers. Some nonprofits don't allocate much money for paying editors, whereas other nonprofits are willing to pay higher rates, so don't assume you can't earn a decent income if you want to focus on working with nonprofits.

- *Authors planning to self-publish:* Considering that 1.4 million self-published titles were sold on Amazon in 2018, self-publishing authors compose a huge target market for freelance editors.[1] True, not all of these authors hire editors, but many do. The services that self-publishing authors are interested in include manuscript evaluation; developmental, substantive, and copy editing; proofreading; assistance in writing back cover copy; typesetting; and even e-book conversion. Though many self-publishing authors are on a tight budget, some are willing to pay above-average rates.

- *Authors planning to submit their manuscripts to literary agents or publishers:* Even with the huge number of authors who self-publish, many authors still aim to get a contract with a traditional publisher. To ensure that their manuscripts have the best chance possible, authors often work with freelance editors prior to submitting the manuscripts to literary agents and publishing houses. These authors may be looking for anything from manuscript evaluation to copy editing. They may also hire freelancers to help craft or edit query letters.

- *Authors writing dissertations, theses, and academic journal articles:* Many academic writers seek editing and formatting help from freelance editors because these authors typically aren't skilled writers or experts in whatever style guide they're required to follow—and they realize they need help. Sometimes they're even required by university or journal reviewers to have the

---

1. Bowker, *Self-Publishing in the United States,* 2013–2018 (Bowker, 2019), https://media2.proquest.com/documents/bowker-selfpublishing-report2019.pdf.

manuscript edited before it will be accepted for publication. That being said, universities typically have guidelines on what type of editing is allowed; copy editing is usually approved, whereas heavier levels of editing aren't. Heavier editing is often okay and needed for journal articles, particularly when written by authors whose first language isn't English.

Of course, you don't need to limit yourself to these areas. A market doesn't need to be large to provide you with a steady flow of work. But the markets above can be good places to focus your attention at first if you don't already have contacts in other, smaller markets.

If you do decide to choose a niche, don't stress about immediately figuring out which one is perfect for you. After all, you're not committing to stick with that area for the rest of your career—you can transition from one niche to another as your interests and vision change. When you're ready to move to a new area, transition slowly to help ensure that your work schedule remains full. The gradual transition will also help you gain the niche-specific experience needed to perform at a high level. During the transition, ramp up your marketing to the target audience of your new niche. Also update your website, LinkedIn profile, and other content to reflect the new niche. As you receive more projects in your new area, you can reduce the number of projects you work on in your former niche.

Now, how do you decide what your niche should be? Start by thinking about what you already have experience in, either professionally or personally. For example, as a long-distance runner I've done a lot of research on sports nutrition and exercise science. I could use that knowledge to focus on editing content in those areas. Maybe you minored in music during college. You could leverage that experience to edit music scores (there really is a market for it) and articles for music-related journals. By choosing a niche in an area of experience, you'll already know that you're interested in it and you'll have less of a learning curve. Sometimes your areas of experience might not come to mind immediately, so consider the following questions to help you brainstorm:

- What topics are you passionate about?
- What subjects did you excel in during school?
- What do you like to do in your spare time?
- What topics do people often ask for your help on?[2]
- If you've volunteered with nonprofits and other organizations, what were their fields of focus?
- What areas do you already have contacts in?

Keep in mind that a niche can also be a service you provide, such as manuscript evaluation, copy editing, indexing, or typesetting. Additionally, a niche can be relatively broad or narrow. For example, your niche could be editing nonfiction books. Or you could narrow the niche to copy editing nonfiction books written by members of an underrepresented group. In deciding on a niche, also consider the vision for your business. Is one potential niche more aligned with your vision than another niche is? As an example, if your vision includes earning enough to work only part-time, you're probably not going to focus exclusively on copy editing trade fiction, because rates in that niche tend to be on the low side.

So far, I've referred to having one niche, but you can actually specialize in more than one—and I recommend doing so. By having multiple niches, you're diversifying your business and thereby reducing risk, such as if work in one of the areas dries up, even if only during

---

2. These first four ideas came from Phon Baillie, "How to Choose a Niche as a Proofreader or Copy Editor," *Art of Proofreading Blog*, March 2019, www .artofproofreadingblog.com/choose-niche-proofreader-copy-editor.

Pros and Cons of Having a Niche

Pros	Cons
• Marketing can be easier because you have a clear target market.	• Becoming well-known can take time, limiting the number of project requests you receive in the short term.
• You can develop a reputation as being an expert in the niche.	• You might not explore other areas of editing that you might really enjoy.
• The reputation might lead to more referrals and higher rates.	• You might get bored working on the same types of projects all the time.
• You'll be able to increase the efficiency and quality of your editing.	

certain months of the year. That being said, it's best not to promote too many niches. Saying you're an expert in ten areas may give people the impression that you're a jack-of-all-trades, master of none. You'll be better off if you select three or so niches to focus on. Of course, you can always list other areas of interest on your website, LinkedIn profile, and other platforms, but don't highlight these areas as niches you have expertise in.

Once you've selected one or more niches, join organizations and groups focused on those niches. (You'll find a lot of options by searching LinkedIn and Facebook.) Identify the style guides commonly used in the niches, and make sure you're familiar with the guidelines. Also seek out ways to continue increasing your knowledge and skills related to the niches, such as by reading published content in the genres you've selected and by reading books, articles, and blog posts on the craft of writing and editing in those areas. Also consider completing formal training offered by relevant organizations.

Finding Clients

If you've selected a niche, you'll have a good idea of who your target clients are and, therefore, whom you should direct your marketing to. If you've decided not to specialize right away, you'll still want to identify a few target markets you'd like to focus your advertising efforts on. You don't have to ignore all other audiences, but narrowing your focus will make the process of finding clients less daunting and will help you tailor your marketing message to the needs of the target audience. Once you've identified your main audience, it's time to reach out to members of the audience—or help them reach out to you. I explain how to do that very thing in the following subsections.

Reach Out to Your Network

One of the first steps you should take is also one of the simplest: let people in your network know about your editing business. Reach out to former employers, and tell them you're available for contract work. If you left the companies on good terms, then you're a safe source for them to turn to when they need to outsource work. They know you have the requisite skills as well as knowledge of the companies, making the process smoother and more efficient for everyone. Also contact former employers' competitors (as long as you haven't signed a noncompete agreement that's still in force). Explain that you're a good fit because you understand the market so well, meaning you can avoid much of the learning curve that comes with starting to contract with a company.

Additionally, make sure to tell your extended family, friends, people you went to school with, and other acquaintances about your business. Some new freelancers are afraid that they'll come off as pushy, but you won't as long as you simply provide information rather than pressure people to hire you or send you referrals. Let the topic of your business come up naturally. When you see friends at a social event or somewhere else and they ask what's new, excitedly tell them that you've been busy setting up or expanding your business. Take a minute or two to describe the services you provide and what projects or business activities you've been focusing on. If your friends ask follow-up questions, answer concisely but with some detail. Let your passion shine through, but don't get carried away talking about your business for fifteen minutes without prompting. If your friends say they or people they know might need an editor, offer a few business cards—enough for your friends and anyone they think might be interested. Express your sincere desire to help others, and then make sure to show interest in your friends' recent activities. By following this pattern, you'll appear friendly and professional, not overbearing.

It's also okay to occasionally mention your business on your personal social media pages. For example, when a book you edited is published, you could post a link to the book and say how excited you are to see it on store shelves and Amazon. In your email signature, include wording that indicates you're a freelance editor; also provide the URL of your LinkedIn profile and the URL of your business website. Simply by including my LinkedIn and website URLs in my email signature, I've received multiple requests for editing.

In all your networking efforts, make sure you're acting with authenticity. What I mean is that when meeting someone, your primary goal should be to learn about the person because you're interested in him or her, not just because the person might become a client or refer other people to you. When you're genuinely interested in the person,

"I've found that the more friends I talk to about what I do, the more clients come my way naturally. Be open about what you do every day for work, and they'll remember you when the need arises."
—*Christina Crossland, freelance editor*

that authenticity shines through and you won't come off as a sales-person interested only in getting more business.

Showing your interest in a person doesn't need to be that challenging. Simply start by asking questions about the person, such as his or her career, goals, or interests. After the person responds, ask follow-up questions to dig deeper and better understand the person's experiences and perspective. Approach the conversation as if you're talking with a friend; that way, you're less likely to feel like the conversation is forced and superficial.

After you've gotten to know some basics about the person, think of ways you can be helpful. Do you have any relevant advice to give? How about resources that the individual might benefit from? Can you connect the individual with someone else in your network who has similar interests? By offering help—in whatever form—you'll be showing that you care about the person, which will encourage the individual to trust and value you. You'll also be establishing a positive reputation for yourself and your business. At some point in the future, the individual might contact you about your editing services or direct another potential client to you. And if not, that's okay. After all, you achieved your goal: to get to know others, benefit from what they share with you, and see how you can benefit them in return—without any money changing hands.

Ask for Referrals

We've just explored how to let people know about your business. Now it's time to go a step further by more directly asking for referrals. I'm distinguishing between these two activities because I don't think you should ask everyone for referrals. If you do, people might think you *are* being pushy. Rather, limit the referrals question to people you've already established relationships with (even if through a brief conversation) and who are likely to have referrals to give, such as writers, people in the publishing industry and in any additional industries you serve, and people who tell you they know of others looking for editors.

Even with people in these groups, keep the request friendly and casual. Let them know that you love helping people and/or businesses fine-tune their writing and that you're interested in making new connections. Even if you're feeling desperate to acquire new clients, don't let the desperation show—it's a turnoff and can encourage people to question your abilities.

The best source of referrals is typically people you've already completed projects for. A great time to ask is after you've returned a project and a client has praised you for your great work. After thanking the client for the opportunity to work with him or her, explain that you'd love to offer your services to anyone else who could use them. Then ask the client to name two or three people who might be looking for an editor. Ideally, the client will connect you with the potential clients via email. Alternatively, the client could provide the individuals with your contact information or might give you the potential clients' contact information.

As an additional reminder that I appreciate referrals, I include the following sentence at the bottom of each invoice I send: "Thank you for the opportunity to work with you! If you know of anyone else who might benefit from my services, please feel free to share my contact information with them."

Perhaps you think that if people want to refer business to you, then they will without your prompting. Some do, but I've found that others need the encouragement. In fact, some people hesitate to refer me because they assume I'm so busy with work that I won't want to take on new clients. Multiple times, I've had people email me with a message like the following: "Suzy, I hope you're not upset, but I gave your email address to someone who's looking for an editor." I assure them that I actually really enjoy receiving word-of-mouth referrals, and then I thank them for thinking of me. If I end up receiving work from someone who was referred to me, then I'll send the referrer a thank-you note. A little message of appreciation can encourage individuals to continue referring people to me, leading to even more work.

Find the Contact Information for Ideal Clients

In addition to informing everyone in your network about your editing business, you should introduce yourself to potential clients. For instance, if you want to be a tech editor, start by listing the tech companies you'd like to freelance for. The big ones will be the easiest to think of but might be the hardest to establish relationships with, so make sure to research smaller tech companies, perhaps starting with ones in your geographic area. Refer to local newspapers, magazines, and other media to learn about small businesses that are just starting or that are growing. They may need assistance with polishing website content, product/service brochures, and so forth.

If you want to work with traditional publishers, then there are some great resources for finding ones that specialize in your areas of interest and experience. I suggest starting with PublishersGlobal .com, which is a free source of information regarding publishing companies in an impressive number of countries. You can narrow your search to certain locations, subjects, media, and languages, and each company entry summarizes the publisher's area of focus and provides the company URL, mailing address, and phone number. (If you pay for a premium subscription, you'll also get access to names and contact information for employees at the company.) Another resource is *Literary Marketplace*, which is an annual publication available in print and online that lists almost all book publishers in the United States and Canada, as well as some publishers in other countries. Since you can limit your search to various topics, locations, and other criteria, searching for ideal clients is relatively easy. Buying a physical copy of the book or an online subscription is pricey, so see if your local library has a copy or subscription. Also consider checking out *Publishers Weekly*'s annual list of the fastest-growing independent publishing companies. Because the companies are expanding quickly, they're likely to be in need of additional freelance editors. Another great resource is a list compiled and updated by editor Katharine O'Moore-Klopf. The list currently includes more than one hundred packagers and editing services that contract with freelance editors.[3]

Don't stop adding to your list until it contains forty (or more) companies. That number might sound overwhelming, but it reflects the reality that response rates are typically low. For every ten companies you contact, three might respond and one might offer you work. So, you'll need to contact a lot of companies in order to fill up your schedule. Yes, the process is time-consuming, but you don't need to contact all forty companies in one day or even one week. And if you do well on the projects you receive, then you can establish long-term relationships with the companies, meaning you won't need to constantly be contacting new companies in the long term.

After you've created your list of target companies, determine the appropriate employee to contact—usually someone in the position of managing editor, production editor, editor in chief, communications manager, or the equivalent in whatever niche you're targeting. Typically, you can find this information by searching on a company's website or on LinkedIn. If you don't hit the jackpot, call the company's main number and ask about who oversees communications, marketing, or whatever other department is most relevant to your focus. (Tell the receptionist, "I am a freelance editor and would like to offer my services. What's the name and job title of the person in charge of freelancers, and what's his or her contact information?") Whatever method you use, try to get the person's phone number and email address so you can try both forms of contact.

---

3. To access the list, go to "Packagers and Editing Services," www.dropbox.com/sh/isusr3iy8au98dx/AACM1B4-bSBVDNL7TvG3RYUfa?dl=0.

Contact Potential Clients

Once you've created your list of potential clients, it's time to contact them. Your three main options are to email, send snail mail, and call on the phone. Emailing seems to be the most common option among freelance editors, but some swear by sending letters or postcards in the mail. The rationale is that since email is predominant today, a letter that arrives in the mail will stand out more and will therefore receive more attention. I haven't personally tried the snail-mail option, so I can't share any evidence of my own, but it certainly wouldn't hurt to try out both options and see whether one has better results for you. You can use the same message in an email and snail mail, so below I'm only going to cover what to include in an email.

EMAIL

I suggest emailing before calling on the phone. Begin by carefully crafting your subject line. According to one study, 35 percent of people decide whether to open an email because of the subject line.[4] So, follow these tips for improving your subject line and, thus, the likelihood your email will be read:

- Keep the subject line short (ideally no more than ten words).[5]
- Include the first name of the person you're emailing or the name of the person's company. Subject lines that are personalized are

---

4. Donna Talarico, "From Inbox to Enroll: Email Marketing Tips," *Recruiting and Retaining Adult Learners* 18, no. 11 (2016): 2–3.

5. Ashish Kumar and Jari Salo, "Effects of Link Placements in Email Newsletters on Their Click-Through Rate," *Journal of Marketing Communications* 24, no. 5 (2018): 535–548; Liz Willits, "2019 Email Marketing Statistics: We Analyzed 1,000 Emails from Today's Top Experts," *AWeber Blog*, January 9, 2019, https://blog.aweber.com/email-marketing/2019-email-marketing-statistics.htm.

22 percent more likely to be opened than are emails with generic subject lines.[6]

· Hint at why you're emailing and the value you provide.

· Consider framing the subject line as a question; most people will automatically think about how they'd answer the question. Because you've piqued their interest, they're likely to open the email.

Based on these tips, your subject line might be something like "Alex, when will XYZ Company next need an experienced freelance editor?" Of course, you'll want to match your tone and wording to the contact's industry. For instance, the example subject line above would work well if you're contacting a marketing manager at a tech company. If you're contacting the project manager at a publishing house, you might want to use a subject line like "High-quality freelance copy editing for XYZ Company." If you're not sure what tone and wording might work best, ask for input from other freelance editors who work in the same niche.

With your subject line ready, it's time to write the body of your message. Again, you'll want to keep the text short. The objective of the email isn't to close a sale; rather, the purpose is to open a conversation by introducing yourself and how you can help the target company. Don't worry that you're not providing a lengthy bio or every reason the company should give you work. Here's a potential outline for your message:

---

6. Stacey Rudolph, "Understanding the Importance of E-mail Subject Lines," Business 2 Community, March 27, 2016, www.business2community.com /infographics/understanding-importance-e-mail-subject-lines-infographic -01492127#za6tqbgOJuwElo71.97.

- Address the person by name.
- In a sentence, refer to your familiarity with the company and its publications. In a second sentence, identify a potential pain point the company or department is experiencing, such as a heavy workload or a lack of editors with a background in the subject area. (You might need to do a little research to identify a probable pain point. In the email, try to incorporate some of the language from the company's website.)
- In a few more sentences, indicate how you can address the pain point through the services you offer. Make sure to highlight the value you provide. For example, you could highlight that you've been editing in the tech industry for ten years and therefore understand how to ensure that the company's communications are clear and engaging to readers. You could then provide a bulleted list of your skills and specific qualifications.
- Provide the URLs to your LinkedIn profile and your website, and mention that you've attached your résumé.
- Present a specific call to action. Do you want to schedule a phone interview? Do you want to complete the company's editing test? Whatever your goal is, make it clear. Don't leave it to the other individual to lead the way. For example, you could state: "I'd like to schedule a phone call with you to see how I can best help XYZ Company [achieve goal or solve pain point]. Are you available on Wednesday or Thursday at 2:00 p.m. EDT?"
- Express appreciation for the time the individual has taken to read your email and, presumably, for the upcoming interview or whatever else you requested in the call to action.
- Close the email with your signature block, which should include your website URL, LinkedIn profile URL, and phone number.

PHONE CALL

If you haven't received a response after a week, then call the person. Keep the conversation brief; you can largely use the same wording as in your email. Before calling, recite your message several times so that you sound friendly, confident, and polished. You want to leave the best impression possible because, in a way, a phone conversation will serve as an interview. If the call goes to voicemail, state your name, reference your earlier email, express your desire to hear back from the individual soon, provide your phone number, and end with an expression of thanks.

Search Job Boards

Another way to find clients is to search job boards and other places that list freelance projects that are currently available. An internet search will lead to a lot of relevant job boards. Here are some examples:

- https://angel.co/jobs
- https://aceseditors.org/resources/job-bank
- https://jobspresso.co
- https://jobzone.publishersweekly.com
- https://remote.co/remote-jobs
- https://weworkremotely.com
- www.mediabistro.com
- www.moonlighting.com

You can also check job-bidding sites. Keep in mind that you're not likely to command high fees for projects you secure on these sites, and some sites take a percentage of your earnings. Nevertheless, the sites can be a place to start, helping you fill your schedule until

Sample Cold Email

Subject: Professional copy editing for Learning to Learn's online curriculum

Dear Derek Tor,

Earlier this year, I saw an ad for Learning to Learn and was impressed with the company's focus on developing online courses that help under-privileged students reach their educational potential. I understand how important it is to help these students succeed, and therefore I consider it essential to ensure that the course content is easy to understand, engaging, and grammatically correct. I'm confident that with my educational background and editing experience, I can help Learning to Learn achieve these goals.

My qualifications include the following:

- I graduated from the University of Illinois with a degree in elementary education.
- I've edited more than fifty academic articles for the Young Prodigies journal.
- I maintained the Young Prodigies weekly blog.
- I'm experienced in APA and Chicago styles.
- I'm proficient in Microsoft Word and Adobe Acrobat, and I have basic knowledge of HTML.

You can learn more about my credentials by reviewing my website, LinkedIn profile, or résumé (attached to this email).

I'd like to schedule a phone call to discuss how I can help Learning to Learn provide students with the highest-quality curriculum possible. Are you available this Thursday or Friday at 1:00 p.m. EDT?

Thank you for your time. I look forward to speaking with you.

Best,
Jane Grammar
janegrammaredits.com
www.linkedin.com/in/janegrammar
207-555-7892

more projects start coming your way from better-paying sources. Here are some of the more well-known job-bidding sites:

- www.upwork.com
- www.guru.com
- www.peopleperhour.com
- www.freelancer.com

You can also find freelance jobs in online editing groups, such as on Facebook and LinkedIn. Another popular group is Copyediting-L (join by going to www.copyediting-l.info). Many of these groups are quite active; while the focus isn't necessarily on freelance projects, opportunities are posted frequently, so it can be beneficial to regularly check in. Further, you can join formal editing organizations that have job boards. These organizations, such as the Editorial Freelancers Association, have membership fees, but some freelancers have found that getting one project from the job board has more than covered the cost of membership.[7]

Team Up with Other Freelancers

Another way to find clients is to team up with freelancers offering complementary services, such as book design, graphic design, and typesetting. This works well if your clients or other people ask you to recommend freelancers who provide these services. First, find freelancers offering these services, and then ensure that the individuals have high-caliber skills (otherwise, you don't want to be recommending them, because your recommendations will reflect poorly on you).

---

7. Your experience might differ, depending on how many of the projects on the job board fit your skills and interests, how many you apply for, what your rates are, how many years you've been editing, and so forth.

Next, contact the freelancers and say something like this: "I'm often asked for referrals for people who design book covers, and I assume you might sometimes be asked to recommend editors. What do you think about referring each other in these situations?" You'll then want to provide evidence that you're a highly skilled editor whom the other person would feel comfortable recommending.

Network

Networking is an additional way to find clients, though this strategy can take some time to produce results. Networking can also feel uncomfortable for people who are introverted and don't like speaking with strangers and mere acquaintances (sound familiar?). I admit that I don't love networking, particularly in settings with a lot of people. But I've experienced the benefits—to the tune of tens of thousands of dollars—so I know that the discomfort is worth the results. You may not choose to make networking one of your top marketing strategies, but if you avoid networking altogether, you'll miss out on a lot of lucrative, personally rewarding opportunities. In fact, research shows that weak connections in our networks provide more referrals in the long run than do strong connections (e.g., family and friends).[8]

Of course, the internet makes it possible to network from the comfort of your own home. Options include social media groups, professional organizations, freelance organizations, and business-networking organizations.[9] Choose just one or a few to actively participate in, because the more you contribute in a single venue or

---

8. Brian W. Powers, Ashish K. Jha, and Sachin H. Jain, "Remembering the Strength of Weak Ties," *American Journal of Managed Care* 22, no. 3 (2016): 202–203.

9. It's easy to find editing groups on Facebook by entering relevant terms in the search bar. To find editing-related posts on Twitter, try searching for hashtags such as #amediting, #ACESChat, and #EditorsChat. Most editing-related groups on LinkedIn aren't that active, but it won't hurt to check out that platform.

organization, the more likely you are to establish connections and reap the benefits.

Though interacting in online groups might be a relatively low-pressure way to start networking, make sure to also network in person. Why put yourself through the pain? For one, it's easier to make a positive lasting impression in person than online. The fact that you're a real person and not just an avatar can speed the process of establishing trust, which in turn can help you develop meaningful, long-term relationships with individuals. Additionally, meeting in person can foster other people's confidence in you.[10] The trust and confidence that result from interacting face-to-face may be why many corporate executives think that in-person meetings are better for sealing business deals.[11]

As for where to network, you have a lot of options. For example, you can attend conferences for editors. Some of the attendees might be managers who hire freelance editors and therefore might be able to directly offer you work. Others might not be in a position to offer you projects, but if you establish relationships with them they might later tell you about project requests they receive but can't take on because their schedules are full. Also consider attending conferences for publishing professionals (not just editors) and for authors and companies in your niche. Attending these conferences has the potential to directly lead to project requests. When talking with other attendees, ask them to summarize their current projects. Provide any helpful information you can think of, bring up any related projects

---

10. Serena Changhong Lu et al., "What Are the Determinants of Interpersonal Trust in Dyadic Negotiations? Meta-analytic Evidence and Implications for Future Research," *Journal of Trust Research* 7, no. 1 (2017): 22–50.

11. Pauline Stamp, Theodore Peters, and Andrew Gorycki, "In Spite of Technology: A Failure in Student Project Ownership," *Organization Management* 17, no. 1 (2020): 36–42; Catherine C. Eckel and Ragan Petrie, "Face Value," *American Economic Review* 101, no. 4 (2011): 1497–1513.

you've worked on, let them know you'd be interested in helping them, and offer your business card. To find conferences, simply google your niche and the word *conferences*, and you'll find a number of conferences to attend around the world.

Of course, conferences aren't your only option. Also search for local business networking meetings. You'll likely find many good opportunities by looking on www.meetup.com and www.eventbrite .com, among other sites. You can also join networking organizations such as BNI and LeTip. (Make sure you fully understand the requirements before joining and paying the dues.)

Finding networking events is the easy part; actually going to them and meeting people is the part that can induce fear. Keep in mind that other attendees are likely feeling uncomfortable themselves, meaning they'll appreciate it if you reach out to them. Start by looking for someone who's standing alone, and then approach the person, smile, and introduce yourself and what you do. After that, you can focus on the other individual, asking him or her a lot of questions to get to know the individual better. See if you can find anything that the two of you have in common. A commonality will help the other person remember you and feel more connected to you, increasing the chances that you'll come to mind the next time the person or someone he or she knows is in need of editing services. As the conversation ends, hand the person a business card, ask for his or hers, and say that you'll follow up (and make sure you do—the follow-up is when you're likely to be offered projects).[12] Then find someone else standing alone, and repeat the process.

If the idea of attending a networking event on your own is terrifying, then invite a colleague or friend to come with you. You might not

---

12. If you're ready to move on but don't know how to end the conversation, say something like the following: "It was great meeting you. I'm sure there are other people you'd like to talk with, so I won't take up any more of your time."

stay together during the entire event, but knowing that you have a wingman or wingwoman can provide the reassurance you need to actually attend the event.

Getting Repeat Business

Once you've found clients you like, try to turn them into repeat customers. Repeat business is ideal for multiple reasons. For one, because you've worked with the clients before, you already know that you enjoy working with them. Additionally, you won't have to go through the onboarding process again (e.g., answering common new-client questions, signing any client forms, and setting up payment details). And you won't need to spend as much time on marketing, since you won't need to bring in as many new clients. You'll also become familiar with the clients' style guides and processes, meaning that over time you're bound to become more efficient in completing the projects.

The first step in getting repeat business is to make sure you wow your clients with the quality of your work and your customer service. What exactly does customer service include? An important part is being professional and polite. Keep in mind that being professional and polite doesn't mean you have to be overly formal. Let your clients set the tone. If they always refer to you as Mr. or Ms. So-and-So, then address them similarly. If they're on the casual side, using emoticons in emails and telling you about the amazing vacations they went on, then it's okay to be more casual yourself (though always avoid crude language and stories, as well as any dirty laundry).

Similarly, be positive and encouraging—in your emails, phone calls, and such, as well as in your comments in files. Even if you're having a bad day, don't let it be reflected in how you interact with clients. And don't let your frustration show through even when you're banging your head against the wall because an author has made the same mistake for the fiftieth time. (I'm not the only editor who's gotten a little worked up about this, right?) Instead, find something to compliment the client on—maybe an insightful idea in the manuscript. And if you're finding it hard to identify something in the manuscript to praise, then thank the client for sending the manuscript on time, responding to your email promptly, or doing something else worth mentioning. (If you can't find a single thing to praise, then you need to phase out this client—the sooner the better.) Make sure to phrase all editorial comments in a kind, encouraging way, so the client sees you as an ally, not an enemy. Express confidence that the client can make the revisions needed to ensure that the end product will be as good as possible.

Also try to be flexible—within reason. You don't need to compromise the business standards and boundaries you've established, but if every now and then a client asks you to, for example, complete a project a little sooner than you said you would, try to accommodate the client. Doing so may earn you a lot of bonus points with the client. And, of course, always complete projects by their deadlines—or even early once in a while, which will add to a client's good impression of you.

Additionally, admit when you've made a mistake. Most clients are understanding; they realize that no one—not even an editor (gasp!)—is perfect. If you make an error, a client isn't likely to swear off ever working with you again, as long as you take responsibility for the error and address it professionally. Is there something you can do to solve the issue immediately? If not—for example, if you introduced an error in a manuscript that's now been printed—apologize and explain how you'll avoid making the same type of mistake in the future. Your apology should be sincere, but you don't need to repeat over and over that you're sorry. If you profusely apologize, you'll likely come off as unprofessional and as making a bigger deal about the issue than is warranted.

Once your clients have seen that you're a delight to work with, it's time to ask whether they have additional projects you can work on. Sometimes, clients will beat you to the question and ask whether you're available for more work. If they don't, take the initiative to inquire about future editing projects. You can also ask whether a client needs help with other publishing tasks, such as typesetting or proofreading; the more you understand the client's work, needs, and challenges, the better able you'll be to suggest additional ways you can provide assistance.

If a client is a company, consider asking your contact whether another department in the company might need your assistance. Since your contact is probably very busy, the best approach might be to have your contact connect you via email with managers in other departments. If a client is an individual, he or she may not have additional content to be edited for a while. But still brainstorm some ideas. For instance, if you've just edited an author's novel, offer to edit any query letters the author will be sending to literary agents and publishers. Or offer to help the client with content on his or her author website (having one really is essential these days).

Reach out to clients every few months so you remain on their radar. You could email specific clients the link to a relevant article or other resource. Or consider emailing the day before a holiday, wishing your clients a great day. It's also okay to every so often directly ask a client for work. After noting that you enjoyed working with the client previously, state that you're firming up your schedule for the next few months and want to see whether the client will be in need of your services. You could also present a project idea. For instance, if you edited a client's dissertation, then later you could suggest that the client convert the dissertation into a book or distill the dissertation into a journal article. Provide some helpful suggestions for getting started on the project, and then offer to help with the process or to edit the manuscript once it's completed. In using these tips, you won't always score projects but you'll receive more than if you don't touch base.

One caution: Getting repeat business is great, but it's best not to rely on just a few clients for your income. If you do, you could be in big trouble if one of those clients no longer sends you work. You'll be safer if no more than 25 percent of your revenue comes from one client.

Key Takeaways

- You don't need to establish a niche right away, but having one can help you narrow your marketing focus.
- You can have more than one niche, and you can change niches over time.
- To find clients, use the following strategies:
  - Tell everyone you know that you've started a freelance editing business.
  - Ask for referrals in a friendly, casual manner. Let clients know that you love receiving referrals.
  - Make a list of at least forty potential clients, find their contact information, and then email them about your services.
  - Search job boards for freelance projects.
  - Make arrangements with other freelancers to refer business to each other.
  - Attend in-person networking events, and engage in online networking activities.
- To obtain repeat business, deliver high-quality work and be a joy to work with. Also get to know your clients' needs, and then suggest additional projects that you can help the clients with.

5   *Marketing like a Pro*

In the previous chapter, we explored how to identify potential clients. In this chapter, we'll focus on how to convert potential clients into customers. We'll also talk about other strategies to increase awareness of your business, with the goal of bringing in additional projects. There are tons of ways to market your business, so we'll focus on the ones I and various other freelance editors have found to be the most effective. Should you implement any additional tactics? Sure, if you really enjoy them or know that they'll bring in business. Otherwise, think twice about spending your valuable time on strategies—especially time-consuming ones—that aren't likely to have high-yield results. Some strategies that you'll find on the internet might be easy to implement, such as participating in online editing forums, but they're not as effective at locking in projects as are some other approaches. So, fight the urge to default to the easy marketing strategies. Instead, focus on the ones that are more effective, meaning you'll be spending less time on marketing and you'll have more time for editing or (even better) nonwork activities.

One caveat: if simply thinking about a specific marketing strategy makes you sick to your stomach, then the strategy probably won't work well for you. You'll probably procrastinate implementing it, and when you do work on it, your efforts will be lackluster. And that means the strategy won't be effective. So, focus on other strategies that are appealing and also effective. After you get more used to marketing in general, you may find that the strategy you used to loathe doesn't seem too bad anymore and that you're ready to give it a shot.

Awareness of Target Clients' Needs

To make your marketing as effective as possible, you need to understand potential clients' underlying problems, needs, and objectives. With that information in hand, focus on crafting marketing messages that explain how you can help solve the problems, fill the needs, and achieve the goals. These messages will resonate with members of your target market, and they'll be thrilled that they've found someone who truly "gets" them and understands what they're looking for. At that point, it'll be a lot easier to secure their business—even if your rates are higher than competitors'.

But how do you figure out what your target clients' pain points are? How do you know what keeps them up at night? The process is actually pretty simple, and you don't have to be a mind reader. Start by talking with current clients. You probably already understand some of their difficulties and how you're able to help address them, but drill deeper. Ask clients what their greatest publishing-related challenges are and what they most want help with (hopefully you're already providing it, but if not, offer to start doing so). Ask clients what motivated them to hire an editor and why they selected you. Ask what their ultimate goals are and why they want to accomplish them. What rewards or benefits are they seeking?

After gathering data from current clients, collect information from your larger network and potential clients. Talk to them at conferences and networking events. Join LinkedIn and Facebook groups that potential clients are members of, and pay attention to their posts and comments. Be bold by directly asking them to describe what their biggest publishing-related challenges are. What tasks would they love to take off their plate and put on someone else's (ideally, yours)? What will accomplishing these tasks and the overall goals enable these individuals to achieve?

Though each person's challenges, objectives, and dreams might be a bit different, you'll likely identify some common themes. Address them in your marketing messages. For example, if your target market comprises doctoral students, you'll likely learn that most of these individuals don't like writing and don't feel skilled at it. The only reason they're writing a dissertation is to earn a doctorate, maybe in hopes of obtaining a better job, a higher salary, or greater social prominence. They know their dissertation won't be approved if it's filled with grammar errors and unclear sentences, but they either don't know how to fix these issues or don't have the time or energy to do it. So, they're seeking an editor's help.

Your marketing message could focus on your ability to correct grammar and punctuation errors, to ensure sentences are clear, and to format citations according to a specific style. That message would likely appeal to potential clients. But it won't resonate with them, and it won't make you stand out. After all, don't all editors undertake these tasks? If all editors are doing the same thing, then it's logical to choose the editor with the lowest prices. What will set you apart is a marketing message that says your goal is to help dissertation authors polish their writing so their dissertations are approved, meaning these hardworking individuals can add "Dr." before their name. This message speaks to the potential clients' underlying desire, and they'll be excited to work with you since your goal aligns with their ultimate goal.

Unique Selling Proposition

In almost all of your marketing efforts, you'll want to include your unique selling proposition (USP). You're probably not familiar with that term unless you have a background in business, so let me explain what a USP is. Basically, a USP is a short statement that describes what you do and how your services are different from and/or better than your competitors' services. The purpose of the statement is to position yourself as the best option when someone is in need of a service you provide. With a strong USP, you can persuade people that you're the most logical choice, even if you charge more than competitors do. You can use your USP as your elevator pitch, and you can condense your USP into a tagline to use on business cards, in your LinkedIn headline, in your email signature, and in other marketing materials.

To create your USP, answer the following three questions:

- What type of services do you offer?
- Who are your target clients?
- What makes you different from or a better choice than competitors?[1]

Answering the first two questions is likely pretty easy; the third question is where some people get stuck. You don't need to come up with something that describes you and no one else. Rather, focus on finding something that makes your services, skills, or approach different enough to distinguish yourself from competitors.[2] Here are some strategies for answering the third question:

- Ask current clients why they chose you instead of competitors.
- Put yourself in your potential clients' shoes. What goals are they trying to achieve? What obstacles are in the way? What help are they looking for?

---

1. Slaunwhite, Savage, and Gandia, *Wealthy Freelancer*.
2. Slaunwhite, Savage, and Gandia, *Wealthy Freelancer*.

- Focus on providing solutions to problems. (A great example is the NyQuil slogan from the late 1980s and early 1990s: "The Nighttime Sniffling, Sneezing, Coughing, Aching, Stuffy Head, Fever, So You Can Rest Medicine.")
- Be specific. For example, instead of "I can edit your manuscript," write "I'll ensure that your manuscript has commas in exactly the right places, flows well, and expresses ideas clearly so that your target audience remains engaged."

Here is an example of what your USP might look like after you've answered the three questions: (1) I'm a freelance editor who specializes in helping (2) doctoral students polish their dissertations. (3) I have edited more than thirty dissertations and have a solid understanding of how to ensure your dissertation is approved, meaning you can achieve your ultimate goal: obtaining the title of "Dr."!

Notice that this USP has a good amount of detail and focuses on the value proposition, that is, how the editor provides value to clients. It's critical to clearly explain what benefits you provide—and that your benefits help solve potential clients' challenges. Otherwise, your USP won't likely resonate with your target audience, and potential clients won't feel compelled to choose you over someone else. To illustrate, let's consider some slogans FedEx has used. One of the early slogans was "When It Absolutely, Positively Has to Be There Overnight." This slogan is effective because it speaks to a problem many people have experienced: needing a package to arrive ASAP, often because of an emergency situation. In a tense moment, it's comforting to know that FedEx understands your plight and will make sure the package arrives on time. So, there's an emotional draw to use FedEx.

A slogan that FedEx later introduced is "The World on Time." This slogan isn't nearly as effective. For one, it's vague and too general. What exactly does the world being on time mean? On time according to whose definition? Will the package be delivered by tomorrow? Another problem is that FedEx can't ensure that everything in the world is on time, so this exaggeration can foster skepticism. And since the slogan doesn't address a specific problem, it lacks emotional appeal.

The main takeaway is that your USP should speak to potential clients' needs. If you can get at the underlying challenges and explain how you'll resolve them, you'll communicate to potential clients that you understand them. And they'll be more prone to choose you from among a multitude of freelance editors offering their services.

Lead Nurturing

Let's say you've had some initial conversations with people at businesses you cold-called, you met at networking events, or you were introduced to by current clients. These leads have expressed some interest in your services (your awesome USP certainly helped), and you're excited by the prospect of scoring new clients. Unfortunately, not all potential clients you talk with will be ready to hire an editor in the short term. But they likely will in the future (sometimes in as little as a few weeks and sometimes as far out as a few years from now— I know from experience). So, if you want potential clients to eventually hire you, make sure to keep in touch with them until they're ready to buy. If you don't, they'll likely go with whoever has talked with them or been recommended to them most recently.

The key is to touch base with leads every two to three months— often enough to remain top of mind while avoiding being spammy and overbearing. The goal of contacting leads should be to provide helpful information and resources, to establish a friendly relationship, and to build trust. That means you shouldn't mention your services every time you contact a lead. Rather, send an email with the link to an article you think will be of interest to the lead. If your target

Sample Unique Selling Propositions

Good	Bad
• With eight years of experience as a researcher and an editor, I can help ensure that your technical documents are accurate, easy to understand, and intellectually engaging.	• If you're looking for a great nonfiction editor, you've found him. Thanks to my editing and your drive, your book will be sure to turn heads!
• I'm a trained copy editor who helps STEM professors and students prepare articles for publication. I've edited more than thirty STEM papers that have been accepted for publication in scholarly journals. My copy editing experience can help you present your research in manuscripts that are understandable, error free, and professional.	• I'm a developmental, substantive, and copy editor as well as a fact-checker, typesetter, and proofreader who provides services for tech companies, technical documents, scriptwriters, website owners, and authors of adult speculative fiction, YA romance, middle grade mysteries, and memoirs. I can help you edit grammar, develop characters, finish world building, strengthen plotlines, improve voice, enrich dialogue, appeal to your audience, and stand out from every other self-published or traditionally published author.
• As a developmental editor, I've worked with many authors who've gone on to win praise and awards for their novels. Whether you're plagued by unconvincing plotlines, underdeveloped characters, or uneven pacing, I'll use my expertise in editing and publishing to help you feel more confident in your writing abilities and in your chances of landing a lucrative publishing deal.	• My older sister introduced me to reading and instilled me with a passion for books. I've read more than two hundred novels since graduating with a degree in English and a minor in psychology. Now I'm offering my experience to help authors with their writing.

market consists of academic authors, send a cheat sheet you created explaining how to format citations. If the lead or the lead's company recently received positive press, send a note of congratulations.[3] Prior to a holiday, send a postcard with a relevant greeting. (As you might have noticed, the suggestions here are similar to the ones in chapter 4 about remaining in touch with past clients.)

Every four or so contacts, it's okay to mention your services directly. If you know that the individual is currently working on a project, such as a novel, then ask how the writing is going and say you'd love the opportunity to edit the project once it's finished. You could also frame the message in terms of your upcoming schedule. Some editors have found it effective to say something like, "I am firming up my schedule for June and will then be taking a vacation the first two weeks of July. If you'd like to get in my queue before I'm out of the office, please let me know."

Make sure to keep track of when you've contacted leads; something as basic as an Excel spreadsheet will do the job. Simply list the person's name, the date of the contact, and what your message consisted of (e.g., a link to a resource). Set a reminder in your calendar to review the spreadsheet once a month so you can determine whom to reach out to in the coming week.

Social Media Platforms

With the prevalence of social media today, you definitely shouldn't ignore it when considering how to market your business. Of all the social media platforms out there, I think LinkedIn is the most beneficial for bringing in business, so I've dedicated an entire chapter to

---

3. To easily learn when individuals and organizations are mentioned online (not including on social media sites), set up Google Alerts by going to www .google.com/alerts.

Sample Lead-Nurturing Email

Richard,

I hope you're doing well and making progress on your novel despite your busy schedule. I came across a great article about how to create characters that readers will care about, and as I was sharing the article with some of my clients, I thought you might be interested too. Here's the link: www.writingyourbookright.com/characters_that_make_readers_care.

Best wishes as you continue working on your book! If there's ever anything I can do to help, please let me know.

Sincerely,
Jane Grammar

using this site. Though LinkedIn should likely be your focus when it comes to marketing on social media, using other platforms isn't necessarily a waste of time. If your target clients hang out on a specific site, then be active on the site. The key is to focus on using one or two platforms so that you don't spread yourself too thin, get overwhelmed, or devote too much time to this single marketing strategy.

Because I recommend prioritizing LinkedIn, instead of giving you detailed steps on how to use each of the other platforms, I'm going to highlight more general tactics that apply to all the platforms. Keep in mind that social media marketing is typically a long-term strategy; since you're not likely to receive project requests after making just a few posts, you need to be committed to this marketing tactic. First, figure out which platforms your ideal clients use. How? Start by asking other editors who work in the same genres that you do. Then, go to each of the sites and search for terms and hashtags that are relevant to or describe your target market. For example, if you want to mainly edit for independent authors, consider searching for #WritingCommunity. Also consider searching for the pages of specific authors and companies you'd like to have as clients. Decide which platform seems to have the largest number of ideal clients who are regularly engaging in discussion. This platform should be the focus of your social media marketing.

Once you've selected the platform, join relevant groups; follow or connect with ideal clients; and also see whom they're connected with, since these connections are probably also potential clients. The next step is to participate regularly, in whatever form that involves on your selected platform. Active participation is essential because it's how people are going to get to know you—and decide they want to hire you. Depending on the platform, participating might involve creating posts with links to relevant articles, industry news, blog posts (particularly ones you've written), and great books you've read recently. You might also want to post grammar tips, inspiring quotations about writing or language, and memes that potential clients are likely to chuckle at (and then share with others, increasing your exposure). Often, posts containing images get more attention, so consider creating visuals using a site such as Canva.

You can also post about your editing services, but don't do so often. You don't want to come off as too salesy, which is a big turnoff. People are on social media to interact in communities, and they want the people in their communities to be genuinely interested in the conversation, not participating solely to get business. When you do mention your editing services, try to do so in a low-key manner. For example, you could share an insight you gained from an article you edited, or you could express excitement about seeing the typeset

"Facebook groups of colleagues have been the most effective [social media marketing tool] by providing visibility among people who remember my contributions and apparent skills."
—*Ruth E. Thaler-Carter, freelance editor*

version of a book you copy edited. Only rarely should you use a more direct marketing message, such as saying you're available to take on new projects.

To save time and stay organized, you can use a scheduling program such as Hootsuite, which lets you upload posts and schedule when they'll go live on the social media platforms of your choice.[4] If you'll be posting only on Pinterest and/or Instagram, check out Tailwind, which will publish your posts when your target audience is most likely to be active. These programs, as well as the social media platforms you use, give you access to analytics on how your posts are performing. Make sure to check out this data to get insights regarding the best days and times for posting content, which types of posts are getting the most engagement, the demographics of the people engaging with your content, and so on. Then, do more of what seems to be most effective in terms of increasing engagement, expanding your following, and encouraging people to contact you about your services.

Of course, publishing your own posts isn't the only way to engage with potential clients on social media platforms. You can also share and like posts created by people you follow. When those people see you've shared or liked their posts, they'll tend to be curious about who you are and they might check out your profile. Additionally, comment on their posts in order to encourage dialogue between you and the posters. Your comments could express agreement with the individuals' posts or could answer questions people have posed. By answering questions, you're providing value and also establishing yourself as knowledgeable about the topic. In doing so, those you in-

---

4. Some editors have reported that when they use scheduling programs, their posts are penalized by social media platforms and are seen by fewer people. Luckily, these penalties are a thing of the past, so don't hesitate to use scheduling programs.

teract with will start to trust you, which is typically an important precursor to someone reaching out to you with an editing project.

Editing and Business Directories

Creating a profile in editing directories can also lead to project requests. You'll find a variety of editor directories online, and some cater to editors in specific geographic locations or with certain specialties or characteristics. Some of the directories you might consider are those hosted by Copyediting-L, the Editorial Freelancers Association, the Society for Editors and Proofreaders, ACES, the Board of Editors in the Life Sciences, the Association of Independent Publishing Professionals, Editors of Color, Reedsy, and PeerWith. Setting up profiles in numerous directories might seem time-consuming, but it shouldn't actually take long, since you'll basically be using the same content for each profile—and you can pull most of the info from your LinkedIn page. Though you may not receive a ton of requests from having directory profiles, scoring even a few projects can make the time spent creating these profiles worthwhile.

Also consider creating a business profile through Google My Business, which will help your business website turn up in search results when people in your geographic location are googling for editing businesses. As part of your profile, you'll select the categories that best describe your business. Unfortunately, Google doesn't have an editing category, so you'll need to search for other relevant categories, such as Desktop Publishing Service, Publisher, Book Publisher, Consultant, and Media Consultant. After completing your profile, you can add other service categories and a business description to more accurately explain the services you offer. As with profiles in other directories, your Google business profile isn't likely to bring in a ton of business, but you should see an increase in traffic to your website and likely some additional service requests. The potential for more business is worth the ten or so minutes it takes to complete a profile.

One note of caution regarding business profiles: editors are frequently the target of email scams, and it seems that scammers often use editor directories to obtain email addresses. Beware of emails from people you've never met who are offering you an editing project, ongoing contract work, or even a full-time job. Usually, scam emails contain a few warning bells. For one, the text often contains multiple spelling and grammar errors. The email might also mention that the individual found you in an editor directory, but you might not actually have a profile in the directory (so keep track of where you've posted profiles).

A further warning sign is that the email contains a file. Though an attachment isn't a guarantee that the editing request is a scam, you do need to be wary of files from people you don't know and trust. If you decide to open the attachment, make sure to run a virus scanner first, to help you avoid putting your computer at risk of a virus. Another danger signal is if the email address of the sender doesn't match the name of the person purportedly sending the email. Or, the domain portion of the email address (i.e., what comes after @) is very close to that of a legitimate company's domain but is off by a letter or includes more or less than the legitimate company's domain. Also beware if the email indicates that the individual wants to set up a Google Hangout meeting with you.

Sometimes, you might not be able to detect the scam until after you've communicated with the individual a few times. The scammer might offer you a project and then say that he or she will send you a check immediately. When the check comes, the amount will be much more than the price you agreed upon. After you've deposited the check, the scammer will ask you to return the extra amount. Once you've done so, the individual will make the check bounce, meaning you'll lose the amount of the check you received—and you'll also be out the money you sent in the reimbursement check for the scammer.

The warning signs I've mentioned are common, but scammers are always trying new techniques, so it's a good idea to stay aware of what's currently going around. Also trust your spidey sense. If the email makes you suspicious, then ask other editors in online communities whether they've received the same or a similar email. Often, they will be able to provide guidance and may even be able to confirm that the email is a scam.

Promotional Pieces

Another great marketing tool is a promotional piece that you've written and that you offer to members of your target market, typically for free. The objectives of creating a promo piece are to provide valuable, relevant content to potential clients while at the same time establishing yourself as knowledgeable on the topic you've written about. When you achieve those two goals, people will be more interested in learning about your services and whether you might be a good fit for an upcoming project. These individuals might also be more likely to hire you because you've offered them something of value for free.[5]

---

5. Various studies show that offering something for free has multiple benefits. Individuals who receive a free product with a paid service have better overall opinions of the company and are more likely to refer friends who later become clients (Samuel D. Bond, Stephen X. He, and Wen Wen, "Speaking for 'Free': Word of Mouth in Free- and Paid-Product Settings," *Journal of Marketing Research* 56, no. 2 [2019]: 276–290). People also feel compelled to buy something or spend more on a product or service offered by a company when they have received something for free from the company (Kapil Bawa and Robert Shoemaker, "The Effects of Sample Promotions on Incremental Brand Sales," *Marketing Science* 23, no. 4 [2004]: 345–363).

You can mention the piece on your website, on your social media pages, in your email signature, in emails to potential clients, on your business card, at networking events, and anywhere else you interact with potential clients. Typically, you'll want to make the document available on your website; you could also print hard copies to give to people at events. Another idea is to send your promo piece to former clients, individuals you're trying to establish relationships with, and individuals who've asked you for a price quote on a project.

For your promotional piece to be effective, it needs to be related to your services and helpful and interesting to your target audience. Start by brainstorming what will be of value to your audience. Think about the challenges they experience. What are their pain points? How can your promotional piece help make their publishing-related pursuits or tasks easier? For example, if you provide editing services for indie fiction authors, you could write a promotional piece about how to avoid head-hopping (i.e., suddenly changing who the viewpoint character is). If you cater to academic writers, you could explain ten common punctuation and grammar mistakes. You don't need to worry that you're giving all the answers away and that potential clients won't need your services; after all, your promo piece won't cover all concerns of your target clients. Rather, you'll be whetting their appetite for your more comprehensive (meaning paid) help.

Along those lines, your promotional piece doesn't need to be long—five to ten pages of content can provide a lot of value without requiring you to spend hours writing the piece. And don't worry if you're not an expert on the topic you're thinking of writing about. It's okay if you need to do some research to become more knowledgeable. You could even interview an expert or two and include their responses in your piece. (But do make sure to include your ideas and input, since you want to present yourself as someone whom potential clients should come to when they need help related to the topic.)

To make the content easy to scan, use multiple headings. If appropriate, also use vertical lists. And add a little visual appeal by using a different color or font family for the title and headings. Depending on your topic, you might want to include graphical elements such as charts, tables, or images.

Another key element is the title. Make it engaging so that people feel compelled to take a look at the piece. I'm not going to dive into the details of how to craft a stellar title—you can find lots of great suggestions online—but here are several strategies that are proven to pique readers' interest. If you can incorporate more than one of these strategies in your title, all the better!

- Include a number in the title (e.g., "7 Ways to Improve Characterization in Your Novel").
- Use "How to" in the title (e.g., "How to Write the Perfect Query Letter in 5 Steps").
- Refer to something readers shouldn't do (e.g., "9 Plot Holes You Need to Avoid").
- Ask a question (e.g., "Are You Making These 10 Common Usage Errors?").
- Use alliteration (e.g., "Polish Your Prose Using These 14 Powerful Tips").
- Include keywords that people would use to search online for information on your topic (e.g., if you're targeting academic writers searching for help on formatting citations according to APA style, your title might be "Using APA Style to Format Citations in Your Doctoral Dissertation").

At the end of your promotional piece, include a brief professional bio as well as your email address and links to your LinkedIn profile and website. Also include a call to action, such as an invitation to visit your website to learn more about your services or an invitation to email you if readers want to know more about the promotional piece's topic or how you can help readers achieve their publishing-related goals.

Books, Training, Podcasts, and YouTube Channels

Of course, you don't need to limit yourself to a short promotional piece; you might also want to write books (whether thirty pages or two hundred) on topics that would be of value to your target clients. The beauty of this option is that you can charge for the books, so you'll be earning some money from book sales while also promoting your editing business.

Similarly, you can market yourself and potentially earn money by offering training, whether on your own or through an organization. Many organizations offer their members professional development opportunities, so search for organizations catering to your ideal audience, and then peruse each organization's website for information on how to apply to provide training sessions. Just a few organizations that offer training are the Freelancers Hub, the Authors Guild, and Writer's Digest. You can also search for opportunities to provide corporate training, such as on basic editing principles or scientific writing. Your best bet is to start by approaching people in your network and asking whether their companies' employees would benefit from training related to writing or another topic you feel comfortable teaching about. Make sure you charge enough for the training to compensate you for your preparation time as well as presentation time. Even if you don't end up being invited to provide training, you might be offered some freelance projects or referrals.

Two other marketing options to consider are podcasts and YouTube channels. You can create your own or seek out opportunities to be a guest on other people's podcasts and videos. Obviously, creating your own is much more time-consuming, so it's a good idea to test the waters by being a guest first. Another benefit of starting on other people's podcasts and videos is that they will already have audiences, so you'll be reaching a larger number of potential clients. If you enjoy your experience, then explore the options for creating your own podcasts or videos. The key with both is to present information that your target clients will find helpful and that will establish yourself as an expert on the topic. At the end, you'll have the chance to briefly mention how people can connect with you to learn more about your services and how you might be able to help people with their publishing-related needs.

I realize that I've covered just the bare bones of each of these marketing strategies. If you're interested in learning more about each, go to http://writingandeditingbysuzy.com/alternate-income -streams-for-freelance-editors. There, you'll get more ideas on how to implement each of these strategies—and even how to make them a source of income separate from your editing work.

Additional Marketing Tips

Here are some additional tips to keep in mind:

- Present yourself confidently—in terms of your abilities and your belief that people will want to work with you. If you struggle with confidence, fake it until you make it.[6]
- Always be looking for more freelance projects. Don't wait until your plate is completely empty to seek out more work. Even when your schedule is full and you don't think you have time for marketing, engage in marketing efforts at least once a week.

---

6. Dana R. Carney, Amy J. C. Cuddy, and Andy J. Yap, "Power Posing: Brief Nonverbal Displays Affect Neuroendocrine Levels and Risk Tolerance," *Psychological Science* 21, no. 10 (2010): 1363–1368.

- Examine how other freelance editors are marketing their businesses. Check out their websites and social media pages. How do these editors present themselves and their services? Are they blogging or posting articles? Do they frequently engage with potential clients on social media or in discussion forums? Don't be afraid to ask other editors for marketing tips; most editors are generous in explaining what works for them. However, don't inundate them with questions; do some research and put in some thought before you ask others for advice.
- To expand awareness of your business and establish credibility, look for opportunities to share your knowledge by writing guest blog posts.
- Be prepared for rejection and bargaining—and don't consider either one a personal insult. Determine what you can learn from the experiences to refine your marketing efforts, and then keep moving forward.
- Be cautious in offering discounts. Some freelancers will offer a discount on a client's first project or will offer a discount if a client refers another person who becomes a client. Those strategies could get your business off the ground, but discounts set a bad precedent: that you're willing to devalue the service you provide and that you might be willing to give discounts in other situations. (That's dangerous territory I'm not willing to enter.) You might also be bringing in clients who aren't willing to pay your regular fees, meaning you won't get repeat business. You're better off finding clients who will pay the full price and who are likely to refer others who are okay with your rates.

Key Takeaways

- Create a USP that communicates the value you provide, and use that USP in your marketing content (e.g., on your website, in online profiles, on your business card, and in cold emails).

- Make sure you understand the challenges, needs, and underlying objectives of your target clients. Then craft marketing messages that speak to those points.
- Keep in touch with potential clients so you'll be the first one they contact when they're ready to hire an editor.
- LinkedIn is arguably the most important social media platform for finding business, but don't ignore other social media sites when it comes to marketing.
- Create profiles in editing directories to increase your exposure.
- Develop a promotional piece on a topic that potential clients care about. Post the piece on your website; mention it on your business card, in your email signature, and in cold emails; and announce it on social media.

6   *Creating Your Website*

As I've talked with other freelance editors, I've been surprised to learn that many don't have a business website. Maybe they're just getting started freelancing, they doubt their tech skills, or they think having a website is unnecessary. Whatever the reason, there's an even more important rationale for having a website: it'll make your freelance business look more legitimate, and potential clients will expect you to have one. There are, of course, other good reasons to have a website, and we'll discuss them in this chapter. I'll also take you through the steps of how to create a website that you'll be proud of. By the end of the chapter, not only will you understand why having a website is an essential marketing tool but you'll also feel confident in building a website that will enhance your freelance business.

Why You Need a Website

If you want to position yourself as a professional freelance editor, then you need to have a website. Sure, your website isn't likely to show up on page 1 of the Google search results when someone types the keywords *freelance editor*, but that's not really the goal of having a website. Rather, for freelance editors, the purpose is to provide a way for people to learn more about you and your services after having met you or heard about you, likely somewhere online. And, yes, you need a website even if you've created profiles on LinkedIn, editing directories, and job-bidding sites, because on your website you won't be limited by the type and amount of content you include.

On your site, you can provide more information about your educational and professional background, the type of work you've completed, and the services you offer. You can also include samples of your work, a downloadable promotional piece (see chapter 5), and client testimonials. Further, on each page you can include a call to action that guides viewers to other important pages of your site and that ultimately encourages viewers to contact you to discuss potential projects.

If those reasons aren't enough, also keep in mind that with a well-developed website, you'll appear more professional and credible. You'll be presenting yourself as the owner of an established business, not as an amateur who might suddenly vanish, perhaps during the middle of working on a client project. Your website can help viewers develop trust in you and feel confident that hiring you for a project will be a good decision. People especially need that reassurance when they're thinking of hiring someone they haven't met in person, which is often the case when they're working with freelance editors. So, use your website to help viewers get to know you professionally as well as a little bit personally (e.g., through your bio page and how your personality comes through from your overall writing tone and style).

How to Build Your Website

The idea of creating a website can feel daunting, because of a lack of web development skills or a lack of funds to hire a web developer. Luckily, you don't need coding skills to create an effective website yourself—and in a relatively short time. Many website-builder platforms make it easy to create a website by choosing from template designs and then adding your customized text and images. Just a few of these platforms include Constant Contact, Squarespace, Weebly, Wix, WordPress, and Yola. Most website-builder platforms work similarly: You select one of the templates and then can tweak it by changing the fonts, images, and other elements. Most platforms offer drag-and-drop tools, meaning you can move an image, a text box, or some other element from one location to another on a page. Typically, you'll work in WYSIWYG (which stands for *what you see is what you get*) and you won't see the HTML coding for what you're designing on the page. However, most platforms will let you toggle to HTML view so you can see the code (and that can be helpful if you have some HTML knowledge and want to do something not offered in WYSIWYG mode). The platforms also provide a lot of plug-ins and widgets you can incorporate into your site, such as to connect your site to social media feeds, add more design features and site components, and increase your SEO (search engine optimization) ranking.

Because of the drag-and-drop tools and the WYSIWYG view, designing a site on a website-builder platform is pretty straightforward. If you do run into any issues, check the platform's user forum and help section. Another good option is to google the platform's name and a short description of what you're trying to do. You'll likely find multiple webpages explaining the steps you need to take.

Most of these platforms allow you to create a basic website for free. Of course, the basic version usually offers limited options and functionality. For instance, with the free version, your URL will have the platform's domain at the end (e.g., www.janegrammaredits .weebly.com) and your site might include ads for the platform's company. You might also be limited in the number of templates and design features you can choose from, and you might have a cap on storage space and bandwidth. Paid versions usually cost around $10 to $20 per month, and in my opinion, the extra options are worth the price. (Keep in mind that the expense is tax deductible.)

If you want more customizability and functionality than is offered by website-builder platforms, your best option is WordPress. It's important to understand that there are actually two WordPress platforms: WordPress.com and WordPress.org. The .com version is the option that's more similar to website-builder platforms. You select a template and then can customize colors, fonts, and so forth. Your site is hosted on WordPress.com, and by upgrading you can customize your domain and access more-advanced design and functionality features. The .org version gives you more control over everything—design, plug-ins, and even what company will host your site.

That last item is perhaps the most important difference to understand. If you use WordPress.org to create your site, you'll need to purchase a domain name (you won't have the option to select a free one with ".wordpress" at the end) and you'll need to pay a web hosting company to provide you with a server to put your site on. Web hosting companies, such as BlueHost and GoDaddy, typically charge $3 to $5 per month for basic hosting. A domain name will cost around $10 to $20 per year. So, for about the same amount you'd pay for advanced features on a web-builder platform, you can get a domain name and web hosting for your completely customizable site created via WordPress.org. However, with the greater freedom comes more responsibility, including installing security updates and backing up your site. So, which WordPress approach do I suggest? Especially when you're just starting out, go with WordPress.com. If you decide later that you want more customizability and are willing to take on the extra responsibility, then read up on what's required and have a go at WordPress.org.

Actually, you should do a little research and testing before choosing any website platform, not just when deciding between the WordPress options. Though site-builder platforms are similar in many ways, they differ regarding the number of templates available, functionality and customizability, customer support, and fees for advanced options. Read some articles that compare and rate website platforms, spend a few minutes perusing templates available on the platforms, and skim tutorials to get an idea of what the setup experience on a platform will be like. Then sign up to create a site on a platform or two, and play around with creating one page on each site. After ten or so minutes, you might discover that you like the user interface of one site better than the other. After you've picked the winner, simply delete your site on other platforms you tested and continue developing your site on the winning platform.

How to Choose and Purchase a Domain Name

As I already mentioned, you can completely customize your domain name (for a fee) or you can use a free domain provided by a website-builder platform. With the latter option, you can customize the first part of the URL, and that portion will be followed by the platform's domain (e.g., ".weebly.com"). Fully customized URLs look more professional, so that option is the better choice. (However, I admit that for many years my website URL was only partly customized, and that fact didn't seem to have a negative effect on my ability to obtain high-quality, high-paying clients.) Another benefit of having a customized domain name is that you can also have an email address that matches your domain (e.g., jane@janegrammaredits.com). You can purchase a domain directly from the website-builder platform you've decided to use, but you might also want to consider purchasing the domain from a domain registrar, since prices will vary, even for the same domain name.

As for what domain name to use, ideally it should match the name of your business so that the domain is easy for people to remember.[1] (See chapter 2 for a discussion of naming your business.) The URL should include at least one keyword (e.g., *editing*), which will help with SEO. After you've picked a few good options, go to your website-builder platform and domain-registrar websites, and in the appropriate field type your desired domain name (without the extension, e.g., ".com," at the end). You'll then see a list of available domain names—including, hopefully, the name you entered as well as similar alternatives.

You'll likely have the option of selecting your extension. I strongly recommend choosing ".com," since it indicates your website is for a business and since this extension is the most common, making your URL easier for people to remember. You could purchase all available extensions (to prevent someone else from having almost the same URL as yours), but I don't think it's necessary, since other editors are unlikely to want a URL so similar to yours. On a related note, check whether your desired URL almost matches that of another active website. If, for example, you see that janegrammaredits.com is available but that janegrammaredits.biz isn't available, check out the latter URL. If someone is already using it, use a different main domain name, such as editsbyjanegrammar.com.

How to Decide on the Website Design

Before you select a design template for your website, look at other freelance editors' websites. Note what you like about those sites and

---

1. If you choose a creative name rather than using your personal name for your business, you might want to purchase a domain that matches your business name and also a domain that matches your personal name. The latter URL could redirect to the domain with your creative name, so if people search for your site using your personal name, they'll make it to the right place. Also, having the domain for your personal name means that no one else can have it and potentially post content you don't want associated with your business.

how they could be improved. Keep those ideas in mind as you peruse the design templates on various website-builder platforms. By choosing a design template on a website-builder platform, you won't need to make too many decisions regarding the design. But don't hesitate to tweak the look to customize your site. For example, you can change the color palette or the fonts used for headings and body text. You can also customize your site by selecting different images to use— and I recommend having an image or other graphical element on each page, to provide visual interest. Most site-builder platforms will offer some free stock photos you can choose from. For more options, go to sites such as www.pexels.com, www.pixabay.com, and www.unsplash .com, which contain huge collections of free images you can use for commercial purposes. If you do tweak your template design, make sure to apply the changes throughout your site so the design is consistent. A uniform design will help with branding purposes and will make your site look more polished and professional.

In choosing a template and customizing it, make sure your design matches the tone of your business and the expectations of target clients. If you're billing yourself as a technical editor, your site should probably look more formal than if your target clients are indie sci-fi authors. It's okay to let a bit of your personality come through in your site design, but make sure your site still looks polished. After all, the purpose of your site is to impress people with your professionalism and skills, in the hopes that visitors will decide to hire you. So, I wouldn't introduce your "editorial assistant" (i.e., your cat) until after you've established a relationship with clients and they've seen your high-quality work.

Pages and Content to Include on Your Website

Once you've figured out the design, it's time to focus on what content to include and where to put it. Your website should include the following pages:

- Home page
- Services page
- Bio page
- Contact page

You might also want to include these pages:

- Testimonials page
- Work samples page
- Promotional piece page

Below, I'll briefly describe the content for each of these pages. But first, here are some tips that you should apply throughout your site:

- Keep the pages relatively short.
- Keep paragraphs relatively short (three to four sentences is a good guideline).
- Use headings to serve as a road map to the page's content.
- Use bulleted lists to help readers scan the content.
- Include internal links (i.e., links to other pages on your site) to guide readers through your site. All pages on your site should lead to your contact page.
- Refer to yourself in the first person.
- In most instances, speak directly to site visitors (i.e., use second person, not third person).
- Make sure your wording is confident. It's okay to brag a bit about the value you provide.
- Include a call to action on each page (e.g., on the home page, encourage readers to visit your services page or to contact you to talk about a project).
- Ensure that each page has tabs or a menu with links to your main pages, including your home page. If your site isn't easy to navigate, visitors are likely to leave.

- Though your website is about you and your services, craft the content so it's focused on your customers—why your business is relevant to them, how you'll provide them with value, and how you'll help them achieve their objectives.
- Make sure to include the terms that potential clients will use when searching for the services you offer. Obvious terms are *editing* and *proofreading*. Also think of terms that are specific to your niches. For instance, if you edit dissertations, you'll probably want to include *dissertation editing, thesis editing, academic editing,* and *APA editor*, among other terms. If you're not sure of which keywords you should be using, you can get ideas by using a tool such as Ubersuggest.

And now on to the page-specific suggestions.

Home Page

Make the name of your business big and bold at the top of the home page. Your business's name should appear above the "fold"—that is, the portion of the screen you see before needing to scroll down. Below the name and any graphical element (most templates include an image above the fold), provide a few paragraphs introducing your business, the services you provide, and your USP. You don't need to go into great depth on the home page. Your goal is simply to pique viewers' interest and get them to move on to other pages of your site.

Services Page

You can take a couple approaches with your services page—or pages. If all your services are closely related, such as copy editing various genres of fiction, then it makes sense to explain your services on one page. If you provide a wider array of offerings, such as editing, writing, and indexing, then consider creating a main services page that briefly describes all your services and that links to additional pages, each one devoted to explaining one of your services in depth. You might also want to use multiple services pages if you specialize in multiple industries. For example, you could have a page about editing services you offer for tech companies, and another page could explain your editing services for academic presses. By having multiple pages, you can tailor your wording to better speak to the realities and needs of a specific target market.

Whether you create one or multiple pages, ensure that somewhere you provide the details of what you do. By getting specific, you'll help calm visitors' fears about whether you have the knowledge and skills needed to do high-quality work. You'll also answer questions visitors might have, meaning you won't be spending as much time answering the questions via email and on the phone.

What specific information should you provide? Perhaps most important is to describe what a certain type of editing includes. Potential clients won't likely know exactly what substantive editing, copy editing, proofreading, or any other type of editing entails. (More than once, clients have told me they wanted something proofread when they really wanted a heavy copy edit.) So, if you say that you offer substantive editing, provide a bulleted list of all tasks you'll complete during the editing process. You might also want to explain how you'll go about editing a document (e.g., using Word's Track Changes and Comment features) and your general process for interacting with clients during the editing process (e.g., whether you'll interact with them regularly or will mainly wait until you've finished editing the project). And make sure to emphasize how your services will help visitors achieve their publishing-related goals.

Bio Page

Your bio/about-you page should include professional information as well as some personal information. Providing the professional information will help establish your credibility, and your personal information will help you appear more relatable, approachable, and trustworthy.

As for the professional information, include relevant education and professional training, internships and in-house jobs, and freelance projects you've worked on (whether in a volunteer or paid capacity). Also mention any awards or professional recognition you've received—after all, your bio page isn't a place to be humble. Particularly when writing about your professional background, keep in mind that site visitors will be reading the information to learn how you can help them and whether you can meet their needs. So, your bio page is a marketing tool, but avoid sounding promotional. Focus on making your writing informative, engaging, and genuine.

In terms of personal information to share, you have a lot of options. You could mention where you grew up, what your hobbies are, and what your favorite books are. Also consider sharing the story of how you got into editing and what aspects of editing you're most passionate about. The overall goal of sharing personal information is to help you appear friendly, to give a hint of your personality, and to help potential clients feel like they know you a little bit. The personal information in your bio can provide assurance to potential clients that you're trustworthy and that they'll enjoy working with you.

Your bio page should also include a professional-quality headshot. Yes, you really do need to post one, even if you're camera shy, as I am. A nice headshot will make your page look more professional and will also help visitors feel more connected with you. You'll come

"When I started my first writing and editing business in July 2008, I made my own little static website. . . . My picture was on the website, and I often heard from prospects that I was 'almost, but not quite' what/who they were looking for. Well! I knew what *that* meant. After a couple of months, I was almost ready to take my picture off my website . . . when first, I got a client from the Middle East who was studying at university in the UK and was so happy to find me. He called me his 'African sister'! Then, I got white clients who just didn't care about anything except that I could do what they needed done. In less than a year, I had clients from all over the world. . . . Over the years, I know I have probably 'lost' some prospects because of who I am, but I have gained so many more."

—*Pam Hilliard Owen, freelance editor*

across as more credible and as not trying to hide anything.[2] In selecting a headshot, keep the following pointers in mind:

- Limit the photograph to a headshot (not a full-body shot). Your face should be large enough for site visitors to see clearly.
- Don't use a photo that you obviously cropped other people out of. (Yes, unfortunately, I've seen people do that.)
- Avoid using a photo with a busy or distracting background.
- Dress professionally. You don't need to be in a business suit if your ideal clients don't dress that formally, but you do need to present yourself as a business owner, not someone who edits as a hobby and doesn't take work seriously.
- Make sure that you're facing forward, that you're smiling, and that there aren't any deep shadows covering parts of your face.

Some freelancers might be wary of including a headshot, fearing they'll be discriminated against because of their ethnicity, gender,

---

2. Chad Edwards et al., "Social Presence on LinkedIn: Perceived Credibility and Interpersonal Attractiveness Based on User Profile Picture," *Online Journal of Communication and Technologies* 5, no. 4 (2015): 102–115.

age, or other factors. However, the prevailing opinion among freelance editors is that the benefits of a headshot outweigh the risk of bias. Some editors have even found that they've gotten business exactly because they're members of a racial minority or another group prone to experiencing discrimination. Though each person's experience will vary, it seems that having a headshot really is the way to go.

Contact Page

Your contact page can be short and simple. If you want to include a contact form, you're in luck: many site-design templates have a built-in contact form, and if your template doesn't, it's typically easy to find a contact-form widget. Even if you do use a form, I strongly encourage you to also provide your email in a prominent spot on the page. Some people (including me) don't like using contact forms because there's no record of the message they sent. That's particularly a problem if the contact form isn't working and you don't receive a response. Directly emailing a person seems a surer guarantee that he or she will receive the message, and providing an email address is a bit more friendly than a contact form is. (I think that a contact form places a barrier between the potential client and the editor.) For these reasons, the majority of people may prefer connecting with businesses via an email rather than a contact form.[3] Maybe you're afraid that including your email address will invite spam emails; unfortunately, contact forms get a good deal of spam as well. If you add your email address to your contact page and do see an uptick in spam emails, try replacing the @ sign with *at* and adding a space on each

---

3. Birgitta Rún Sveinbjörnsdóttir, "Are People Still Using Contact Forms? A UX Research Case Study," UX Collective, December 13, 2018, https://uxdesign.cc/your-users-do-not-trust-contact-forms-but-what-do-they-use-instead-a89bee668e48.

side (e.g., "jane at janegrammaredits.com"). To reduce your chances of receiving spam through a contact form, try adding a captcha plug-in to your form.

In addition to providing your email address, you might want to provide a phone number. That being said, you certainly aren't obligated to share your number, and you may not want just anyone to have it. It's reasonable to share your phone number only after a potential client has contacted you via email and has requested to speak with you on the phone. If you're leery of sharing your number, you could set up one through Google Voice.[4] Any calls made to your Google Voice number will forward to your real phone number, and your real number will remain confidential. You can stop the forwarding at any time.

Your contact page should also include links to your profiles on social media platforms. At a minimum, link to your LinkedIn profile. Also consider linking to any business pages you have on Facebook, Twitter, and other sites or to your personal pages on those sites if you use your personal profiles mainly for business.

Testimonials Page

Though you can get by without a testimonials page, having one is a good idea. The testimonials can give potential clients greater confidence that they'll have a good experience working with you. So, think about creating a testimonials page after you have several projects under your belt. A great time to ask for a testimonial is after you've completed a project and a client has expressed appreciation for your work. If the client praised you in an email, ask for permission to include the praise on your testimonials page. Otherwise, ask the client

---

4. Currently, Google Voice is available only for residents of the United States. Most calls made to numbers in the United States and Canada are free.

if he or she would be willing to write a brief testimonial. Most will be happy to do so. You could suggest characteristics to mention, such as the quality of your editing, your promptness in responding to emails, your communication skills, and your ability to meet deadlines. If you know that a client is especially busy and you have a strong relationship with the client, you could even draft a testimonial and ask him or her to approve it or make any revisions desired. You can also use recommendations that people have posted on your LinkedIn profile.

Once you have five testimonials, you have enough to publish your testimonials page. In addition to listing each testimonial, at a minimum provide the client's name. You'll add credibility if you include a descriptive phrase after the person's name (e.g., "author of *XYZ Book*"). You could also link to the client's LinkedIn profile or website. Some sources recommend also including a photo of the client. While it's true that photos can add credibility and are visually appealing, I personally wouldn't want my photo next to a recommendation I've given someone, so I'm not about to ask clients for permission to use their photos. Of course, if you mainly work with companies, then asking to use the company's logo is a good idea.

Until you create a testimonials page, you could include a couple testimonials on your services page. Even after you have enough blurbs for a testimonials page, you might want to keep some of them on the other page. Doing so can increase the perceived credibility of the content on your services page, perhaps providing the final encouragement someone needs before deciding to contact you.

Work Samples Page

Particularly if you offer services such as writing and design, it's a good idea to post some samples of your work. You'll be demonstrating that you indeed possess the skills you say you have. It's more tricky to post editing samples since your clients may not want you displaying their unpolished work. It doesn't hurt to ask clients, especially independent authors, for permission to post one-page excerpts of documents you've edited, but don't be surprised if your request is turned down.

If clients don't give you the green light, what are your options? You could ask a friend or family member to let you edit and then post one page of something he or she has written. Or you could dig up a paper you wrote during school (and before you learned most editing principles) and then edit and post that. You could also find content in the public domain to edit and post (for a large number of options, try www.gutenberg.org). If you don't like any of those options, you could indicate that you'll provide a free sample edit for potential clients, but I don't recommend that strategy since you're essentially giving away work for free without any guarantee that you'll get the individual's business. Alternatively, post writing samples and state that your editing skills are evident in your clean writing. Or include links to publications you've edited, and encourage viewers to check out the content.

If you do post samples, how many should you post? I recommend including at least three. If you cater to different target markets (e.g., murder mystery authors and faculty members writing journal articles), then post a couple samples relevant to each market. The same goes if you offer multiple types of services. If you provide different levels of editing, then post a couple samples of each type.

Promotional Piece Page

If you decide to create a promotional piece, then highlight it on its own webpage. That way, you can include the page's URL on business cards, in your email signature, on social media platforms, and anywhere else you want. You can display your promotional piece directly on the page, or you can offer it as a downloadable PDF. With either

---

Website Checklist

- Purchase a domain name.
- Choose a website platform.
- Choose a website design, and then customize it to your business and personality.
- Create a home page, services page, bio page, contact page, testimonials page, and work samples page.
- If desired, create a page for your promotional piece.
- If desired, create a blog.
- Include a call to action on each page. For example, the home page could encourage visitors to click on the link to the services page.
- Focus on explaining how you can meet the viewer's needs.
- Use search engine optimization (SEO) keywords.

---

option, add a plug-in or app to the page so that people must provide their contact information before being able to access the promotional piece. You can then use the contact information to reach out to the individuals as part of your strategy to turn potential clients into paying customers.

The Debate about Blogging

If you've wondered if you need a blog on your website, you're not alone. With a quick Google search, you'll find numerous articles arguing that a blog is an essential aspect of marketing in today's world. A blog certainly can be a way to draw more traffic to your website and establish credibility and trust, potentially leading to more clients and projects.[5] But blogging is also time-consuming: you should be post-

---

5. Ji Young Kim et al., "Use of Affect in Blog Communication: Trust, Credibility, and Authenticity," *Public Relations Review* 41, no. 4 (2015): 504–507.

ing new content at least every other week. Plus, blogging is a long-term marketing strategy; it probably won't lead to a lot of new work for months (or even years—if ever). Many other marketing strategies are more effective in landing new projects, so I don't recommend blogging unless you really enjoy the process of creating content and you've found at least some evidence that your target clientele reads blog posts on topics you'd be writing about.

If you do decide to blog, keep some things in mind. To be an effective marketing tool, your blog posts should be directed to potential clients, not to your colleagues. Focus your posts on addressing problems and questions that members of your target market experience. For instance, if your niche is YA fiction, cover topics such as how to resolve issues with character development, point of view, and setting. After you've spent some time working in your niche, you'll know some of the main problems your potential clients experience. For additional ideas, join online discussion groups frequented by members of your target market and make a list of the questions being asked. Some of your posts can also address questions that potential clients have sent you about editing in general and about your editing process in particular.

If you decide to venture into blogging territory, consider writing a few posts at a time so that you get into blog-writing mode and can be more efficient. Once you've polished and proofread them (an essential step, even for editors), schedule when you want each post to go live on your site. It's a good idea to publish on a consistent schedule, such as every Tuesday at noon or every other Friday at 9:00 a.m. That way, readers will know when to expect the posts to be published and will look forward to seeing them. In addition to writing posts for your own site, consider writing guest posts for other blogs. Identify ones that are of interest to your target clients, and examine the blogs to determine whether they include guest posts. If they do, contact the blog owners or managers and pitch blog post topics. Make sure to

Tips for Blogging

- Focus your posts on content that will be helpful for your target market.
- Write a few posts at a time.
- Schedule your posts to publish at regular intervals.
- Conduct research and use web analytics to determine the best day of the week and time of the day to publish posts in order to reach your target audience and achieve your goals for the posts.
- Announce your posts via email and social media.
- Invite individuals to write guest posts, and volunteer to write guest posts for other blogs.

follow the blogs' norms, such as regarding word count and tone. You could also invite guests to write posts for your blog.

After you've published a post, make sure to announce it through various media; don't rely on people to discover the posts without your help. Announce the post on your social media pages (use a program such as Hootsuite to automate the process of announcing posts on multiple social media platforms). Also make sure your blog has a subscribe option so that people can receive a notification each time you publish a post. And consider emailing past and potential clients the links to specific posts that will be of particular interest to these individuals. You can also include a few links in cold emails; again, make sure to select the blog posts that are most relevant to whomever you're emailing.

Key Takeaways

- Having a business website is essential. It serves as an electronic business card and a way to establish your credibility.

- Website-building platforms make it easy to create a website even if you're a novice when it comes to web design.
- For a fee, you can access advanced website design tools and can customize your website URL.
- At a minimum, your website should include a home page, a services page, a bio page, and a contact page. You might also want to include a testimonials page, a work samples page, and a promotional piece page.
- Your website can benefit from having a blog, but blog only if you're going to enjoy it. Blogging can be time-consuming, and it won't likely be an effective marketing tool if you don't post regularly.

7   *Maximizing the Benefits of LinkedIn*

Of all the social media platforms, LinkedIn can be the most powerful for advertising your business and gaining new clients. Why? Because more than 645 million people use LinkedIn[1] and the focus is on business—people are there to further their careers and to look for individuals who can add value to their companies. Of course, merely having a profile isn't enough. You need to approach your profile as a marketing tool, using wording that will help your profile turn up in search results and wow viewers. Simply because I have optimized my profile with targeted wording and have participated in a few discussion threads, I have been contacted by multiple individuals and have received thousands of dollars of work. And I'm definitely not the only freelancer who's benefited from having a LinkedIn profile.

It's important to fill out all areas of your profile, but the most important parts are your headshot, headline, and "About" section, so we'll discuss them first. Though the other components aren't as critical, you should still complete them because doing so will improve your ranking in search results and can add credibility. And that's why

---

1. LinkedIn, "Statistics," 2019, https://news.linkedin.com/about-us#statistics.

we'll also cover those components in this chapter. Then we'll walk through the process of connecting with people and searching for freelance work via LinkedIn.

Components of a LinkedIn Profile

Headshot

Including a headshot is essential. According to LinkedIn, profiles with a headshot are fourteen times more likely to be viewed than are profiles without a headshot.[2] Forgoing a headshot suggests you haven't completed your profile (and, by extension, aren't that serious about receiving work) or that you have something to hide. So, set aside any hesitations, and upload a photo. Make sure that the photo you upload is professional looking; LinkedIn isn't the place to post selfies. When choosing a headshot, keep in mind the pointers I provided in the "Bio Page" section in chapter 6.

In addition to including your headshot, you can customize the banner image behind your headshot. Changing the banner image can make your profile stand out from others, though you won't necessarily receive more work as a result. If you do decide to customize the image, select one that coordinates well with your headshot. Also consider selecting an image that's related to your services or niche. Alternatively, you could create an image by starting with a plain background (e.g., a single color) and then adding your business logo if you have one, your tagline, and your contact information.

---

2. Lydia Abbot, "10 Tips for Picking the Right LinkedIn Profile Picture," *LinkedIn Talent Blog*, August 5, 2019, https://business.linkedin.com/talent-solutions/blog/2014/12/5-tips-for-picking-the-right-linkedin-profile-picture.

Headline

Your headline is just as important as your headshot because your headline tells people at a glance what you do and how you provide value to clients. Your headline can be up to 120 characters, including spaces. Use the space well by writing an engaging description that entices viewers to learn more about you through reading your "About" section. Also make sure to use relevant keywords in your headline, since they'll help you turn up in search results on LinkedIn. For that reason, your headline isn't a place to be creative in describing what you do. People aren't likely to search for the term *grammar guru*. Rather, they'll use a search term such as *freelance editor*. So, use the exact terms your potential clients will most likely enter into the search bar. Be specific; if you focus on technical editing, then use the term *freelance technical editor* in your headline.

After you've specified your role, indicate the value you can provide to clients. For example, your headline might be "Experienced Freelance Technical Editor Helping Companies Communicate Clearly." I'm guessing you'll agree that this headline is more compelling than the headlines most freelance editors use, which are short and lack a value statement (just a few examples include "Editor," "Freelance Copy Editor," and "Editor and Writer"). If you were looking for a freelancer, I bet you'd want to learn more about the ones whose headlines identify how you could benefit from working with those freelancers. Make sure your headline does just that.

"About" Section

Because you grabbed viewers' attention with your headline, they'll be more likely to read your "About" section. This section should expand on the ideas you presented in your headline. Describe your services, present your skills and qualifications, and explain how you help clients overcome their challenges and achieve their goals. By default, LinkedIn shows only the first few lines of the "About" section (you have to click "see more" for the rest to appear), so those lines should have the most punch. They need to be compelling so that viewers will want to see the rest of the section. These lines of text also need to sufficiently summarize your services and value so that if viewers don't expand the section, they'll still understand why they should consider contacting you. A great option is to include your USP (or a modified version of it) in the first three lines.

Some people keep their "About" section quite short—just a few sentences in a single paragraph. But that's a wasted opportunity. A much better approach is to include several paragraphs of content. One reason is that you'll have numerous opportunities to include keywords that your target clients are likely to enter in the search bar and are looking for in freelancers' profiles. With a higher percentage of relevant keywords in your "About" section, you'll appear higher up in the search results. You'll also present yourself as someone who knows what potential clients are looking for and as someone who can meet their needs.

How exactly do you determine which keywords to include? Many of them are straightforward because they're directly related to who you are and what you do—for instance, *editor, copy edit*, and *proofread*. Others are related to soft skills; these terms include *project management, attention to detail*, and *self-motivated*. Don't forget to include niche-specific terms, going as detailed as, say, *Regency romance novels, construction management articles*, and *horticulture books*. After you've brainstormed a list of terms, you can get more ideas by looking at other editors' profiles (especially editors who work in the same niche as you) and by looking at job descriptions for freelance and full-time editors at the types of companies you want to have as clients.

As you write your "About" section, keep your focus on how you provide benefit—that's what potential clients really care about. Make sure to support your statements with evidence, such as by describing your relevant education or work experience. This evidence will make you appear more credible.

The end of this section should include a call to action. What do you want viewers to do? Send you InMail? Visit your website? Call you? Make that action clear, and connect it with one final statement about why viewers should want to take that action. For example, you might write: "If you want to ensure your manuscript is polished before sending it to a literary agent, contact me at jane@janegrammaredits.com."

Here are some additional tips:

- Write in the first person.
- Make your tone conversational but professional. Use contractions, but avoid slang.
- Keep paragraphs short (approximately three sentences).
- When possible, use vertical lists to make content easy to scan. Since LinkedIn doesn't have a built-in list format, use an asterisk or paste in a bullet symbol at the start of each list item.

"Featured" Section

The "Featured" section enables you to highlight content you've published on LinkedIn, to upload content (e.g., your promotional piece), and to link to sites displaying or promoting your work. Not everyone includes content in this section, but why not take advantage of this additional chance to impress people viewing your profile?

"Experience" Section

Don't neglect the "Experience" section—it's an additional place to establish your credibility and qualifications. Though this section may

Sample LinkedIn Headline and "About" Section

Jane Grammar

HEADLINE

Skilled Freelance Editor Helping YA Fiction Authors Get Published

ABOUT

For five years, I've worked directly with YA fiction authors to help them refine their manuscripts for publication, whether through traditional publishing or self-publishing. I'm skilled at considering the big picture as well as the details, meaning that I can assist authors at every stage of the editing process, from developmental editing to proofreading. For example, with my knowledge of the principles involved in great fiction writing (story structure, character development, conflict, etc.), I've been able to help authors ensure that their stories are engaging to readers. Through applying my copy editing skills, I can ensure that authors' books are free of typos that might distract readers.

In addition to providing high-quality work, I have a reputation for providing impeccable customer service. I pay attention to each client's unique needs and publishing goals and then partner with the client to make these goals a reality. Because of my dedication to helping authors succeed, they return to me after writing additional novels and also refer other authors to me.

I truly enjoy helping authors refine their work so that it's polished for publication. If you're ready to take that step or want more details on what it will involve, feel free to connect with and message me. I'm happy to answer questions and provide guidance to help you in the editing and publishing process. My ultimate goal is to help you achieve the best results possible.

seem time-consuming to complete, it's really not that bad if you have an updated résumé. Simply copy your job-experience section from your résumé, and paste the content into your LinkedIn profile. Make sure to describe each position; use bulleted lists so that the content is easy to scan. It's okay to list nonediting jobs; just highlight the skills and accomplishments that are relevant to your editing services (e.g., customer service and time management). If you've completed just a few freelance projects, list them separately. If you've completed five or more and also have other types of work experience, consider grouping your freelance projects under one job title, such as "Freelance Editor." Under that title, list the freelance projects (or categories of projects).

"Education" Section

In the "Education" section, list any higher education you've completed, as well as any certificates related to the services you offer. Get even more specific by listing courses in your degree or certificate programs that are directly related to your services; you'll be validating that you have the skills you say you have.

"Skills and Endorsements" Section

The "Skills and Endorsements" section is another opportunity to highlight your skills. People who fill out this section "receive an average of 13 times more profile views than those who don't,"[3] at least in part because the skills serve as keywords that are used to determine whether and how high up your profile will appear in search results.

---

3. Mathieu Bastian, "Your Skills Are Your Competitive Edge on LinkedIn," *LinkedIn Official Blog*, October 16, 2014, https://blog.linkedin.com/2014/10/16/your-skills-are-your-competitive-edge-on-linkedin.

So, don't skimp on the number of skills you list (you can select up to fifty of the more than forty-five thousand skills in LinkedIn's database). After you've added your skills, make sure they're listed in the order of importance because only the top three are shown on your profile unless a viewer clicks on "show more." Plus, these three skills are the ones that LinkedIn will typically prompt people to endorse you for when they view your profile.

Don't stress that it'll take a while to rack up endorsements of your skills. Though endorsements serve as social proof, they've also received a good amount of criticism because people can endorse you for a skill even if they don't know whether you actually have it. As a result, many people don't put much stock in endorsements. That being said, if fifty or more people have endorsed you for a skill, then it's reasonable for viewers to assume you do in fact have it.

To get endorsements, look no further than your clients. You can ask them after you've received positive feedback from them or when they offer to refer you to other people. Another strategy is to visit the profiles of people you're connected with and then endorse them for skills you know they have. When those people see you've endorsed them, they'll likely return the favor by endorsing you. Since endorsements aren't that important, don't spend too much time endorsing people in hopes of reciprocation. Just set aside ten to fifteen minutes one day per month to review a few people's profiles and endorse them for skills. You'll slowly see an increase in the number of endorsements you receive.

"Recommendations" Section

Also keep the "Recommendations" section in mind. You don't need a lot of recommendations—even just a few can provide enough support. (Think along the lines of recommendations required for full-time jobs—most companies require only two or three letters of recommendation.) As with endorsements, a good time to ask for recommendations is after you've completed a project and received praise or expressions of appreciation from a client. When you ask people for recommendations, you can help them out by suggesting a few qualities and skills to include in the write-ups. Of course, make sure to vary these suggestions so that different recommendations highlight different qualities; combined, the recommendations will present a fuller picture of your characteristics and the value you offer (particularly in terms of how you help clients achieve their goals).

"Accomplishments" Section

The "Accomplishments" section provides an additional opportunity to wow viewers with your accomplishments and gives you another chance to use keywords that can improve your ranking in search results. You can list publications you've edited or otherwise contributed to, awards you've received, foreign languages you speak, and organizations you belong to, among other items of interest.

"Interests" Section

The "Interests" section shows any companies and schools you're following and any LinkedIn groups you're a member of. You might be wondering what the purpose of this section is. I see two potential uses. First, it's a way for you to indicate that you walk the talk. For example, if you say that you're a skilled technical editor, you would presumably be interested in following some tech companies and would join some groups for people in the tech industry. If you follow only fiction publishers and are a member of sci-fi writer and editor groups but no tech groups, then viewers might doubt that you're serious about tech editing. Conversely, if you reach out to a tech company about your freelance services and your contact sees that you're following the company on LinkedIn, you might win some brownie points.

The second potential use of the "Interests" section involves looking at this section in other people's profiles. See what organizations and groups are listed in the profiles of people you want to establish relationships with. You could use a commonality as a way to introduce yourself ("Hey, So-and-So, I see that we both follow XYZ Organization . . ."). Also consider joining some of the groups that these individuals are in. Doing so could provide you with the opportunity to engage in forum discussions with these people, make connections with other members of the groups, learn what potential clients are struggling with and how you can help, and establish your expertise by providing helpful comments in discussion threads.

URL

Make sure to customize the URL for your profile. When you create your profile, LinkedIn will generate a URL for you—it will start with "linkedin.com/in/" and will be followed by your name and an alphanumeric code. To change the URL, click on "Edit Public Profile & URL" on the right side of the page. Tweak the URL to include only your name after "linkedin.com/in/." If that URL is already in use, then get a little creative, such as by adding a hyphen or underscore between your first and last name. You could also add a word such as *editor*.

How to Connect and Network with People on LinkedIn

Connecting with people on LinkedIn is important, not only because the number of connections you have affects your credibility but also because the more connections you have, the more likely you are to meet people who'll become your clients or refer people to you. Connect with people you've met in person and online, but don't stop there. It's okay to connect with people you haven't met. When you send a connection request, include a message explaining why you'd like to connect with the person—maybe because you have common professional interests or because you're interested in learning more about the organization the person works for. Also consider connecting with the people who've viewed your profile or liked or commented on your posts but who aren't yet connected with you.

Most people will accept your connection request if your message seems reasonable and your profile indicates that your professional interests relate in some way to those of the people you want to connect with. The key is to not come across as spammy and to not ask for projects right away. Think of it this way: If a stranger contacts you and immediately asks to be hired to revamp your website, refinance your home mortgage, or provide some other service or product, are you likely to respond with "Sign me up!" right on the spot? Probably not. Similarly, you probably won't have good results if you search LinkedIn for people with *author* in their headline and then send a connection request with a message stating that you'd like to offer your editing services. (And it's not any better if you send that message right after a person accepts your connection request.) Instead, spend time getting to know the person, learning what he or she might need help with, and establishing trust. You'll be showing that you're sincerely interested in the person and not just trying to make money off of him or her. When the individual is ready for the services you offer, you'll likely get the job.

In addition to sending connection requests, be open to accepting the ones you receive. I rarely turn down a connection request, even if the person doesn't seem to have anything in common with me. My perspective is that at some time in the future, the person might need an editor or might know someone who does. Accepting the connection request will increase the likelihood that I'll receive project inquiries. For this reason and because the focus of LinkedIn is on professional networking, not on people's personal lives, I see little harm in accept-

"Targeted networking and staying focused on one's market(s) are what it's all about. I have at least one LinkedIn window open all day, where I monitor the feed as well as responses to my own posts and comments.... Every comment I make—anywhere on the platform—means another exposure (my headshot plus the front-loaded portion of my tagline). Just like inescapable soda advertising, it all serves to build my brand and credibility as someone having a degree of authority. Unknown prospects get to know me over time, making a subliminal assessment as to whether they'd like to engage me for their assignments. More than one client has come to me by way of my inbound marketing on LinkedIn."

—Chris Morton, freelance editor

ing connection requests. After all, the majority of professional opportunities come through weak connections—people you don't regularly interact with.[4] So, connecting with people you aren't familiar with initially could lead to lucrative freelance opportunities. If it turns out that you don't want to be connected with someone, you can simply remove the connection. (Of the twelve hundred or so people I'm connected with, I've only needed to do that once, when it turned out that the person in question apparently thought LinkedIn was a dating site.)

After connecting with people, stay in touch with them by congratulating them on new jobs and anniversaries. (LinkedIn will conveniently send you notifications about these milestones.) Every week or so, skim your news feed to see what articles and other resources your connections have posted. If you find a resource to be helpful, comment on the post and share it with others. Also publish posts of your own: you can share brief updates about your professional activities, as well as articles, images, or videos that you've created. You can also post links to content you've found on the internet. When people comment on your posts, make sure to respond.

---

4. Laura K. Gee et al., "The Paradox of Weak Ties in 55 Countries," *Journal of Economic Behavior and Organization* 133 (2017): 362–372.

Another way to network on LinkedIn is through joining and participating in groups. You'll likely benefit from joining groups for editors, particularly in your niche area. Through participating in discussions, you'll strengthen your knowledge and skills and might also learn about freelance projects that are up for grabs. If you've established yourself as a knowledgeable editor by providing insightful comments in group discussions, group members might even reach out to you about freelance opportunities these members are unable to work on. In addition to editing groups, join groups that your potential clients are members of. If you can impress members by providing valuable input, they just might contact you when they or their companies need a freelance editor. Also proactively reach out to members you'd like to work with; if you've established your credibility and congeniality through your participation in group discussions, members will likely respond to private messages you send.

Another very easy strategy is to join the alumni group for your alma mater. Search for a group post that asks members to introduce themselves and what they do for work. If you can't find such a discussion, start one yourself. Either way, add a comment that explains in a sentence or two the services you offer and how you provide value to clients. Then invite people to message you if they'd like to learn more about how you can help them achieve their goals. Several years ago, I spent two minutes writing such a comment and afterward was offered an ongoing freelance gig that netted me tens of thousands of dollars—now, that's an awesome ROI!

How to Search for Jobs on LinkedIn

Networking on LinkedIn is a long-term strategy for getting freelance work. A more direct and quicker strategy is to search for and receive notifications about freelance jobs on LinkedIn. You can do that through using LinkedIn's search function.

How to Network on LinkedIn

- Send connection requests, including to people you've met in person and in online forums, people who've viewed your profile, and people you want to meet because they have connections at organizations you'd like to freelance for.
- Accept connection requests, even from individuals who aren't in publishing or other target markets.
- Comment on people's posts.
- Post content, and respond to people who comment on your posts.
- Join and participate in LinkedIn groups.
- Send private messages to group members you'd like to network with on an individual level.

First, use LinkedIn's search tool. Enter a search term, such as *free-lance editor*;[5] then, on the results page, click on "Content" near the top of the page. Now you'll see posts that people have made that mention your search term. The results won't be limited to posts from people looking for an editor, but you should see some posts along those lines. You have a better chance of landing one of these gigs because fewer people will see these posts than will see the postings listed in the "Jobs" category (which we'll discuss next). The final step is to sort the postings by "Latest" (the default is "Relevance"). Scroll through the results, and take note of posts about freelance projects that you'd be a good fit for. Sometimes the post will contain a URL to a page with more information or the email address of the person to contact. Sometimes a post will merely indicate that you should contact the poster. If that's the case, send a connection request if you aren't already connected. Next, send a message introducing

---

5. To avoid getting results that mention video editors, after typing your search term, type "NOT video editor."

yourself, noting that you saw the post, and explaining why you're a good fit for the project. Make sure to emphasize the value you'll provide and how you'll help the person achieve the underlying objectives for the project. Also consider asking to set up a time to discuss the project on the phone. Make sure to convey confidence in your skills and enthusiasm about the project.

Repeat the search process with several different search terms, since not everyone will use the same words in their posts and some people may not know what the correct search term is (e.g., *proofreader* vs. *copy editor*).

After you've checked out the results in the "Content" section, search the "Jobs" section of LinkedIn. You'll see a lot more results and typically they'll be for ongoing contract work, but you'll be competing against many more sets of editorial eyes. To narrow your search, use the filters, such as to sort the posts by most recent and to include only contract positions. One of the great things about LinkedIn's job postings is that they contain more details and features than do postings on a lot of other job sites. For example, a posting on LinkedIn will indicate how many people have applied for the position via this site, the approximate number of employees in the organization, and whether any of your LinkedIn contacts have connections with the organization—if your contacts do, definitely ask them whether they can facilitate an introduction with the hiring manager. Receiving a personal introduction could significantly increase your chances of being offered the project, especially if a lot of people have already applied. Also consider turning on the job-alert feature so that you'll receive emails when a new position that meets your search criteria is posted.

When you apply for a contract position, you'll likely need to follow the standard protocol of submitting a résumé and cover letter. Make sure that they're both tailored to the position and that your cover letter emphasizes how your services will help the organization achieve its goals (hopefully you're seeing a pattern here—no matter the format you pitch your services in, always talk in terms of how you'll assist the client in accomplishing the project's aims).

Key Takeaways

- LinkedIn is perhaps the most effective social media platform for obtaining freelance business—if you've completed your profile and focused it on demonstrating how you can help clients.
- The most important components of your profile are your headshot, your headline, and your "About" section. Focus on presenting yourself as a professional who's approachable.
- Don't be afraid to connect with people you want as clients or who might help you make connections with people you want as clients.
- Be open to accepting connection requests from people you don't know; they just might send business your way.
- Participate in group discussions to help other members, to establish your credibility, and to establish relationships with potential clients.
- Search for freelance projects and contract work through using LinkedIn's search tool.

8   *Winning at the Pricing Game*

I admit it: the pricing aspect of being a freelancer can be tricky. And uncomfortable. What if the client thinks your pricing is too high? What if you underestimate the time you'll need to spend on a project and consequently underestimate the cost? How do you even know what's reasonable to charge? Though you might not ever come to love the pricing component of freelancing, this chapter will help you feel more confident in determining how much to charge, what pricing method to use, and how to overcome price objections, along with other pricing-related topics. You'll learn how to win at the pricing game rather than feeling like you're always on the losing side.

Figuring Out How Much to Charge

The first step in the pricing process is to figure out how much you need to earn per hour to cover your monthly living costs as well as to put money in savings for occasional expenses (e.g., yearly car registration renewal), tax payments, emergencies, and retirement. To make that calculation, you need to know what your expenses are. If you haven't already started using a monthly budget and tracking your expenses, now's the time to begin. To develop a good understanding of what your typical monthly expenses are, you'll need to document what you spend for several months. (Ideally, you'll want to consider how expenses vary by season. For example, is your electricity bill a lot higher in December than in May? If so, make sure to take this range into account.) Make sure to record everything: utilities, food, gas, entertainment, gifts, and so forth. Average the totals of several months to get an idea of what your typical monthly outgo is. Then multiply that number by twelve to determine what your monthly expenses will likely be for the year.

Next, think of costs that come up only a few times a year, such as subscription renewals, business expenses, vacations, and holiday gifts. Total these costs, and then add the number to your estimate of your yearly expenses. After that, you'll need to calculate how much to save for taxes, general and emergency savings, and retirement each year (see chapters 12 and 13). Add that amount to the yearly expenses you already calculated. You'll now know the minimum you need to earn during the year to cover your costs. Write down that number; we'll be coming back to it soon.

Now, determine how many hours you'll spend on billable work each week. Be realistic—if you plan to work forty hours a week but will be spending five of it on marketing, then you'll only be getting paid for thirty-five hours of work. Then factor in days you don't plan to work, such as holidays, sick days (for you and any dependents), and vacation time. Again, be realistic; even though you might think you'll be okay working on a holiday or two, when those days come, you likely won't feel much motivation. And if you get sick, you won't want to feel extra stress because you haven't given yourself any sick days. Let's say you decide you want six vacation days, five sick days, and nine holidays, for a total of twenty days—in other words, four weeks of work. In that case, you'll be working forty-eight weeks a year. Now, multiply the number of weeks by the number of hours you plan to work per week to determine how many billable hours you'll be working annually.

After completing these calculations, you're ready to calculate the minimum hourly rate you need to charge. Simply divide the amount you need to earn during the year by your number of billable hours per year. The result will be the amount you need to earn per hour.

Okay, I realize we've just breezed through a lot of information, so let's consider how we'd apply it to editor Jane Grammar. (The dollar amounts for Jane might be a lot higher or lower than for you, depending on your location and other circumstances, so focus more on the overall concept.) Jane's looked at her expenses for the last six months, and her average monthly outgo is $4,000. She's also averaged her less frequent expenses; spread out over twelve months, these costs total $300 per month. And she wants to save $2,000 a month (including for tax payments). To break even, she needs to earn $6,300 per month. Multiplying that number by twelve, she needs to earn $75,600 during the year to cover all her expenses.

Next, Jane decides that she's going to work thirty-five billable hours per week, and she's planning to work the equivalent of forty-eight weeks during the year. So, she'll be working a total of 1,680 hours annually. Jane then figures out how much she needs to earn per hour by dividing her annual expenses ($75,600) by her total billable hours (1,680) to arrive at her minimum hourly rate of $45.

Of course, it's important to keep the following in mind: Especially when you're new to freelancing, you might not have enough work to fill up all the time you've allocated for billable work. So, you might actually need to earn more per hour than the rate you calculated using the steps above. Or, you might need to be prepared to work more than your ideal number of hours during weeks when you have more projects in your queue so that you reach your total number of billable hours per year. Further, your minimum hourly rate might be higher than you can reasonably ask for because of your level of editing skills, your years of experience, and your target market.

I'm not going to go into detail regarding what you might expect to earn per hour, since the number will vary widely because of factors I mentioned above (plus others). If you talk with other freelance editors, you'll discover that they earn vastly different amounts, from around $20 per hour to more than $100 per hour. For rough estimates of what freelance editors earn for different types of work, you can check out the rates chart that the Editorial Freelancers Association provides at www.the-efa.org/rates. However, keep in mind that the chart lists median rate ranges and doesn't identify different rates based on genre and industry. The chart does suggest different rates for different types of services (e.g., developmental editing vs. copy editing), but I personally don't like this approach because it suggests that your time is less valuable when providing some services than when providing other services. In my opinion, my time is my time no matter what type of work I'm providing, so I'm going to charge the same amount (or at least have a baseline I won't go below). Overall, my take is that the chart can give you a basic understanding of common rates, but they're not hard-and-fast numbers to stick to.

You'll have an easier time earning higher rates in some genres and industries than in others. For instance, book packagers and traditional publishers are well-known for paying freelancers low rates. In contrast, companies in the technical and medical industries typically pay freelancers more. Also, many self-publishing fiction authors have limited budgets to pay editors, whereas nonfiction authors writing on business topics often have more money to spend on editing. What's the main takeaway from all this information? No single source lists how much to charge for a specific type of editing in a specific genre or industry—there's just too much variability. You'll need to talk with other editors working on the type of project you're creating a quote for, use your Google-fu skills to look for information on what rates to charge for that type of project, and learn by trial and error (e.g., increase your rate for the next project and see whether the individual accepts that amount).

Now, what if you're not able to earn the minimum hourly rate you calculated above? If you're focusing on genres and editing services that typically are associated with lower rates, then switch your focus to higher-paying genres and services. You don't need to entirely give up your ideal projects, but you can decide that they won't be your bread and butter. In other cases, you'll just need to wait until you're more established and skilled as an editor. With more experience, you'll be able to justify higher rates.

As you're working on getting better-paying projects, in the short term you might need to put in more billable hours than you had initially planned when calculating your minimum hourly rate. Maybe you need to spend two more hours per week on project work, or maybe you need to reduce the number of vacation days you want to take. Alternatively, you can look for ways to reduce your costs. Instead of going to the movie theater once a month, rent a movie to watch at home. Look for coupons and sales before making purchases. Cancel subscriptions for things that you don't regularly use or don't really need. Additionally, it's likely that you'll decrease your costs simply by quitting a full-time job and working from home, since you won't be commuting to an office, won't need to purchase and clean business clothes, and probably won't be going out for lunch as often.

Don't get discouraged if at first you don't earn the income required to support the lifestyle you desire. Remember that it takes time to achieve goals. Then, focus on taking the steps needed to reach your financial target.

Choosing a Pricing Method

Another essential aspect of pricing is deciding whether to charge by the hour, by the word, or by the project. Each method has its advantages and disadvantages, but in general I recommend using a project fee. Let's look at each method in more depth, including when and why you might want to use a certain method.

Hourly Fee

The overall concept of an hourly fee is straightforward: you bill clients for the amount of time you spend working on a project (whether editing, communicating with the client, or creating an invoice for the work). Your hourly fee should be based on multiple factors: (1) what you've determined you need to earn per hour to cover your expenses, (2) your experience level and the value you provide, and (3) what clients are willing to pay.

When using an hourly fee, you won't need to tell a client beforehand what the exact cost of the project will be. But you will need to provide an estimate of the hours required, so the client has a basic idea of what the project will cost. After all, wouldn't you want an estimate before agreeing to pay a plumber, auto mechanic, or other service provider for something you need? (To estimate how long the project will take, follow the steps in the section titled "Developing a Project Fee.") Many editors who use an hourly fee will present the estimate as a range, telling the client that the project will take approximately eight to ten hours, for example. With this estimate and your hourly rate, the client will be able to calculate a price range for the project. If it turns out that you're able to complete the project in less than your estimate, then the client will be pleasantly surprised when you submit an invoice for a lower amount.

In theory, with an hourly fee you won't ever be paid less for a project than the hours you spend on it. (In contrast, if you use a word or project fee, you could underestimate the time required and therefore end up earning less per hour than you want.) But what if the time estimate you give a client turns out to be way too low? You certainly don't want to surprise the client by submitting an invoice for a much higher amount than you estimated before starting. Sometimes, an editor will eat most of the additional hours in order to avoid upsetting a client, especially if the editor simply made a mathematical error in estimating the hours required (rather than encountering a major issue in the manuscript that required a lot more time and attention). In other situations, it might be appropriate to ask the client whether he or she is okay with your spending more time—and therefore charging more money. The client may give you the green light, or you and the client may need to determine how you can work more quickly, such as by not changing most passive-voice constructions to active voice.

The hourly fee approach can be the most beneficial pricing method when a project is loosely defined, isn't limited to a certain number of pages, or will involve a lot of collaboration between you and the client. Under these circumstances, it can be difficult if not impossible to develop a realistic project or per-word fee. In such cases, you might be able to arrive at a very rough estimate of the time required. Or your client might understand that it's not practical and, as long as your hourly rate seems reasonable, might give you the go-ahead to spend whatever hours are required.

Except for these types of projects, using an hourly fee isn't ideal. The main reason is that you'll be inviting the client to judge whether you're worth the amount you're charging per hour. The client will likely compare your hourly rate to what he or she earns per hour, and your rate will probably be higher if your client isn't a freelancer and therefore receives subsidized health insurance, doesn't need to pay self-employment tax, and so on.

Let me give you an example of the price-per-hour hang-up: Years ago, as I talked with a potential client on the phone about his project, he asked what my standard hourly rate for editing was. I told him that I used project fees instead of charging by the hour and that I'd develop a project quote after briefly reviewing his manuscript. After he asked a few more times what my hourly rate was, I told him I usually charge around $XX per hour. In response, he said that my hourly rate was higher than he was expecting. I replied that I'd still be happy to give him a project quote and that if it was more than he had budgeted, I'd give him the contact information for some other editors who might be in his price range.

After developing a price quote, I talked with the potential client again. I emphasized why my experience and skills were a great fit for his project, and then I gave him the price quote. He responded that I could have charged him twice that much and he would have paid it because a mutual acquaintance had highly recommended me and because I had demonstrated I would be a valuable contributor to his project. But he still preferred an hourly fee structure, and I agreed to it because in this second conversation the scope of the project had expanded and become much fuzzier. I told him I'd charge my hourly fee of $XX, which is what I based my project fee on. At that point, he stalled. He just couldn't seem to get over the high hourly rate, even though he knew it was the basis of the project fee that he'd just said he'd pay the double of. He had a hard time moving past the emotional reaction and seeing the logic that if he was okay with my project fee, he should be okay with my hourly fee. Finally, after more discussion, he accepted my hourly rate. Moral of the story: When you use a project fee, clients won't be judging whether *you* should earn a certain amount of money per hour. Rather, the only consideration is whether your project fee is within the budget set aside for the project.

Project Fee

As I already mentioned, in most cases a project fee is a better choice than an hourly fee. When you use a project fee instead of an hourly fee, clients won't be judging whether they think you're worth your hourly fee. Instead, they only need to evaluate whether your project fee is within their budget. Along those lines, clients will know before the project starts how much they'll need to pay, and that knowledge can reduce anxiety. If you were to use an hourly fee system, you'd need to give an estimate of how much time you'd likely spend, so why not go a step further and simply use that estimate to come up with a project fee?

Another benefit of using a project-fee approach is that you won't be charging less for a project as you become more efficient. For instance, if you charge by the hour and over time increase the number of pages you can edit per hour, then you'll be earning less on a project than if you worked at a slower pace. Sure, you'll have time to take on more projects, but you'll be a slave to the ticking clock rather than reaping benefits from your increased efficiency. In contrast, if you charge by the project and become more efficient, then you're effectively increasing your hourly rate. With the additional time you've freed up, you can start on another project to bring in additional income or you can use the time for nonwork activities. (How about cracking open that book your friends have been raving about?)

The benefits of project-fee pricing mean that you have much greater earning potential than when using an hourly fee. You won't be penalized for working faster, and you won't be limited by how much clients think you're qualified to earn per hour. If you effectively communicate the value you'll be providing, then clients (particularly businesses) will be willing to pay much more than they would if you

"I prefer to charge by the word/project fee so that I don't have to track every second of working time. It allows me a lot more flexibility in my schedule so I can do bits of work while I wait for the microwave or am in a room full of distractions and not have to treat my time like it's 100 percent either/or. For me, schedules are constricting and make me less productive than if I can just casually pick a project up at various moments throughout my day. Especially when life is hectic and schedules are subject to change."
—*Anonymous freelance editor*

charged by the hour. Further, you can increase your rates without having to announce the change. You simply quote a higher project fee the next time around. Most clients likely won't even notice the increase, and the only real consideration for them will be whether your fee is within their budget.

Despite the benefits of project-fee pricing, many editors continue to use an hourly fee approach. Why? My guess is fear—fear that they will underestimate the time required to complete a project and will consequently earn less than if they'd charged per hour. I understand this fear, because on occasion I've made the mistake of underestimating. But on some other projects, I've overestimated the time required and thus earned more than my desired hourly rate. The underestimating and overestimating tend to balance each other out, so overall I'm still achieving my desired hourly rate—a rate I probably wouldn't be able to command if I were charging by the hour.

Of course, you'll want to get really good at accurately estimating the time required. A lot of editors are prone to underestimating the amount of time they'll spend on a project, perhaps for multiple reasons. For one, it can be difficult to identify all the problems in a manuscript when you're quickly reviewing it. The problems might not become apparent until after the client has signed the contract and you're a third of the way through the file. A good rule of thumb is to assume that every project is going to have some unexpected elements that'll slow down your progress. For that reason, always add extra time to your estimate. (See "Developing a Project Fee," later in this chapter, for more advice on arriving at an accurate estimate.)

What if an issue comes up that'll greatly increase the time you need to spend on a project? You can always try to renegotiate the project fee, explaining to the author why the project is more time-consuming than you'd expected it to be. The client might consent to a higher fee, or you might agree to scale back your tasks in the project. As a note, I wouldn't try to renegotiate the fee very often, or you might get a reputation for not being an experienced editor or for being dishonest by trying to lure in clients with prices that you intend to increase after the project starts.

A related reason editors might shy away from using a project-fee approach is the fear of scope creep—in other words, that the project will grow in one or more ways after you and the client have agreed on the price and signed the contract. Maybe the client decides that chapter 5 needs to be fleshed out more and sends you seven extra pages of content to edit. Or maybe the client starts calling you once a week to talk about the manuscript. Maybe the client asks you to supply the information that you pointed out is missing from reference-list entries. And maybe the client is doing all of the above—and more! Even one of those tasks could reduce your earnings to minimum wage.

What's an editor to do? Grin and bear it in the name of customer service? Definitely not. Rather, you make sure that your contract specifies everything that the project fee includes and stipulates that anything beyond the scope will be charged an additional fee (either an hourly fee or a project fee, depending on what's involved). For example, you could specify in your contract that the project fee includes thirty minutes of phone-discussion time; any additional phone time will be charged at $XX per hour. Or, if the author sends you more or revised content to be edited, respond that you'll be happy to edit that content for a fee of $XX (in addition to the previously established project fee).

Another reason editors might underestimate is that they're afraid to present a potential client with a higher fee, thinking that the individual will decide to hire an editor who'll charge less. Yeah, that might happen, but I don't think it's as common as many editors assume. In fact, I've often been surprised at how quickly clients will agree to my fees even when I think I might be pricing myself out of their budgets. So, don't shortchange yourself by underestimating the time required. If you do, you'll likely feel stressed and frustrated while working on the project, knowing that you're making less per hour than you wanted—and maybe needed—to. But what if you're still afraid that you'll lose business because of your higher prices? Then check out the section below titled "Overcoming Price Objections and Negotiating a Rate." As I'll explain there, a little price resistance isn't necessarily a bad thing, and it certainly doesn't mean you've lost the project.

Per-Word Fee

Some editors base their fees on the word count of a manuscript. Doing so does avoid the issues involved in using an hourly fee, but a per-word approach has its own problems. The main one is that this method doesn't consider the condition of the manuscript. Two documents could have the same number of words, but one might be a lot easier and faster to edit because it's in better condition and you don't need to change as much. Another issue is that a per-word fee is less flexible in terms of the level of editing you'll provide. For example, what if the client wants basic copy editing as well as fact-checking of specific content? Since your basic copy editing service doesn't include extensive fact-checking, your per-word rate for copy editing won't be appropriate for this situation, so you'll need to create a customized per-word rate for the project. If you're going to customize the rate for a project, why not present a project fee? Clients will probably appreciate that you're doing the math for them.

Setting the Stage for Presenting a Fee

During your initial discussions with a potential client, it's important to ask for specific information and to share some information of your own. Doing so will help you set the stage for presenting your fee for the proposed project. Now, what information do you need? You obviously

Pros and Cons of Project, Per-Word, and Hourly Rates

Project Fee	
Pros	*Cons*
• The client will know before the project starts how much you'll be charging.	• You might underestimate the time required to complete a project.
• The client's decision to hire you will be based on whether the project fee is within his or her budget, not on whether you deserve to earn a certain amount per hour.	• The project could grow in scope after you and the client have agreed on the price and signed the contract.
• The client will likely be willing to pay more than he or she would if you charged by the hour.	• The project might not be well-defined, making it hard to estimate how long you'll take to complete the project.
• You won't be penalized for becoming more efficient and editing faster.	
• You can increase your rates without having to announce the change.	

Per-Word Fee	
Pros	*Cons*
• You can avoid the issues that using an hourly fee involves.	• You can't raise or lower the rate according to the condition of the manuscript.
	• This method is less flexible in terms of the level of editing you'll provide.

Pros and Cons of Project, Per-Word, and Hourly Rates
(continued)

Hourly Fee	
Pros	*Cons*
• You won't need to tell a client the exact cost of the project before completing the work. • You'll be paid for the number of hours you work, so you won't end up earning less per hour than you planned on.	• The client will likely compare your hourly rate to what he or she makes per hour. • You'll be inviting the client to judge whether you're worth the amount you're charging per hour. • You'll need to provide an estimate of the hours required. • You might submit an invoice for a much higher amount than you estimated before starting.

need to know the details of the project—the word count, the type of editing involved,[1] the deadline, and the like. In addition, you need to find out what the potential client's underlying goal for the project is. The surface-level goal is probably obvious, such as to ensure the manuscript is free of grammatical errors. But you need to understand the person's deeper motivations. Does the individual hope that the editing

---

1. Don't assume that individuals who say they want proofreading, for example, really do want proofreading. Not even editors agree on how to define levels of editing, so how can we expect other people to know what term to use in describing the level of editing they want? When I talk with potential clients, I always specify what my copy editing, substantive editing, and other services entail so that the individuals can accurately tell me what type of editing they want me to provide.

will give the manuscript a better chance of piquing an agent's or a publisher's interest? Or does a pharmaceutical company need to ensure that the description of a drug is accurate and easy to understand? Whatever the goal is, make sure to uncover it. Ask what the potential client plans to do with the manuscript after it's edited. Also ask how the editing will help the individual achieve his or her ultimate goal.

After you've uncovered the underlying objective, it's time for you to explain how your skill set and experience will help achieve this objective. By providing this explanation, the potential client will likely feel a connection to you and feel assured that you "get" him or her. You'll be distinguishing yourself from other editors whom the potential client has spoken with—editors who talked only about how they could ensure the grammar was correct. To strengthen your connection with the potential client, acknowledge the hard work the individual has already put in and the difficulties he or she has likely faced and will face until the goal is achieved. For instance, if you're talking with a doctoral student, note that you understand how challenging it is to write a dissertation and how many obstacles have to be overcome. Then assure the individual that your focus is on fine-tuning the grammar and clarity of the writing so that the dissertation is approved and the individual will achieve the coveted title of "Dr."

Conclude your discussion by summarizing how your skills and relevant experience will enable you to help the potential client, and then identify the next steps. Here's an example: "Because of my experience copy editing dissertations, I'm confident that I can help you polish your dissertation so you can move on to your oral defense and earn your doctorate! I'm going to review your dissertation file, and then tomorrow I'll email you price quotes for a few editing options. I look forward to the opportunity to work with you."

If you've followed the steps above, the potential client will likely be excited to receive your email the next day and for you to get started on the project.

Sometimes an individual will ask for a rough price estimate before providing the manuscript for review. When that happens to me, I explain that I'll create a customized quote after reviewing the project. I prefer not to name a price yet because I first want to get a feel for the document, what I'll need to do in it, and what the client's needs and expectations are. Usually my response satisfies the individual, but if he or she continues to ask for an estimate on the spot, I'll provide a ballpark range. I can do that because I know my average speeds for different types of editing per 250 words. Let's say I can copy edit 250 words in six to nine minutes. If the client's manuscript is 25,000 words, then I should be able to edit the manuscript in six hundred to nine hundred minutes (ten to fifteen hours). If I want to earn $50 an hour, then my ballpark estimate for the project will be $500–$750. I make sure to sound confident when I give the estimate; that confidence helps the potential client feel more confident that the price is reasonable and is an amount other people are willing to pay me.

If the potential client is okay with the ballpark range, I'll ask to see the manuscript so I can calculate an exact project fee. If the client says the range is more than expected, then I'll ask what range the individual was forecasting. Next, I'll emphasize everything that I'll be doing for the price (correcting grammar and punctuation, formatting according to the specified style, etc.) and then highlight how my services will help the individual achieve his or her underlying goal. Sometimes, those steps are the only ones needed, but if the potential client still has concerns, I'll implement the strategies I describe later in this chapter (see "Overcoming Price Objections and Negotiating a Rate").[2]

---

2. Note for editors using hourly or per-word rates: Because it's so important to understand the potential client's needs and to establish the value you'll offer, I don't recommend posting your rates on your website or in other locations. Individuals who aren't willing to contact you unless you have rates on your website are likely hunting for low-cost editors; therefore, these individuals probably aren't your ideal clients.

When discussing a potential project with a company, I try to let the company lead the way in discussing fees, since companies that contract out editing and writing work often have standard ranges or budgets, which may be higher than I'd normally charge. To avoid looking inexperienced or missing out on a higher rate, I'll ask what the company's typical budget is. If the individual doesn't want to provide the number (either because of really not knowing or because of wanting me to be the first to name a number), then I'll say something like the following: "I'm just looking for a very basic idea—along the lines of whether the budget is in the range of $100, $1,000, or $10,000." The response will tell me whether my rates are too far above the budget for me to even consider the project, whether I can probably negotiate a fee that will work for me and the company, or whether I can earn a rate much higher than my standard fare.

Developing a Price Quote

Whether you use the hourly fee method or the project-fee method, it's essential that you carefully estimate how long a project will take to complete. Otherwise, you and your client could be in for a big surprise—and not one to celebrate. So, let's walk through the steps of estimating the time required to finish a project. First, ask to see either the entire manuscript or a section of it. If you'll be receiving only a section, make sure it's not the beginning or the end, because authors usually spend more time refining those parts than everything in between. You'll want to review the messiest part so you can get a more accurate understanding of how quickly you can edit the content.

After reviewing multiple pages, complete a sample edit of a page and note how much time you spent. If you spent ten minutes, for example, then hypothetically you should be able to edit six pages per hour (i.e., sixty minutes in an hour divided by ten minutes per page). Also factor in whether the manuscript contains a lot of graphics (tables, charts, images, etc.) or references that need to be formatted. Are they in good shape, or will they need a lot of TLC? Figure out whether they'll slow down your pace or speed it up. Another thing to consider is the level of editing. Did you copy edit, per the potential client's request, but notice that the document would benefit from substantive editing too? If so, estimate your overall pace for a substantive and copy edit.

Once you've estimated your overall pace, you'll want to build in a little extra time to account for the unexpected issues that almost always come up in a manuscript. Depending on the length and complexity of the manuscript, you might want to reduce your pages-per-hour estimate by one full page. (The one-page difference has worked pretty well for me; over time, you'll get a feel for what's most accurate for you.) Let's say you reduce the pages-per-hour estimate to five. You'd then divide the total number of pages by your estimated pages-per-hour rate to determine how many hours you'll likely spend editing the manuscript. So, if the manuscript is two hundred pages, you'll need to put in forty hours of editing.

There's one more step before you're ready to finalize the number of hours: you need to estimate whether you'll spend time on tasks that don't involve editing. For instance, do you expect that you'll be talking on the phone with the client biweekly? Or will you be corresponding a lot via email? After you've sent the client the edited manuscript, will the client revise and then send you updated text to review? If you foresee these tasks being part of the project, make sure to estimate the time required and add that amount to your time estimate. (Also list these tasks in your contract, and specify that any additional work will be charged a separate fee. See chapter 9 for additional information on what to include in a contract.)

After you've estimated the time required for any additional tasks, add that number to your editing estimate to arrive at an estimate of the total time required for the project. Assuming you've decided to use the

Sample Email Presenting a Price Quote

Richard,

I hope you're having a nice day. I've briefly reviewed your article and found the topic to be very interesting. Based on my review of the article and your goal to publish the article in *XYZ Journal*, I recommend selecting one of the following levels of editing:

Advanced: $540.00

- Resolve grammar issues
- Correct misspelled words and inconsistent spellings
- Address any punctuation issues
- Ensure clarity of meaning in sentences
- Format the file according to APA style
- Ensure that each paragraph focuses on one main topic
- Increase the flow between sentences
- Point out organizational issues

Basic Editing: $430.00

- Resolve grammar issues
- Correct misspelled words and inconsistent spellings
- Address any punctuation issues
- Ensure clarity of meaning in sentences
- Format the file according to APA style

Of course, I can customize the services further according to your preferences, so please let me know which option you prefer and whether you'd like me to add/remove any tasks from the option.

With my strong understanding of APA style and academic writing, I've helped various other researchers fine-tune their articles before submitting them to journals. It's always satisfying when I learn that the articles were accepted, and I'm excited to help you achieve this goal too. So, as soon as you let me know which level of editing you want, I'll send you a contract for the project and add your project to my schedule.

Sample Email Presenting a Price Quote *(continued)*

If you have any questions, please let me know. I look forward to hearing from you soon.

Best,

Jane Grammar

project-fee method, all you need to do now is multiply the total time estimate by your hourly rate to determine what your project fee will be.

Applying a Rush Fee

At some point, a client may ask you to complete a project that you won't have time for in your normal work schedule, either because the client needs a quick turnaround or because your schedule is nearly full already. If the client doesn't want to extend the due date, you can either decline the project (and, ideally, recommend another editor) or offer to complete the project for your normal price plus a rush fee. Some editors charge a flat rate as a rush fee, whereas others charge a percentage of the project price. The percentage approach makes more sense to me because it takes into account the size of the project and the degree of inconvenience you'll experience in order to fit in the project. If you instead charge a flat fee, such as $100, that amount might not be sufficient if you'll need to work ten extra hours per week for the next two weeks in order to complete the project. If you use a percentage, the rush fee will scale with the circumstances of the project.

Overall, the key is to pick a fee that will make the extra hours (likely on weeknights and weekends) worth it. And that means you might vary the percentage of the rush fee depending on the project. If working on the project will cut into family time, the amount of sleep you get, or another important commitment, then it's reasonable to charge a higher percentage, maybe 50 percent; if you'll simply need to postpone your lunch date with a friend until the following week, then perhaps 25 percent is reasonable. I wouldn't charge less than a 25 percent fee; any lower, and it might not deter clients from consistently asking you to complete rush jobs. And, of course, you can charge more than 50 percent—some editors charge as much as 100 percent of the project fee, though 25–50 percent is more common.

Depending on the size of the project, some clients will be more than willing to pay the extra amount in exchange for receiving the work back by the desired deadline. In contrast, other clients will decide that the "urgent" project isn't so urgent after all and that they can wait longer to receive the final product if it means they won't need to pay a rush fee. In some cases, a client might decide to work with another editor—one who has more availability and therefore won't charge a rush fee. However, according to my experience and that of various other editors, your risk of losing this business is low, particularly if you have already established a relationship with the client and have demonstrated the value you provide. So, don't be afraid to charge a rush fee that fairly compensates you for the trade-offs you'll have to make in order to complete the project.

Presenting Your Price

After you've developed your price quote (actually, price quotes, as I'll explain shortly), you're ready to email it to the potential client. Why email? I prefer it over a phone call, even if I initially spoke to the potential client on the phone or face-to-face, because via email I can present the pricing options in more detail and in a format that better emphasizes all that my services will involve and that enables the individual to review and carefully consider all the information. Presented orally, there's simply too much information for the individual to be able to absorb it all, meaning that the likelihood of confusion is greater. Having everything in writing also gives you a source to point back to when it's time to create the contract.

Structuring Your Message

Here's how I structure the email. (Since I use the same format every time, I've created an email template; I simply tweak the details to fit the project, and I'm ready to hit Send.)

GREETING

First, I greet the potential client and state that I've completed my review of the manuscript in order to prepare a price quote. I also note something positive about the manuscript—for instance, that I'm personally interested in the topic or that I like the author's writing style.

PRICING OPTIONS

Next, I explain that as a result of my review and understanding of the individual's goals, I've developed a few service options to choose from. I present multiple options even if the individual has already specified what level of editing or what services he or she wants. The first option offers more comprehensive services (e.g., substantive and copy editing if my review of the document indicates that both services are needed), whereas the second offers fewer services; sometimes I offer a third option, which is the most pared-down version. And, of course, the price goes down as the number of services decreases.

Let's consider some of the benefits of offering options. For one, people appreciate having a few options and the opportunity to choose the one that's the best fit. The options also make it more likely that one of them will be within the individual's budget (I typically offer a third option only when I know that the potential client's budget is quite limited). Additionally, presenting the highest-priced option first serves as a benchmark that the other price will be compared to. If the first price looks high to the individual, the lower price will look much better; in fact, research shows that sales of a product increase when it's presented next to a higher-priced option.[3] Of course, individuals won't always choose the lower-priced option: sometimes they'll want the more comprehensive one, even if it's much more expensive (believe me—it happens). So, always provide options, and always present the most expensive one first.

It's important to detail everything that each option involves. I do so in a bulleted list, which makes the items easy to scan and which also takes up more vertical space, emphasizing the many tasks I'll be completing. As an example, my copy editing option might include the following list:

- Correct spelling errors and ensure consistency when more than one spelling is acceptable
- Fix punctuation errors
- Correct grammatical issues
- Ensure clarity of meaning in sentences
- Change passive voice to active voice when appropriate
- Format according to Chicago style

After presenting the options, I note that I'm happy to further customize the options upon request. I explain that my goal is to meet the individual's needs, whatever they be.

---

3. See, for example, Rashmi Adaval and Robert S. Wyer Jr., "Conscious and Nonconscious Comparisons with Price Anchors: Effects on Willingness to Pay for Related and Unrelated Products," *Journal of Marketing Research* 48 (April 2011): 355–365.

CONCLUDING PARAGRAPH

Follow the service options and prices with a brief paragraph reminding the potential client of your skill set and experience and how you'll help him or her achieve the underlying objectives of the project. Express your interest in the project, and then note that after the individual selects an editing option, you'll create a contract for the project. (That's right—be confident and assume that the person is going to hire you. Your confidence may be the final motivation someone needs before deciding to give you the green light.) Also state that you look forward to hearing back from the individual and that you're happy to answer any questions. Close the email with your signature block, and you're ready to send the email.

PS

If you want, you can include a postscript mentioning a resource that you've included in the email (either as an attachment or a link) and that you think the potential client will find useful. The resource could be the pdf of a promotional piece you've written, a link to a post on your blog, a link to a YouTube video you posted, or something else you've created that will demonstrate your knowledge and that will be of benefit to the individual. When a business offers something for free, potential customers are more likely to become paying customers—they feel compelled to reciprocate, often through purchasing the business's service or product.[4]

Following Up

If you don't hear back from the individual within forty-eight business hours, send a follow-up email. Keep the message brief: state that you

---

4. Bawa and Shoemaker, "Effects of Sample Promotions."

want to ensure the potential client received your price quotes and that you look forward to starting on the project. If you don't receive a response to your follow-up email, wait a day longer and then call the individual if you have his or her number. It's possible that your emails are going to a spam folder or are getting lost in cyberspace (both have happened to me before). If you get the person's voicemail, leave a message similar to that of your follow-up email.

If you don't receive a response to your email or voicemail, go ahead and feel disappointed for ten minutes, but then shrug off the feeling and focus your attention elsewhere—either by working on current projects or by marketing your services to other potential clients. What if you do hear back from the individual but he or she expresses concerns about the pricing? I'll explain exactly what to do in the next section.

Overcoming Price Objections and Negotiating a Rate

Whether you're experimenting with a higher fee or using your current rate, some potential clients may express concern about your proposed fee, stating it's higher than expected and perhaps higher than what other editors are charging. You can often avoid this issue simply by following the principles discussed in the section titled "Presenting Your Fee," but you'll still probably encounter resistance every once in a while (and if you don't, you probably need to increase your rates). The situation isn't fun, but it doesn't mean that you've lost the project—or that you immediately should lower your price. In this section, you'll learn numerous strategies for overcoming price objections and negotiating a fee that both you and the client are happy with.

When someone indicates your fee is too high, start by acknowledging the person's concern and explaining that the fee is typical of what professionals with your experience and skills charge for a project like the one under consideration. Then state that you're confident you and the individual can come to a mutually beneficial arrangement.[5] This response shows that you're respectful and flexible, which can put the individual at ease rather than on the defensive. Next, ask the individual what his or her budget for the project is.

Use the person's response to develop some options regarding what tasks you can complete within the individual's budget. For example, maybe the person wants you to copy edit and improve the flow of the document; you determine that if you copy edit the document but don't address flow, you can stay within the desired budget. Or you could complete a lighter overall copy edit and then improve the flow of the sections the individual is most concerned about. Or, if your initial quote included two rounds of editing, you could offer only one round for a lower price. The more you understand about the potential client's goals, the better able you'll be to present options he or she will be happy to accept. (Of course, presenting options will work only if the budget is somewhat reasonable to begin with. If the person wants a 250-page manuscript edited for $200, you'll need to kindly explain that this amount is lower than what a professional editor would charge and that you won't be able to take on the project.)

Another way to reduce the work you need to complete—and thus reduce the amount you'll charge—is to identify tasks that the potential client could complete before or after you work on the project. For instance, if during your initial review of the project you noticed that the reference list is missing essential citation information, you could ask the author to add the information before you start editing. Or you could agree to only add comments on citations that are missing information rather than to find and add the information.

Another option is to offer to complete an additional service for the original fee you proposed. The key here is to choose a service that

5. Hat tip to Slaunwhite, Savage, and Gandia, authors of *The Wealthy Freelancer*, for this idea.

will be valuable to the client but won't be time-consuming for you. For instance, if the project is a dissertation, tell the potential client that as part of the fee, you'll update the table of contents (TOC) after the individual has made revisions based on your edits and feedback and before he or she submits the final file for university approval. Since you can create an automated TOC when you format the dissertation, you'll need only a minute to update the TOC later on. Whereas the time investment will be negligible for you, most doctoral students don't know how to create or update an automated TOC, and they dread updating it manually. So, they'll assign a high value to your offer to update the TOC.

If the project is long, you could suggest dividing it into phases, with each phase paid for separately. Or, you could suggest a payment plan in which the client has more time to complete the final payment. As an example, instead of requiring 50 percent up front and 50 percent upon completing the project, you could require 50 percent up front, 25 percent upon completing the project, and 25 percent thirty days after completing the project. (I don't recommend reducing the up-front percentage; from my experience, if the client isn't able to afford the 50 percent before I start, he or she is more likely to have problems paying the balance later on.)

As a further strategy, you could offer to finish your work sooner than you would otherwise. This proposal could be appealing to individuals who want to finalize a project as soon as possible; in return, they might be willing to pay your initially proposed fee. Alternatively, you could offer to lower your fee if you can have extra time to complete the project. I'd extend this offer only if having the extra time would make your life easier, if you don't have other projects scheduled during the extended time frame, and if you don't expect to have other projects come in during that time. If you'll personally benefit, the lower rate might be okay; otherwise, you'll simply be giving a discount, which I don't recommend doing. The problem with giving discounts is that you're setting the precedent that you're willing to work for less. The individual may then expect to get a discount on a future project or might tell others that you'll give discounts when pressed. Giving discounts also suggests that your services aren't as valuable as your standard rate indicates, since you're willing to lower it. For these reasons, I strongly recommend presenting options that allow you to earn your standard hourly rate while also meeting the client's needs, such as by using the strategies I've already discussed.

If you decide you want to offer discounts anyway, consider doing so only for the following reasons:

- The client agrees to pay the entire fee up front.
- The client agrees to send you more than one project *at the same time.* I've emphasized those words because a promise to send more work rarely pans out, not necessarily because the client is purposefully being dishonest but because plans change. For example, maybe the next project never comes to fruition, or maybe the client no longer has the funds to pay for your services. Unless you receive the projects at the same time, create a contract for them, and receive payment for them, it's not safe to assume that offering a discount will lead to additional work from the client.

When presenting any of the options I've discussed above, make sure to reemphasize your experience related to the individual's specific genre/industry, the value you'll provide, and how you'll help the individual achieve his or her underlying objectives. Also offer to provide the contact information for previous clients who would be happy to vouch for your skills. Following the strategies in this section will help you overcome many price objections.

If you and the individual can't settle on a price and services that are mutually agreeable, don't take it personally. Some people don't understand the value of editing or freelancers' need to earn a livable wage. And some people simply don't have the funds to pay for professional editing. Not landing a project doesn't mean that you're an unskilled editor or that you won't win other projects. Acknowledge that you and the individual aren't a good fit, and then move forward with your marketing activities so you can secure clients who are willing to pay your rates. Be proud that you respect yourself enough to not accept prices that are below your standard.

So far, I've provided suggestions based on the assumption that you've been asked to provide a project quote, rather than that a company has presented you with rates that it pays freelance editors. When the company is dictating the rates, you may be more restricted in terms of negotiating, but don't assume that your only options are to accept the offered rate or to turn down the work. Companies often have some wiggle room, so don't hesitate to ask for 25 percent more than the offered rate. The company might not agree to the full 25 percent but might agree to 15 percent, for example. You can then decide whether the new amount meets your needs.

One final consideration: You may be wondering whether it's ever okay to accept rates that are lower than your standard. My answer is *perhaps*. If you're just starting on your freelance adventure and your main focus—and need—is to simply bring in work, expand your client base, and spread the word about your business, then accepting rates that are somewhat lower than your ideal might be okay. Similarly, if you want to expand into a new niche, accepting lower-priced projects could enable you to get some experience in the niche, and experience is often a prerequisite to commanding higher rates. So, consider accepting a few lower-paying projects as a stepping-stone to gaining experience, establishing your credibility, and obtaining more clients—particularly ones who are willing to pay higher rates. You might also agree to a lower fee if you're passionate about the project's topic and goals or you're a staunch supporter of the client's organization (e.g., a nonprofit championing a cause you firmly believe in).

In all these circumstances, you should still expect to earn a reasonable amount per hour; you shouldn't ever feel obligated to work for free or for less than minimum wage. Of course, you could offer your services gratis, particularly to support a cause that's important to you, but you should make it clear that you're choosing to volunteer your services and that you're making a special exception. Don't give the impression that you're willing to work for free or for pennies whenever someone asks—or whenever someone shows resistance to your prices.

Increasing Your Rate

As a freelancer, you are the boss and are therefore responsible for deciding when to give yourself a raise. At a minimum, you should increase your rate annually to keep up with inflation and costs of living. An annual raise is typical for businesses, and that guideline applies to businesses of one. If you use project fees, increasing your rate is simple: the next time someone sends you a project, you use your new hourly rate to calculate the fee. You don't need to announce the rate increase to clients.

Increasing your rate can be trickier if you charge by the hour or the word because you should inform existing clients in advance that you're increasing your fee. Many freelance editors are hesitant to make such an announcement, fearing that clients will balk and perhaps even find a less expensive editor to work with. True, you might face one or both of those responses from time to time, and I'll explain later how to address each, but many clients will accept the rate increase if you present it appropriately. Companies and individuals typically understand that business prices increase over time, and though your clients won't likely celebrate the increase, they'll probably accept it, especially if the amount of the increase seems reasonable. And what's reasonable? Typically, you'll be safe with an increase of 5–10 percent.

To help your announcement be well received, consider sending it via email two months before the increase will go into effect. (An effective date of January 1 is particularly logical and easy to remember.) Start your email by stating that you enjoy working with the client and providing value in a specific way, and then express appreciation for your continued business relationship. Next, state that on XYZ date you'll be increasing your rate to $XX per hour or per word and that any projects the client sends before that date will be charged at your current rate. Indicate that you'd be happy to answer any questions the client has, and then conclude by stating you look forward to working with the client in the future. Your message might be phrased something like the following:

Dear Client,

I've really enjoyed working with you this year to polish your articles before submitting them for publication. Thanks for keeping me updated on when the articles have been accepted by the target journals! In working on the articles, I've learned more about the construction industry than I ever expected to, and the information came in handy recently when I worked with contractors on some home-renovation projects.

With the new year, I'll be increasing my hourly rate to $XX an hour. Any projects you send me before January 1 will be billed at my current rate. If you have any questions, please feel free to ask.

I look forward to continuing to work with you—and to learn from your great information!

Best,
Jane Grammar

Notice that the message doesn't mention the reason for the rate increase. You don't need to justify the reason, just as grocery stores don't justify the reason for increasing the price of apples. Likewise, you shouldn't apologize for the increase or ask whether the client is okay with it. Instead, present yourself as a confident business owner. You'll set the right tone by keeping the message short but friendly. Your email may even bring in more business in the short term, since clients may want to squeeze in some projects before your rate increases.

Now, what about those occasions when clients do resist the price increase? You have a couple of options. You can negotiate the increase, perhaps agreeing to a 5 percent raise instead of the 10 percent you initially presented. You could also agree to stick with your current rate for now but reevaluate the situation in six months. Or perhaps the client explains that he or she won't be able to afford the rate increase at any point in the foreseeable future. In any of these situations, you could agree to the client's terms for now, particularly if you need the client's projects in order to achieve your monthly earning goals. But you should also start looking for new clients willing to pay your higher fee.

As you get projects from the new clients, you can phase out the lower-paying clients, explaining that you won't be able to take on as many or any of the projects because you need to focus on higher-paying projects. If the old clients are paying you very low rates and you have enough other work to satisfy your financial obligations, then it might be best to end your business relationship even before you find better-paying clients. That way, you'll have time to market yourself to the clients who are able and willing to pay your rates. Cutting ties with a client doesn't mean you can't remain on good terms; it just means that you and the client are no longer a good fit. As a kind gesture, you could give the client the contact information for a few editors who would be willing to work for the amount the client will pay.

In addition to increasing your rates for current clients, experiment with increasing your rates when preparing quotes for potential clients. In other words, use rates even higher than the new ones you introduced to current clients. A great time to experiment with higher rates is when your schedule is already full for the next month or so. That way, if you pitch a higher fee to a potential client and the individual chooses not to work with you because your fee is too high, then it's not a big deal. You haven't lost income that you need this month in order to pay the bills.

You may think that losing any projects is a bad thing. That could be true in some situations, such as when you're just starting out or when you won't be able to cover basic expenses without the projects. In other cases, you should be pickier, focusing on scoring projects that are of interest to you and that meet or exceed your earning expectations. You don't need to be content accepting whatever amount a client is willing to pay you. And you don't need to cap your hourly rate at the dollar amount that you calculated will enable you to meet your financial obligations. So, definitely do experiment with higher figures. You'll likely be surprised at how much people are willing to pay you. (I've experienced that surprise myself.) In fact, if every person you give a project quote to immediately accepts your fee, you probably should be charging more. You should charge enough that you're experiencing some resistance.

Further, charging a higher fee can make your services appear more valuable and desirable because people tend to assume that the more expensive something is, the better quality it is.[6] If you charge a

---

6. Jung Eun Lee and Jessi H. Chen-Yu, "Effects of Price Discount on Consumers' Perceptions of Savings, Quality, and Value for Apparel Products: Mediating Effect of Price Discount Affect," *Fashion and Textiles* 5, no. 1 (2018): 1–21.

low price, people will tend to conclude that you're inexperienced and won't produce high-quality results. I learned this lesson for myself when I approached a contact at a multibillion-dollar tech company. I'd previously collaborated with her on a project through another company that I contracted with, and now I was interested in contracting directly with the tech company. Our discussion was going well until she asked what my hourly rate was and I responded with a number that was a little higher than I typically charged. Cue an uncomfortable silence. When she finally replied, I realized that I had undershot and had consequently lost credibility. As I later discovered, this company's contractors often charged twice as much as the amount I proposed. Because I hadn't done my research and had pitched too low, I lost the opportunity to work with the company.[7] Lesson learned: make sure to always research what the typical rates are for freelancers in the sector you're marketing your services to.

So far, I've talked about situations in which you have control over how much you charge. But in some contexts, freelance editors' fees are largely determined by the clients. In particular, traditional publishers tend to dictate the rates they'll pay, and freelance editors who aren't willing to work for those rates will need to look elsewhere for projects. That being said, some freelancers who work for publishers have asked for and received rate increases from publishers. So, if you really want to freelance for a traditional publishing house, you might be able to negotiate a slightly higher rate—after you've proven yourself to be a highly skilled, reliable editor. Some editors who are paid flat rates for projects have become faster editors over time (e.g., by using macros—see chapter 10 for more information), so they've increased their hourly earnings even without the publishers raising

---

7. Though you shouldn't shortchange yourself, do make sure your skills warrant your fee. If you're still developing basic editing skills, you shouldn't be charging expert-level rates.

their rates. You'll never earn big bucks if you work only for these publishers, but some editors are willing to accept the limited earnings because they're working on their ideal projects and receiving steady work from the publishers, decreasing the amount of marketing these editors need to do.

One final note: When you're just starting out as a freelancer, you'll likely be charging less than you'd prefer and you're more likely to be in a position of accepting rates offered rather than presenting your rates to clients. That's okay. Rest assured that as you establish your reputation in your market and receive word-of-mouth referrals, you'll gain a stronger position and you'll be able to increase your rates and phase out low-paying clients.

Reducing Income Uncertainty through Establishing Retainers

If you frequently receive project requests from a client you enjoy working with, then you might want to talk with the client about establishing a retainer agreement. With a retainer, the client agrees to pay you ahead of time for a certain amount of work you'll complete during a specific period, often a month. In return, you agree to be available to put in the agreed-upon hours. If you work for more than those hours, you'll bill for the extra time at the end of the period.

Let's consider an example. Jane Grammar typically spends about fifteen hours a month editing documents for a law firm. The firm accepts her proposal to enter a retainer agreement for fifteen hours of work a month at her standard rate of $75 an hour. So, at the start of each month, the law firm pays her $1,125 (fifteen hours × $75). The first month, she spends fourteen hours working on the documents she receives from the firm. She doesn't have to refund the money for the hour of work that wasn't required, and the extra hour isn't carried forward to the next month (i.e., she doesn't need to work sixteen hours the next month). At the start of the second month, she again receives $1,125, and she puts in seventeen hours of work during the month. She then submits an invoice for $150 to account for the two extra hours she worked.

Sounds pretty nice, right? Retainer agreements can be advantageous for everyone involved: You'll benefit from a guaranteed amount of income. The client will benefit because you're guaranteeing that you'll set aside time for the client's projects; in a way, the client is getting priority access to your time. Of course, that fact could be a disadvantage for you. Because you're giving this client priority, you might have a harder time juggling his or her projects with your other projects. And you might not be able to accept some projects—perhaps better-paying ones—because of your commitment to work on the retainer client's projects. The limited time for other projects is one reason you shouldn't agree to lower your hourly rate for the retainer client. Sure, the guaranteed income is nice, but your hourly fee should take into account the opportunities you might have to forgo because of the retainer agreement.

Make sure to specify all the details of the agreement in a contract. For example, include what your hourly fee is, how many hours you guarantee to set aside for the client each period, how long each period lasts, and how long the retainer agreement lasts. Also specify any reasons that the agreement can be terminated. It's likewise important to indicate how quickly you'll return documents to the client. You might want to provide a range of turnaround times based on document length and the type of editing required. Make sure the turnaround times are realistic given how busy you are with other clients' projects. Though you'll want to prioritize the retainer client's projects, you don't want to agree to turnaround times that will make your life stressful because you're struggling to meet all clients' deadlines. Remember: the retainer agreement is supposed to be a positive arrangement for you; if you and the client can't reach mutually beneficial terms, you're better off not entering a retainer agreement.

Choosing Payment Methods

Editors often wonder which payment methods they should accept. My view is that the more methods you offer, the better—you want to make it easy for clients to pay you. As a result, they might pay you sooner. That being said, I prefer that clients pay me via bank transfer so the money appears in my bank account without any extra work on my part. Some editors are hesitant to share their account information with clients, but you're sharing that information whenever you write someone a check. With your account and routing numbers, the only thing clients can do is put money in your account; they can't take money out, so there's little risk to this payment option. A check in the mail is almost as safe, but there's the risk that the check will bounce when you deposit it. (For that reason, your contract should specify that the client is responsible for paying any fees you're charged for a bounced check.) If you're still leery about providing your bank information, you can receive a bank transfer through Zelle. This company partners with most large banks in the United States, and if your or your client's bank is a Zelle partner, then your client can pay you by simply entering your email address or cell phone number into the system. Usually, the money is available within a few minutes.

Additional payment methods include ones connected to accounting systems, such as Wave and QuickBooks. If you're already using one of these systems to manage your finances, using the payment tool can further streamline your accounting. Other online options include PayPal, Stripe, and Square, all of which can integrate with your website, meaning that clients can submit payment right on your site. Despite the convenience of collecting payment through these online accounting and payment systems, I don't like using them, since I'm charged a transaction fee for receiving money; instead, I prefer payment methods that add the transaction fee to the client's cost. Per PayPal's terms and conditions, you're not allowed to add the amount of the fee to the client's total amount due, so if you're going to use PayPal a lot, you probably should increase your editing prices overall to account for the expense of using this payment service. Of course, the fees that PayPal and similar systems charge are business expenses, so they're tax deductible, but you won't recoup the entire amount come tax time. As a result, I believe you're better off increasing your rates by 5 percent for all clients or simply not accepting payments through these systems.

One benefit of PayPal, Stripe, Square, and similar payment platforms is that you can receive money from clients in other countries. But these platforms aren't your only options. Many people have had good experiences using Wise and Western Union, both of which add the transaction fee to the client's payment rather than deducting the fee from what you receive. Be aware that with Western Union, the money might not be sent to your bank account; instead, you might need to go to a Western Union location. So, Western Union isn't ideal if you don't live close to a location or don't want to receive payment in cash (and then make a trip to your bank to deposit the money).

Occasionally, clients ask to pay me via systems I haven't previously heard of. In such cases, I google the name of the system and check out its website and a couple other sites that describe the system. My goal is to make sure that the system looks legit and that people who use the system don't typically experience problems in receiving payment. If my five minutes of research suggests that the system works okay, then I'll accept payment through it.

Key Takeaways

- To determine how much you need to charge for your services, figure out how much money you need to earn to cover your monthly expenses and incidentals and to set aside money for savings and retirement.

- The three main approaches to pricing are hourly fees, project fees, and per-word fees. Typically, using project fees is the most beneficial for freelancers.
- When estimating how long a project will take to complete, always build in extra time for the unexpected.
- When talking with a potential client and presenting price quotes, be confident, highlight your experience, and emphasize how you'll help the individual achieve his or her underlying objectives for the project.
- When an individual asks for a lower fee, focus on finding a solution that's mutually beneficial, such as by reducing the services you'll provide so you can stay within the client's budget.
- Increase your rate at least annually, and experiment with different rates to see what individuals in your target markets are willing to pay.
- If you frequently work with a specific client, suggest establishing a retainer agreement.

9 *Using Contracts and Invoices to Get Paid and Protect Yourself*

On the surface, contracts and invoices might not seem like a barrel of fun, but they're actually some of the most exciting parts of your business. Why? Because they lay out the plan for how and when you get paid. They also help to clarify expectations with your clients and protect you in the rare case that something goes sideways with a client. This chapter covers the basics of contracts, the important role that they play in your business, and the elements you should include in contracts and invoices. Unfortunately, using contracts and invoices won't completely remove the risk of payment problems, so this chapter also discusses how to handle payment issues when they rear their ugly heads. By the time you finish the chapter, you still might not love thinking about contracts and invoices, but you'll know how to use them to your advantage, including in terms of avoiding payment issues.[1]

---

1. Just as a reminder, I'm not a lawyer. In this chapter, I'm presenting legal information, but I'm not providing formal legal advice.

What You Need to Know about Contracts

Why You Need a Contract

Admittedly, when I started on my freelance journey, I didn't always create a contract for each project. And things went okay . . . until they didn't. I was shocked the first time a client tried to get out of paying me for work I'd completed (this first occasion, I was due $1,000). I think the client assumed she could evade paying me because we hadn't signed a contract. (I'll talk more about the story later in the chapter.) After a few more troubles collecting payment for projects I hadn't established contracts for, I'd learned my lesson. Now, I won't start working on a project until the client has signed and returned the contract (and I've received partial payment).

Let's be clear: I don't think most clients are trying to bamboozle their editors. And like I said, I'd gone without a contract multiple times without issues. But having a contract is like locking your front door. You don't do it because you think a thief is going to try to break in every night. Rather, you lock the door as a precaution so that you're protected on the one night a thief does try to turn the knob.

Of course, contracts are important for other reasons too. Using a contract helps you present yourself as a professional. Even more important, a contract helps ensure that you and your client understand and agree to the details of the project. Without a contract, the details

"Contracts are not instruments of doom; they are a road map to help both parties perform their side of an explicit bargain. Without the guidance of a contract, both parties act on unspoken assumptions that can be wrong. When honest people feel that their expectations have not been met in a business context, they might feel cheated or exploited when the real problem was that there was not a meeting of the minds. A well-drafted contract helps ensure that both parties know what their rights and responsibilities are, which leads to a fulfilling outcome for both."
—*Karin Cather, freelance editor*

and expectations of a project can be hazy. You might have one set of expectations, while the client has a different set. Consequently, one or both of you might end up frustrated about how the project progresses or about how it turns out. For instance, the client might ask you to complete more work than you initially expected and, therefore, more than you based your fee on. You can do the extra work without charge, which will lead you to feel shortchanged. Or you can tell the client that there will be an extra fee for the extra work, and the client might be upset, believing you have hidden costs and are trying to take advantage of him or her. Having a detailed contract can help you avoid these issues and many others.

What Constitutes a Contract

Typically, when we think of contracts, we think of ones that are labeled as such, that are printed out or in an electronic file, and that contain each party's signature. But contracts can be less formal, consisting of a verbal discussion or an email conversation in which one person agrees to pay the other person for a service or product. That type of contract could be considered binding in a court of law, but you'll be better off if you have a formal, written contract that you and your client have signed. A formal contract will likely be a lot more detailed, helping you ensure you haven't left out any information. A formal, written contract can also put you in a better position if you end up suing a client.

With the first client who tried to avoid paying me, I didn't have a written contract, but I did have a string of emails in which the client and I discussed the parameters of the project. In the email string, the client also indicated that she was excited for me to start working on the project. In a later email, she stated that she had mailed my payment (a statement I later learned wasn't true). So, when I eventually sent her a demand letter declaring that she needed to pay me or else

I'd take her to court, I didn't have a formal contract as evidence but I did have the emails, which served as an implied in-fact contract. After my client consulted with her lawyer, she agreed to pay the amount due.

Clients may not be aware that a verbal or email agreement is legally binding, so they may not take these informal contracts as seriously—yet another reason to use a formal contract. A formal contract should be signed by you and the client, and you have a variety of options for signing. Of course, you can sign a printed copy, scan and email it to the client, and then have the client complete the same process. Another option is to save the contract as a pdf, use Adobe Acrobat to add your signature, and then send the client the pdf to sign. You can also use an online program such as DocuSign or Hello-Sign. (Some of these programs let you send a few contracts a month for free.) The method I use, which I think is simplest, is to type my name in the Word version of the contract. I then email the client the file and direct the client to sign in the same way. With this method, I don't have to worry about whether the client has Adobe Acrobat, and I keep the contract files stored on my computer, not in a cloud program that I might not always have access to. And signing in Word is 100 percent legally valid.

Even if you understand the importance of having a contract, you probably don't look forward to creating one yourself. In the next section I'll discuss components to include in a contract so you can create your own, but another option is to use one of the many contract templates online. You can also build a contract through using AND.CO's free system.[2] Just make sure that you're using a reputable source. You can find a lot of helpful contract information, including specific wording to use in a contract, at Nolo.com.

---

2. To get started, go to www.and.co/the-freelance-contract.

Components of a Contract

When creating a contract or modifying a contract template someone else created, you get to decide what components to include and how detailed to be. You probably don't want to end up with a ten-page document (wouldn't you be a little alarmed if you were the client?), but you do want to cover all your bases. Otherwise, you might be leaving yourself open to trouble later on. This section lists the most common (and essential) contract components, as well as ones you might want to include to give yourself more protection.

First, here are the elements you really should include:

- The names of the parties involved in the agreement—you, the client, and anyone else
- The name of the project (A descriptive name is fine if the project doesn't have an official title.)
- The word count
- A description of the work you'll complete (Be detailed. For example, instead of simply stating that you'll copy edit the document, state that you will correct grammar, punctuation, and spelling errors and will revise for clarity. Specify whether you'll format the document, including any citations, and whether you'll fact-check the document. Also indicate whether the project fee includes any phone consultation time. Make sure to fully describe the scope of your work. Also specify that if the scope of the project increases, you'll create a contract addendum or a new contract for the additional work.)
- The date by which the client must send any materials you need for the project
- A clause stating that if the client doesn't send the materials on time or doesn't respond to project-related questions in a timely manner, you may need to extend the project due date

- The date and time of day the project is due (Specify the time zone.)
- The method (e.g., email or file transfer service) you'll use to return the completed work
- The total project fee (Specify the currency if your client is in a different country than you.)
- The date each payment installment is due
- The payment methods you accept
- A late-payment clause (Specify that you'll charge a fee for late payments. You can charge either a flat fee—say, $50 for every thirty days late—or a percentage of the payment due. If you choose the latter, you must charge simple, not compound, interest, and you must specify the monthly and annual interest rates. Additionally, most states limit the percentage you can charge; you should be okay if you charge a maximum of 10 percent per year, which equates to 0.8333 percent per month. Also specify what will happen if the payment is more than sixty days late. For example, will you send the account to collections or file a lawsuit?)
- A bounced-check clause (State that the client is responsible for compensating you for any late fees you're charged if a check the client sends bounces. Specify that the late fee will be in effect if the amount that bounced isn't repaid by the payment due date.)
- Your and the client's phone numbers, mailing addresses, and email addresses
- Your and the client's signatures and date of signing

Beyond the basic components above, you probably should include the following in your contract:

- The date that the offer—that is, the unsigned contract—expires (The main purpose of this clause is to prevent someone from signing the contract a year or more after you send it and expecting you to honor the project fee presented in the contract—after all, you should be raising your rates every year.)

- A termination clause (State the conditions under which you or the client can terminate the contract. For example, my termination clause specifies that the contract can be canceled within forty-eight hours after the client has returned the contract to me and that the cancellation notice must be sent via email. My clause also specifies that I'll be paid for any work I completed prior to the cancellation. I know some editors who choose to make the amount of the first payment nonrefundable if the client cancels the contract. The reasoning is that if the client cancels, you'll have a gap in your schedule that you might not be able to fill immediately.)
- An acknowledgment clause (Specify that you reserve the right to review, edit, and approve any acknowledgment the client wants to give you in the manuscript.)
- A warranty clause (State that you can't guarantee 100 percent accuracy in editing and can't guarantee that the manuscript will be accepted by a publisher, will be approved by a dissertation committee, etc.)
- A clause specifying the method for amending the contract (For example, will it be sufficient for you and the client to agree to the change via email? Or will you require a written addendum that you and the client must sign?)
- An indemnification clause (State that the client will indemnify you from any claims that the manuscript violates copyright laws, contains defamatory language, or in some other way provides the grounds for legal action. Also state that you aren't responsible for any legal fees the client must pay in a lawsuit resulting from any content in the manuscript.)

- A jurisdiction clause (Specify the geographical location where any legal disputes will be resolved. If you don't specify a location, you'll typically be required to file a lawsuit in the client's geographical jurisdiction.)
- A clause regarding attorney fees and collection agency fees (Specify that in a legal dispute, the party who loses is responsible for paying the winning party's attorney fees and other costs incurred as part of the dispute. Also specify that the client will be responsible for paying any collection agency fees.)

Some editors also include a copyright clause, specifying that they own the copyright to the edited manuscript until the client pays for the work completed. I don't include this clause, partly because I haven't seen evidence that this clause would hold up in court.

Client-Provided Contracts

If your client is a company, the client might have created a standard contract for independent contractors and might require you to sign it rather than using your own contract. There's nothing wrong with using the company's contract—as long as it covers the essentials and doesn't include any unreasonable requirements. Make sure to read the contract carefully so you understand what you're being asked to agree to. For instance, the contract might state that you must have liability or other types of insurance, but such requirements don't make sense for freelance editors, who (presumably) work from home, don't have clients come to the home, don't go to the client's office, and don't have employees. So, what do you do? Simply strike out the content and add your initials in the margin. When you return the contract, explain why you crossed out the content. To accept your deletion of the clause, the client should add his or her initials in the margin. If the client won't budge, then you'll need to decide whether

Sample Contract

EDITORIAL AGREEMENT

This agreement is between Jane Grammar Edits LLC and Richard Writer ("Client") and concerns the following manuscript: Doctoral Dissertation

Length of total manuscript: 40,000 words

1. Editorial Tasks

Jane Grammar Edits LLC agrees to do the following:

- Resolve grammar issues
- Correct misspelled words and inconsistent spellings
- Address any punctuation issues
- Ensure clarity of phrasing
- Format according to APA style

Additional tasks (e.g., submitting new content after the contract is signed, asking Jane Grammar Edits LLC to complete more than one round of editing, or scheduling meetings to discuss the project) will incur an additional fee and may require due dates to be adjusted. Any proposed changes to the parameters of the project will be addressed by Jane Grammar Edits LLC and the Client. As appropriate, an addendum will be added to this contract.

2. Delivery

Client Due Date

The Client is to deliver the unedited manuscript as a Word file to Jane Grammar Edits LLC by 11:59 p.m. EDT on August 1, 2021, by means of an email.

Jane Grammar Edits LLC Due Date

Jane Grammar Edits LLC is to deliver the edited manuscript as a Word file to the Client on or before 6:00 p.m. EDT on August 15, 2021, by means of an email, provided that the Client has done the following:

Sample Contract *(continued)*

- Submitted the unedited manuscript as a Word file by 11:59 p.m. EDT on August 1, 2021
- Paid the first 50 percent by August 1, 2021
- Responded to project-related questions within three days of the questions being emailed to the Client

If the Client does not meet these conditions, the due date for returning the edited manuscript may be delayed.

3. Payment

Total Cost

The project cost is $2,030.00.

Payment Schedule

- 50 percent ($1,015.00) is due by August 1, 2021.
- 50 percent ($1,015.00) is due by September 29, 2021.

Payment Method

The Client is to pay Jane Grammar Edits LLC via one of the following methods:

- Bank transfer via Zelle
- Check in the mail
- Western Union

Late-Payment Fee

Any payment not received by the due date is subject to a 0.8333 percent late fee per thirty days late.

Bounced Check

If the Client submits payment via check and the Client's account has insufficient funds to pay the amount of the check, the Client is responsible for compensating Jane Grammar Edits for any late fees incurred by Jane Grammar Edits. If the repayment is not made by the established due date, the established late fee will be put into effect.

Sample Contract *(continued)*

4. Expiration

If the Client does not sign this contract within sixty days of Jane Grammar Edits LLC emailing it to the Client, the offer will expire. After this time, if the Client chooses to reengage with Jane Grammar Edits LLC, a new contract will be generated and sent to the Client.

5. Confidentiality

Jane Grammar Edits LLC agrees to keep the contents of the manuscript confidential and will not share the content with any third parties.

6. Termination

This agreement may be terminated by either party in the event of material change of circumstance, with forty-eight hours' notice sent in writing to the other party at the address shown below. If Jane Grammar Edits LLC terminates the agreement, Jane Grammar Edits LLC will be paid by the Client for work done up to the date of termination. If the Client terminates the agreement, Jane Grammar Edits LLC will be paid by the Client for the work done up to the date of termination.

7. Acknowledgments

The Client must receive approval from Jane Grammar Edits LLC before acknowledging Jane Grammar Edits LLC in any way in the Client's manuscript.

8. Indemnity

Editing is intrinsically a process of offering advice and suggestions to the Client. It is the Client's responsibility to decide whether to accept or reject the edits and suggestions provided by Jane Grammar Edits. Although Jane Grammar Edits LLC will make every effort to bring questionable material to the attention of the Client, the Client agrees to indemnify and save harmless Jane Grammar Edits LLC from any and all claims or demands, including legal fees, arising out of any alleged libel or copyright infringement committed by the Client in creating the work.

Sample Contract *(continued)*

9. Warranty

Editing involves some subjectivity. The Client has the discretion to accept or reject any or all of the changes made by Jane Grammar Edits LLC. Disliking or rejecting the changes is not grounds for refusing to pay part or all of the fee established in this contract.

Jane Grammar Edits LLC will strive to correct all errors in the document but cannot guarantee 100 percent accuracy. The Client is ultimately responsible for all content in the manuscript.

Jane Grammar Edits LLC does not guarantee that the manuscript will be accepted or approved by a publishing house, an academic committee, or any other organization/group. Failure to receive acceptance or approval by a publishing house, an academic committee, or any other organization/group is not Jane Grammar Edits LLC's fault and is not grounds for reducing the agreed-upon fee for the editorial services described in this contract.

10. Dispute Resolution

This contract is entered into in Cabot Cove, York County, Maine, which is the sole place of business of Jane Grammar Edits LLC. Any legal action brought to enforce or terminate this contract or any term of this contract must be brought in a court of the State of Maine located in Cabot Cove, York County, Maine, which the parties to this contract agree is the proper venue and the court that has jurisdiction over any dispute regarding this contract. Further, Maine law is the law governing this contract. Service of process will be effective if it is served by the usual court-ordered process to Jane Grammar Edits LLC at the address below Jane Grammar Edits LLC's signature and, in the event that such service is unsuccessful, to the secretary of state for the State of Maine as agent for Jane Grammar Edits LLC. Should the court rule in Jane Grammar Edits LLC's favor, the Client is responsible for paying Jane Grammar Edits LLC's legal fees and associated costs.

Sample Contract *(continued)*

This contract may be changed only by written agreement between Jane Grammar Edits LLC and the Client.

11. Signatures

Signed by the parties to this agreement:

Editor's electronic signature: Jane Grammar
Date: July 15, 2021
Address: 698 Candlewood Ln., Cabot Cove, ME 04046
Phone #: 207-555-7892
Email: jane@janegrammaredits.com

Client's electronic signature: Richard Writer
Date: July 15, 2021
Address: 322 Maple St., Mayberry, NC 27030
Phone #: 336-555-1492
Email: richard@richardwriter.com

you want to pay for the insurance or put up with other unnecessary requirements. In deciding, consider both the time and money you'll spend as a result of agreeing to the client's terms. If you're not comfortable reviewing contract wording on your own, consider consulting with a lawyer or someone else you trust to get his or her opinion on the fairness of the contract. You could also ask the client to sign your contract; doing so will help ensure that you're including any important components not addressed in the client's contract.

What You Need to Include in Invoices

To help ensure that you're paid for a project—and in a timely manner—it's a good idea to send an invoice each time a payment is pending. An invoice is a reminder of the payment due date and of accepted payment methods and also serves as important documentation if a client doesn't pay on time (more about that in the next section). You can use an online program to generate invoices, or you can create your own template and just fill in the details for a specific project. Here's the information I include:

- My business's name, mailing address, email address, and phone number
- The client's name
- The date of the invoice
- The services provided
- The payment amount due
- The payment due date
- The payment methods I accept

Below this information, I thank the client for the opportunity to work on the project. Then I encourage the client to share my contact information with anyone else who might benefit from my services. I save the invoice as a pdf and attach it to an email I then send to the client.

It's a good idea to note in your calendar when the payment is due. Alternatively, you can track payments in a project tracker (see "Use a System to Track Projects" in chapter 10). Either way, it'll be easy to keep track of when you're supposed to receive payments—and whether they actually come in.

How to Address Issues in Getting Paid

In my experience, most clients will pay you—and typically on time. But I've also heard horror stories from editors who've experienced long delays in being paid . . . or who never ended up being paid. I've had a few experiences like that myself. So, though not every client

---

Sample Invoice

INVOICE FOR SERVICE RENDERED

Jane Grammar Edits LLC

698 Candlewood Ln., Cabot Cove, ME 04046

jane@janegrammaredits.com

207-555-7892

Bill to: Richard Writer
Date: August 3, 2021
Service provided: Copy editing of doctoral dissertation
Amount due: $2,030

Payment options:

- Bank transfer via Zelle
- Check in the mail
- Western Union

Please submit payment within 14 days.

Thank you for the opportunity to work with you! If you know of anyone else who might benefit from my services, please feel free to share my contact information with them.

---

will present payment problems, it's important to understand how to address these issues when they come up.

Two of the best ways to avoid payment issues are to use a contract and to require partial payment up front. The contract shows that you mean business—you and the client are entering a legally binding agreement, including the part about paying you by a certain date. And the late-payment clause can motivate clients to pay on time. The up-front payment likewise shows that you're taking the business relationship seriously, and the payment also lowers your risk because if you later have problems getting paid by the client, at least you've already received part of the money. I've found that individuals who can't afford to pay the partial amount up front are more likely to have trouble paying the balance later.[3] So, I've become strict on requiring 50 percent before I start working (unless either I have worked with a client for a long time and am confident that I'll be paid or I am working with a company that insists on paying afterward). If a client asks to pay a lower percentage up front, I suggest that we divide the project into smaller ones, each with its own contract and payments. With that option, I receive 50 percent before I start on the project, with the remainder due after I return the work. Then, the client can send me the next section of the project, with 50 percent again due up front.

Another way to avoid payment issues—and client issues in general—is to tune into your spidey sense. When you're in initial discussions with a potential client, look out for any warning signs. Is the individual rude or impatient? Does the individual try to low-ball you or pressure you to complete more work for the same price? Does the person take a long time to respond to you? These and other behaviors can signal that you're in for even more trouble if you agree to work with the individual.

First Steps

If you don't receive a payment by the due date, send a friendly email to the client, noting that you haven't received the payment and that

---

3. I realize that this stance might seem harsh. I'm not trying to discriminate against people who have limited funds. Rather, I'm taking a business perspective and avoiding risk. If people with limited funds want to hire me, then I recommend that they save the required money and then contact me again. If saving the required amount isn't feasible, then these individuals would be better off working with an editor who charges lower fees. I believe that most people who sign a contract are intending to pay the agreed-upon amount, but if financial hardship strikes, it's easier to not pay an editor than to not pay the mortgage or the electricity bill.

you want to make sure the payment didn't get lost in transmission. The client will likely apologize for the delay and make sure the payment arrives quickly. If it still doesn't come, be persistent in reminding the client about the delinquent payment. Every one or two weeks (depending on how aggressive you want to be), email a new invoice, with *LATE* in the file name. At the top of the invoice, include *LATE* in red letters. Also include the late-notice number (e.g., "Fourth Notice"), how late the payment is, and what the current late charge is. Sending the invoices in the postal mail as well as via email can make it even clearer that you're serious about being paid.

Particularly if your client is a company, try calling to discuss the situation. You might have better results if you call the accounting department rather than your contact, who might have little control over when payments are made. If you live close by, it can be even more effective to visit the company's office and speak to someone in person. Some companies have standard payment time lines of sixty or even ninety days after receiving an invoice, and you may have little luck getting payment sooner. (Make sure to address this issue in your contract. Even if the company won't budge on the payment time line, at least you'll know beforehand—and can decide whether you're willing to work with the company after all.) As always, make sure to remain calm and respectful. Yelling and demanding won't motivate people to help you. Also resist the urge to explain why you need the payment ASAP (rent, medical bills, etc.); keep the conversation business focused.

If a client admits that he or she hasn't paid because of a lack of funds, collaborate with the client to develop a payment plan. Though you might not get the money as soon as you'd like, the payment plan increases your chances of receiving the money, and you won't have to put as much time and energy into constantly reminding the client of the payment that's past due. The payment plan should be realistic for the client's situation but shouldn't be too lenient. For example, you could suggest breaking up the balance into two to four payments, due every two or four weeks, depending on the dollar amount due and the client's situation.

More Serious Options

What if you haven't received payment by ninety days after the due date (or perhaps even just sixty)? And what if the client point-blank refuses to pay? Then you have a decision to make: Do you write off the money, or do you escalate the issue, such as by threatening to take the client to court? If the client owes you a small amount (and *small* is different for different editors), then the best option might be to write off the debt so you can spend your time on moneymaking projects rather than on trying to get the delinquent client to pay. Writing off the debt might also reduce your stress level, and better emotional health can be worth the amount you're writing off.

If the amount you're owed is more than you're willing to give up, then it's time to take stronger action than simply sending additional invoices. One strategy—if you're okay burning all bridges—is to post about the late payment on the client's social media pages. Briefly present the facts in a professional, objective manner, and ask the client to contact you so you can work out the issue. The embarrassment from being called out on social media could motivate the client to pay—or to feel angry and even more resistant to paying, so definitely be careful when using this option. (If you state only facts, without any opinion or name calling, you won't be guilty of libel.)

You might also consider taking the client to court or sending the account to a collection agency. Sometimes, simply telling the client you're going to do one or the other will persuade the client to pay. And that's really what you should hope for, because resorting to litigation and/or a collection agency creates more hassle (and no guarantee you'll actually get the money).

Whichever option you choose, start by sending the client a demand letter. You can hire a lawyer to write the letter, but if you want to save a couple hundred dollars, you can write the letter yourself. Here's what to include:

- State the date you're writing the letter.
- Explain that the client breached the contract by not paying by the established due date.
- State when the payment was due and the number of days late the payment currently is.
- State the original amount owed and any late charges that have been applied.
- Specify what you've already done in an attempt to obtain payment (sent invoices, made phone calls, etc.). Include dates of any contact.
- Explain what the client needs to do to resolve the problem. You can be specific, such as by stating that the client must pay $XXX by so-and-so date. Or you can be more general, stating that the client must arrange a payment plan that's agreeable to you and that the client must follow through with the plan by so-and-so date.
- Explain that if the client doesn't resolve the problem, you'll have no other option than to send the account to a collection agency and/or to file a lawsuit.

Email the client the letter, and also send it via certified and regular mail. Why certified *and* regular mail? Because using both methods shows that you're making an appropriate effort to reach the client (this effort is important to establish if you decide to go to court). If the client doesn't answer the door when a carrier delivers the certified letter, then it will be returned to the post office and will remain there until the client chooses to get the letter. With the regularly mailed version, use USPS tracking so you know it was delivered to the client's address, even though you won't have proof that the client personally received the letter.

If the client doesn't respond to your demand letter or doesn't remedy the issue by making the payment, then it's time to decide whether you want to follow through on your threat to send the account to collections or whether you want to take the client to court. Let's examine what each option involves.

COLLECTIONS

If a collection agency is able to collect money from the client, the agency might not collect the total amount. For example, the agency might negotiate a settlement of 75 percent (or even less) of the total amount the client owes you. Then the agency will take a percentage of that percentage (often 25–45 percent), so you'll recoup even less in the end. Also, if the client refuses to pay the collection agency, the agency can't garnish a person's wages unless the case has gone to court and the judge has ruled in your favor. The agency might pay for a lawyer to take the case to court, or you can do so yourself. If you have the agency's lawyer handle the case, be prepared to pay for the service.

On that note, be aware of other fees the agency might charge you. Do your research before selecting a specific agency to work with. Read the details of how the agency operates, check out users' reviews of the agency, and see whether any complaints have been registered with the Better Business Bureau. Then think carefully about whether working with an agency makes sense for your situation.

COURT

Your other option is to take the client to court. You'll want to choose small claims court unless the amount your client owes exceeds the maximum amount your state allows to be considered in this type of court.[4] The reason to opt for small claims court is that this route is typically less expensive and faster to complete than are other types of litigation. The main cost savings comes from not needing a lawyer—the process is typically easy enough to handle on your own, and the filing fee is low. Here's how the process generally works (the specifics vary state by state):

- You file a complaint in the justice court for the location in which the client lives (or for the jurisdiction specified in your contract) and pay the filing fee.
- The complaint is served to the client via certified or first-class mail or by a court official or other approved individual.
- The client will have a certain number of days to respond to the complaint. If he or she doesn't reply within the specified time frame, the client will receive a default judgment, meaning you win the case.
- The court sets a date for the trial.
- You prepare your evidence (e.g., print out contracts, email correspondence, invoices, and demand letter).
- You present your case at the trial. If the client doesn't come to the trial, the judge will rule in your favor (via a default judgment).

Even if you win, you'll still need to collect the money; the court won't collect for you. The client will hopefully decide to pay, even if only to avoid having an unpaid judgment against him or her, which could affect the client's credit and ability to borrow money. Typically,

---

4. For a list of the max allowed in each state, see Ann O'Connell, "50-State Chart of Small Claims Court Dollar Limits," Nolo, Legal Topics, January 24, 2020, www.nolo.com/legal-encyclopedia/small-claims-suits-how-much-30031.html.

if the client doesn't pay within thirty days, you can go back to court to order a wage garnishment or to get a lien on the client's property.

Key Takeaways

- Always, always, always use a contract. A contract helps ensure that you and the client are on the same page, discourages payment issues, and provides protection if you need to take legal action against the client.
- Sending an invoice can encourage prompt payment and remind clients that you appreciate referrals.
- If a client doesn't pay by the due date, regularly send new invoices that indicate the original amount due as well as the late fee being assessed.
- If a client refuses to pay, you can send the account to collections and/or can sue the client. However, neither option ensures that you'll receive the full amount due.

10 *Managing Time like a Pro and Increasing Productivity*

If I could have a super power, it would involve not needing to sleep—just think how much more I could do each day! Because that power hasn't developed yet, I've focused on managing my time and boosting my productivity so that I can accomplish a lot in the sixteen or so hours I am awake and also fit in some down time.

As I'm sure you already know, productivity is important. But you might not realize how essential it is in maintaining a successful business. In fact, productivity is as critical as marketing and bringing in clients, because if you don't manage your time efficiently, you won't be able to maximize your profits and you might feel like you're working all the time and can't fit in personal responsibilities and pursuits. To help you become a pro at productivity, in this chapter I'm going to share numerous tips on how you can manage your time and maximize your productivity. I'll start with general tips and then focus on editing-specific strategies to become more efficient. I'll follow those ideas with suggestions on how to manage your project schedule and how to avoid procrastination.

General Strategies to Improve Your Time Management and Productivity

Invest in Yourself

To be productive, you need to invest in yourself—in terms of completing job-related training, learning how to manage your business, and taking care of your physical and emotional health. This investment will likely require time and money, but you'll get a good return on investment in the long run because you'll be able to perform more efficiently, earn more per hour, and enjoy a better overall quality of life. Also keep in mind that a lot of free online resources are available and that investing in yourself doesn't require hours at a time. For example, maybe once a week you spend fifteen minutes studying a section of *The Chicago Manual of Style* and then completing one of the Chicago Style Workout quizzes at https://cmosshoptalk.com/chicago -style-workouts.

Take Breaks

It may seem counterintuitive, but taking breaks can help you accomplish more and at a higher level of quality than if you try to power through a workday without stopping. Breaks have many benefits: they can help you feel more energized and motivated, be more creative, think more clearly, develop solutions to problems, and make better decisions.[1] The key is to be laser focused during the work

---

1. John Pencavel, "Recovery from Work and the Productivity of Working Hours," *Economica* 83 (2016): 545–563; Ze Zhu, Lauren Kuykendall, and Xichao Zhang, "The Impact of Within-Day Work Breaks on Daily Recovery Processes: An Event-Based Pre-/Post-experience Sampling Study," *Journal of Occupational and Organizational Psychology* 92, no. 1 (2019): 191–211; Ron Friedman, "Schedule a 15-Minute Break before You Burn Out," *Harvard Business Review*, August 4, 2014, https://hbr.org/2014/08/schedule-a-15-minute-break-before-you-burn-out.

session; if you aren't, you likely won't be able to accomplish more work than if you didn't take a break. So, when you're working, you shouldn't look at your phone, check social media, or do anything else unrelated to your work task. Don't even look at work emails.

Various sources recommend different lengths of work and break time; some of the common recommendations are a twenty-five-minute work session and a five-minute break, a fifty-two-minute work session and a seventeen-minute break, and a ninety-minute work session and a twenty-minute break. I personally recommend working for fifty minutes and then taking a ten-minute break. With that combo, it's easy to schedule your day in hourly increments. Additionally, if you stop more frequently—say, every twenty-five minutes—you might not reach a state of flow when editing. Of course, you need to figure out what works best for you, and it might change depending on the project. For instance, a proofreading project won't likely take as much brain power, so you'll be able to work on it for a longer stretch, whereas a really complex project in need of heavy editing will be more mentally taxing and you might need to take breaks more often than usual.

What if working for even twenty-five minutes without a break seems daunting? (That's understandable considering the barrage of interruptions and distractions created by notifications on our cell phones, the lure of social media, and incoming emails, all of which can make it harder for us to stay focused.) The key is to evaluate how long you can currently focus and then to slowly increase your focus time. If you're currently starting to lose focus after twenty minutes, set a goal for next week to work for twenty-two minutes before taking a break. The following week, increase your work sessions to twenty-five minutes each. Continue strengthening your focus muscle until you've reached fifty minutes (or whatever focus time you're targeting).

Now, what should you do during your breaks? A great option is to get up and move around, such as for a short walk outside. Exercise can increase your productivity (as I'll explain in more detail below) and will also bring physical health benefits, especially if you tend to sit all day long. Aside from exercising, simply going to a different room in your home can be helpful because of the change in scenery, helping you think of something other than work. Consider completing a crossword puzzle, folding laundry, checking your Twitter feed, or texting a friend. Just make sure to pick something that will get your focus off your work—doing so is as important as remaining focused on your work during your focus session. Even though you won't consciously be thinking about your current work project, you likely will be on a subconscious level; when you start your next focus session, you might realize that you now know how to fix that sentence that had stumped you before you took the break.

Automate Processes and Tasks

Whenever you find that you're repeating the same tasks or steps over and over, see if you can automate some or all of the process. For example, if potential clients typically email you to request information about your services, then create a standard reply to use as a template. Follow your email provider's steps for creating and saving an email template and then inserting the template into an email. After you've inserted the template text into your return email to a potential client, all you'll need to do is customize the text to the individual (e.g., inserting the person's name). Create another email template for the message you include when you send a project contract, when you return an edited file, and so forth.

In addition to email templates, create Word templates for contracts, invoices, and any other documents you typically send to clients. In each template, highlight any areas in which you need to insert customized information, so it's easy for you to ensure you don't forget anything. Beyond creating templates, see what other processes you can automate—especially the ones you don't like do-ing because they're tedious. Not sure whether you can automate a process? Simply google a description of what you're trying to auto-mate. You might be surprised to find a variety of programs and other options that will meet your needs.

Use Free (or Paid) Business Tools

As you search the internet for ways to automate processes, you might come across some of the numerous business productivity tools avail-able—many of which are free or have free versions. Here's a sampling of what you can benefit from (free options are listed in parentheses):

- Project time tracker (e.g., Toggl and Clockify)
- Project management tool (e.g., Trello, Freedcamp, and Asana)
- Invoicing and accounting software (e.g., Sunrise, Waveapps, and Zipbooks)
- To-do list (e.g., Microsoft To Do, Todoist, and Any.do)
- Password manager (e.g., LastPass and Dashlane)
- Social media scheduler (e.g., Hootsuite and Buffer)
- Calendar (e.g., Google Calendar and Microsoft Outlook)

There really are a lot of options, even for one type of tool, so if you try one company's version and don't like it, try a competing com-pany's offering. The key is to choose something that you'll actually use and that will save you time and/or keep you organized.

Turn Off Notifications

To avoid distractions, turn off email notifications on your phone and your desktop. Also consider using your cell phone's Do Not Disturb setting so you won't be interrupted by social media notifications, phone calls, and texts. If you don't want to silence calls and texts from specific people, such as immediate family members, just add them to your phone's priority contact list. (But you might want to let them know that the only time they should contact you during your work hours is when there's an emergency.)

Schedule When You'll Check and Respond to Emails

A huge way to be more productive is to limit the number of times you check and respond to emails each day. A lot of people frequently check their inbox as a way to procrastinate (perhaps unintentionally) and because seeing a new email can trigger the release of dopamine, a hormone that creates a feeling of happiness.[2] But checking your inbox numerous times a day increases stress and distracts you from the project you're currently working on. And, as with all types of distractions, it takes time for you to get back on task—twenty-three minutes, according to one study—and your brain has to work hard to focus again on the project and reach maximum efficiency.[3] Further, you're more likely to make errors when you do start working again.[4] So, pick just two times a day that you'll go to your inbox. I recommend checking your inbox at the start of your workday and then toward the end

2. Pierre Berthon, Leyland Pitt, and Colin Campbell, "Addictive De-Vices: A Public Policy Analysis of Sources and Solutions to Digital Addiction," *Journal of Public Policy and Marketing* 38, no. 4 (2019): 451–468.

3. Gloria Mark et al., "Email Duration, Batching, and Self-Interruption: Patterns of Email Use on Productivity and Stress," in *Proceedings of the 2016 CHI Conference on Human Factors in Computing Systems* (New York: ACM, 2016), 1717–1728; Kermit Pattison, "Worker, Interrupted: The Cost of Task Switching," *Fast Company*, July 28, 2008, www.fastcompany.com/944128/worker-interrupted-cost -task-switching.

4. Duncan P. Brumby, Christian P. Janssen, and Gloria Mark, "How Do Interruptions Affect Productivity?," in *Rethinking Productivity in Software Engineering*, ed. Caitlin Sadowski and Thomas Zimmerman (Berkeley, CA: Apress, 2019), 85–107.

of your workday. That way, you'll be able to respond promptly to emails but won't be distracted by them during most of your workday, when you'll want to focus on editing.

Identify What Motivates You

Particularly when you're feeling tired or would rather be doing something other than working, focus on what gets you in a good mood, energizes you, and motivates you to be productive. That thing could be as simple as lighting a candle with a fabulous scent, listening to one of your favorite songs (and singing along or dancing to it), or repeating a mantra or affirmation (see chapter 3). You could even start each workday with that motivating element so that it becomes a trigger that helps your mind get into work mode.[5]

Also establish rewards for accomplishing tasks, projects, and goals. Decide what type of reward will motivate you to press forward even when you don't want to. For the best results, match the size or significance of the reward to the size of the task, project, or goal. A small motivation might be to check out a friend's must-read list, whereas a bigger motivation might be to buy something for your workspace. A big motivation might be a conference registration or a vacation. Whatever you decide on, think of it whenever your enthusiasm starts to wane.

Identify What Times of Day You're Most Productive

If you don't already know when you're most productive each day, now's the time to find out. Then, schedule your work, particularly the

---

5. See, for example, Wendy Wood and David T. Neal, "Healthy through Habit: Interventions for Maintaining Health Behavior Change," *Behavioral Science and Policy* 2, no. 1 (2016): 71–83.

mind-draining tasks, during your most productive hours. Don't just assume that you're at max productivity from an hour after you wake up until four hours later, for example. You might indeed be efficient that first hour or two, but then you might have a slump until a few hours later, when you feel another burst of energy. (And if you're like me, you'll feel another burst at night.) Or maybe you need a few hours to warm up your brain before you're ready to tackle the hardest tasks. There's no right or wrong pattern, so work with your natural rhythms instead of trying to force yourself into a schedule that someone else says is best.

To determine when you're the most productive, for at least one week (two weeks is better) note in a notebook or on a calendar how you feel every hour that you're awake. On a scale of 1–10, how energetic do you feel? On that same scale, how motivated are you to be working or doing anything else that requires brain power? How sharp is your thinking? How much did you accomplish the previous hour? Don't be surprised if your answers vary somewhat from day to day. You might also find that you're generally more productive on some days of the week than on others. For example, if you tend to get to bed late on Wednesdays because you're attending a child's sporting events, then you might be less productive on Thursdays than on other days, when you've gotten more sleep the night before. Perhaps you could work an extra hour earlier in the week so that you work one fewer hour on the day you're not as productive. Or maybe you can schedule less demanding tasks for that day. The key is to work with your reality instead of trying to fight it. That being said, you might also notice that some of your habits are decreasing your overall productivity—habits such as regularly getting little sleep, drinking alcohol, or not maintaining a nutritious diet. If any of your habits are hampering your overall productivity, consider making the needed changes.

Create a Comprehensive Schedule

At the start of each week, I create a schedule of everything that I'll be doing that week, whether for my business or in my personal life. I start with the nonnegotiables, which include a certain number of work hours, exercise, and religious practices. Then I fill in the rest of my available hours with other important items, followed by things I'd like to do if I have time. I also make sure to leave some empty time in my schedule so that if something unexpected comes up (and something usually does), I'm more likely to be able to fit it in without taking away time from other items, particularly the most important ones. This practice has definitely been a stress reliever for me.

Aim to schedule your work time during your most productive hours. Of course, this might not be possible if you have family obligations or other responsibilities involving schedules you don't control. (See chapter 11 for tips on balancing work with family and other responsibilities.) You don't need to have the same work schedule every day. Go ahead and take that 2:00 p.m. art class on Thursdays if you want—flexibility is one of the benefits of freelancing! But maintaining a fairly regular schedule can help you be in work mode when it's time to work and can make it easier for clients, family members, and others to know when you're typically available and when you aren't. Speaking of family, make sure to include on your calendar any activities that family members are involved in that you need to be aware of.

Establish a Plan for Working with Others Around

If you'll be working from home and you live with other people, it's essential to establish a plan for how to be productive when others are around while you're working. As part of your plan, establish boundaries—when is it okay or not okay for housemates to interrupt you? Is it okay for them to blast music or the TV from the next room? Will you be in charge of taking kids to extracurricular activities? Discuss these and other questions with those in your home (and potentially with family members who live elsewhere but regularly interact with you). Make sure they understand the importance of your business and what's required in order for you to succeed. Also get their input. What compromises can you all make so that everyone's needs are met? If you don't agree on a plan, you're all likely to experience ongoing frustration and stress.

Even after you've created a plan that everyone agrees to, expect that it will take a while for everyone to establish new habits. You can create reminders to gently help everybody remember what you've agreed on. For example, when you start working for a block of time, post a sign on your office door that indicates you're busy. You might even want to note when you will be taking your next break and will be available to talk. You could also display a project tracker on the door so housemates can see what you're currently working on and can track your progress on projects—and hopefully cheer you on along the way.

Organize Your Workspace

I'm a neat freak and can focus on work much better when my workspace is clean and clutter free. Even if you don't consciously crave a

"It's challenging to work from home with family members around. It helps to communicate in advance the hours I'll be working and ask not to be interrupted during that time. Having a dedicated workspace with a door that locks helps me stay focused. (I realize not everyone has that luxury.) Figuring out how many pages per day I need to get through helps me know if I am truly done for the day or if I need to work more after the kids go to bed. When my kids were younger, I hired a babysitter to entertain them for a few hours so I could focus on work."
—Scarlett Lindsay, freelance editor

clean space, research suggests that you do at least subconsciously. Various studies indicate that clutter can increase a person's feelings of stress and anxiety; can lead to procrastination; and can decrease the ability to focus, make good decisions, and be productive.[6] So, at the end of the workday, take a few minutes to organize your workspace so that when you return the next day, you'll feel calm rather than overwhelmed before you even start working.

You might also want to add some decor to your space, whether with plants, photos, motivating quotes, or something else that appeals to you. Making your workspace aesthetically pleasing can increase productivity and happiness.[7]

As a side note, you may wonder whether you need a dedicated workspace. Having one can help you stay organized (you'll know where to find your style manuals and other resources) and can help you separate work time from leisure time. When you go to that space, you'll be telling your brain that it's time to start working. Personally, I have an office to work in, but I also take my laptop with me to other areas of my house so that I can have a change of scenery, eat a snack, or sit on my couch when I feel like it. Switching things up now and then is nice, but I still like having a home base where all my reference materials and other work items are located.

---

6. Elizabeth Sander, Arran Caza, and Peter J. Jordan, "Psychological Perceptions Matter: Developing the Reactions to the Physical Work Environment Scale," *Building and Environment* 148, no. 15 (2019): 338–347; Catherine A. Roster and Joseph R. Ferrari, "Does Work Stress Lead to Office Clutter, and How? Mediating Influences of Emotional Exhaustion and Indecision," *Environment and Behavior* 50 (2019): 86–115; Joseph R. Ferrari et al., "Procrastinators and Clutter: An Ecological View of Living with Excessive 'Stuff,'" *Current Psychology* 37 (2018): 441–444.

7. Craig Knight and S. Alexander Haslam, "The Relative Merits of Lean, Enriched, and Empowered Offices: An Experimental Examination of the Impact of Workspace Management Strategies on Well-Being and Productivity," *Journal of Experimental Psychology* 16, no. 2 (2010): 158–172.

Exercise

You already know that exercising is important for your health, but did you know that exercising can also improve your work productivity? Various researchers have documented how physical activity can increase people's efficiency when working. For example, exercising before you start working or during a work break can improve your ability to think clearly; increase your energy level, focus, and time management; reduce stress; and improve your mood.[8]

A medium to long session of higher-intensity physical activity is great, but it isn't enough—or your only option. However you choose to move, and that could be simply walking, you should also avoid sitting at your computer for hours on end. Even if you regularly exercise, sitting for long periods increases your risk of chronic diseases, such as diabetes, heart disease, and some cancers.[9] To combat these risks, one group of experts has recommended setting a goal of standing and/or walking for a total of two hours during the workday and eventually increasing to four hours per workday.[10] You might be wondering whether even two hours is doable. I can confirm that it is—even four hours is, as I've tested out myself. For years, I've alternated between sitting and standing while working. Typically, I'll stand for about forty-five minutes and then sit for about fifteen. Often, standing makes me feel more alert and clearheaded than I feel when I'm

8. Candice L. Hogan, Jutta Mata, and Laura L. Carstensen. "Exercise Holds Immediate Benefits for Affect and Cognition in Younger and Older Adults," *Psychology and Aging* 28, no. 2 (2013): 587–594; Joanne C. Coulson, Jim McKenna, and Matthew Field, "Exercising at Work and Self-Reported Work Performance," *International Journal of Workplace Health Management* 1, no. 3 (2008): 176–197.

9. Neville Owen et al., "Too Much Sitting: The Population-Health Science of Sedentary Behavior," *Exercise and Sport Sciences Reviews* 38, no. 3 (2010): 106–113.

10. Anna Puig-Ribera et al., "Impact of a Workplace 'Sit Less, Move More' Program on Efficiency-Related Outcomes of Office Employees," *BMC Public Health* 17, no. 1 (2017): 455–466.

sitting. Sometimes I'll even walk on my treadmill while working (usually on easier, less brain-draining tasks). You have a lot of options in terms of creating a workspace in which you can stand. You can go the more expensive route and buy a standing desk, or you can be like me and configure one yourself. As for walking on my treadmill, I lay a board on the treadmill's arms and then place my laptop on the board. (For numerous DIY ideas, google "DIY standing desk" and "DIY treadmill desk.") Even if you don't build up to two hours of standing or walking, let alone four hours, however much time you do rack up will benefit your health—and likely your productivity.[11]

Outsource Tasks

I'm a DIY kind of person. I typically make my meals rather than buy them at a store or restaurant, I mow my lawn rather than hire a neighborhood teen, and I complete basic home maintenance myself rather than pay a service company. But I've also learned over the years that there are benefits to outsourcing some tasks so that I can focus on more important, more enjoyable, and/or more profitable activities. That's one reason I no longer prepare my annual tax return. Paying a professional tax preparer to file my taxes saves me considerable time—time I can instead spend working on a freelance project that will pay more than I pay my tax preparer. Think about what tasks you can pay someone else to do so that you have more time to invest in moneymaking activities. Focus on the tasks that you don't enjoy, that aren't your specialty, or that you can pay someone else to do for less per hour than you earn per hour.

---

11. I realize that some people have health conditions that prevent them from standing much, let alone moving around much. My intent is to highlight good practices for the general population; please make sure to do what is best for you personally.

Perhaps early on in your freelancing career, you won't have the funds to outsource any tasks. But at some point it will make more business sense to outsource certain tasks rather than complete them yourself. And you might reach that point sooner than you'd expect, because sometimes you need to invest before you get the results you want. As an example, paying someone to do your yard work could give you more time to market your services to ideal clients or to complete a longer project that you otherwise wouldn't be able to fit in with your other projects. Taking on that project could lead to repeat business or to additional referrals. And when you've reached or exceeded your earning goals, outsourcing some tasks could simply give you more time to spend with family and friends and to focus on your hobbies.

Strategies to Improve Your Editing Efficiency

I'm a big proponent of using computer tools to increase editing efficiency (and accuracy), so many of the tips below focus on these tools. But don't limit yourself to the ones I discuss. Make it a goal to regularly look for additional ways to increase your effectiveness when editing.

Create Word Shortcut Keys

You're likely aware of many of Word's shortcut keys, such Ctrl + C (or Cmd + C on a Mac) to copy text, and hopefully you use them. But are you using shortcut keys for other commands and tools? For example, Ctrl + Shift + E will toggle track changes on and off. Ctrl + M will add a comment to any text you've selected. Over time, using these and other shortcut keys instead of mousing to the commands on the toolbar will speed up your editing. Numerous shortcut keys are preprogrammed into Word (for a list of common shortcut keys, search on

Google; you can also google instructions on how to generate a list of all shortcut keys in your version of Word). Check them out, and write down the shortcuts you use regularly and will want to memorize.

You can save even more time if you create shortcuts for tools you regularly use but that don't already have shortcuts assigned. For example, I use the Compare tool frequently, so I created a shortcut key for this feature. Creating your own shortcuts is simple, but the steps vary somewhat based on the version of Word you're using; to find what steps you need to take, google "create shortcut Word [enter version number]."

Use Word's Advanced Find and Replace Features

I'm sure you use Word's basic Find and Replace tool to locate words and phrases and to replace them with something else. But do you use the advanced search options, which let you make your search case sensitive, limit your search to whole words only or words with specific formatting, and confine your search to a variety of other conditions? For example, you can use the options to specify how to format any text you enter into the Replace With box. The Find and Replace tool is even more powerful—and time-saving—when you use the wildcards function.

If you're not familiar with how to use these advanced features, watch a few tutorials on YouTube and then try out the features for yourself. (While you're practicing, use a copy of a document you're currently editing, not the version you'll eventually send to your client. You'll likely save yourself heartache and hours of fixing any problems you introduced.) To become a wildcard power user, consider reading Jack Lyon's short book *Wildcard Cookbook for Microsoft Word*. The time you spend learning the ins and outs will pay dividends in the long term. You'll learn that by using wildcards and other advanced Find and Replace features, you'll be able to make global

Preprogrammed Word Shortcuts for Editors

The key combinations shown below are for Windows operating systems. On Macs, the same shortcuts are usually available by using Cmd instead of Ctrl.

Ctrl + A: Select all text in document

Ctrl + Alt + D: Insert endnote

Ctrl + Alt + F: Insert footnote

Ctrl + Alt + H: Highlight selected text

Ctrl + Alt + M: Add a comment to the selected text

Ctrl + B: Toggle between bold and no bold

Ctrl + C: Copy selected text

Ctrl + Enter: Insert page break

Ctrl + F: Open Navigation pane (including the Find tool)

Ctrl + H: Open Find and Replace box

Ctrl + I: Toggle between italics and no italics

Ctrl + N: Open new document

Ctrl + O: Open existing document

Ctrl + S: Save

Ctrl + Shift + =: Toggle between superscript and nonsuperscript

Ctrl + Shift + A: Toggle between capital and lowercase letters

Ctrl + Shift + C: Copy formatting of text

Ctrl + Shift + Spacebar: Insert nonbreaking space

Ctrl + Shift + V: Paste formatting of text

Ctrl + Shift+ E: Toggle on and off track changes

Ctrl + U: Toggle between underline and no underline

Ctrl + V: Paste selected text

Ctrl + Y: Redo

Ctrl + Z: Undo

Ctrl + - (on Numeric Keypad): Insert en dash

Ctrl + Alt + - (on Numeric Keypad): Insert em dash

Ctrl + =: Toggle between subscript and nonsubscript

Ctrl + ↑: Move cursor up one paragraph

Ctrl + →: Move cursor one word to the right

Ctrl + ↓: Move cursor down one paragraph

Ctrl + ←: Move cursor one word to the left

Esc: Cancel a command

F12: Save file with new name

F7: Open spell check

Shift + F7: Open thesaurus

changes in a document—changes that if you made manually one by one would take considerable time (not to mention that you might miss a place where the change is needed).

Use Macros

Macros can be even more powerful than Word's advanced Find and Replace features. Simply put, a macro is a series of commands that are grouped together; when you run the macro, the commands will automatically be completed in the order you've specified. A macro can be short and simple or long and complex.

Let's look at one I created. First, the background: I once edited a multivolume book that came to me chapter by chapter, and I needed to apply a project-specific template to each file (more than seventy!) so that I had the correct styles. The process to switch the template is pretty straightforward but requires navigating to several places and making a good number of clicks. All in all, the process takes about thirty seconds per chapter. The manual method became tedious very quickly, so I decided to record a macro to automate the steps, and then I assigned a shortcut key to the macro. Now, with just one keystroke and less than a second of time, I can switch the template for a file. Just like that, my editing became more efficient. The more macros you use, especially for longer, more complex processes, the more productive you'll become.

Macros can increase not only your editing speed but also your editing accuracy. For example, I run a macro to determine whether a paragraph has an odd number of double quotation marks (which in most cases indicates I need to add an opening or closing quotation mark somewhere). I also run a macro that lists all proper nouns in a file; if two proper nouns have very similar spellings, suggesting that one is a misspelling, the words will be highlighted in the list. Using this macro has helped me identify many misspellings,

particularly in foreign names I'm not familiar with and I therefore
don't easily notice when they're spelled inconsistently. (Catching
such errors can earn you bonus points with clients—and, no, you
don't need to let them in on the secret of how you did it.)

The quotation mark and proper noun macros are only two of the
hundreds that Paul Beverley has created and that he freely shares at
www.archivepub.co.uk/book.html. If I'm looking for a macro to automate a process, I turn to his book of macros first. In addition to providing the macros, he's created text and video tutorials explaining
macros, good ones to start with, and how to use various macros. If
Paul doesn't have a macro to do what I'm looking for, I'll google
"Word macro for [insert task]" or I'll record my own macro (google
"record Word macro" for instructions). To boost your editing speed
and accuracy, make it a goal to regularly use macros. Perhaps try out
one new macro a month, so that you slowly add to your tool kit but
don't feel overwhelmed by all the options. Another good time to
try a new macro is when you're completing a monotonous, time-
intensive task. Instead of plodding through the process, spend a few
minutes looking for a macro. Then use the time you saved to complete an extra work task—or to dive into your latest library find (yep,
you've earned that latter option).

Use Word's Comment Feature to Make Notes for Yourself

As you're editing a document, you might come across a sentence that
doesn't make sense and that you're not sure how to revise. Or maybe
you think a sentence should be moved to a different paragraph but
you're not sure which one. Instead of dwelling on the sentences too
long (and therefore halting progress on the manuscript), add a comment on the sentence. In the comment, type your name and a brief description of the issue or question. Then move on to the next sentence
so that you keep the forward momentum on the manuscript. After

you've finished the section, the chapter, or another component of the manuscript, return to the problematic sentences by entering your name in the Find bar. When you return to a sentence, you'll likely be able to resolve the issue relatively quickly because you've gained helpful, clarifying information as you've moved farther along in the manuscript and because your brain has been subconsciously thinking about the issue in the meantime and has formed some possible solutions.[12] If you're still stuck, revise your comment so it's directed to the author.

Learn Best Practices for Using Other Programs You Work In

Though editors typically spend a lot of time working in Word, this program isn't the only one you might use for your projects. If you regularly use other programs—PowerPoint, InDesign, Acrobat, and so forth—then take a bit of time to learn how to use the programs effectively. For example, check out what shortcut keys are available and how to use advanced features of any find and replace tools. Play around with the program's display settings to figure out which options allow you to work most effectively. To learn to use programs efficiently, start with a few of the free tutorials that are available online. You can also register for paid courses that are run by other editors and various organizations.

Use a System to Track Your Projects

To maximize efficiency and productivity, you need to be organized, especially when it comes to tracking your projects. So, it's important

---

12. For research on the connection between unconscious thought and decision-making, see J. David Creswell, "Neural Reactivation Links Unconscious Thought to Decision-Making Performance," *Social Cognitive and Affective Neuroscience* 8, no. 8 (2013): 863–869.

to set up a system for tracking information about current and upcoming work. I prefer to use an Excel spreadsheet, since I can customize it to include exactly the information I want and I can access the information offline. But you certainly can use a higher-tech option, including cloud-based programs, such as Trello and Asana. (Note that many editors think such programs have a high learning curve.)

If you choose to create your own tracker, you'll likely want to include the following categories:

· The project's name
· The client's name
· The client's contact information
· The projected date that the client will submit the project
· The date the project is due back to the client
· The fee or hourly rate
· Details of the service provided
· The style guide
· The number of pages/words
· The estimated time required to complete the project
· The actual time required to complete the project
· The date(s) payment is due
· The date you sent the invoice
· The date(s) payment is received

By tracking this information, you can use Excel to calculate various stats. For example, by documenting the project word count and hours spent, you can set up a formula in Excel to automatically calculate how many words you edited per hour. (If you're not familiar with how to use Excel formulas, google "create formula in Excel" to find numerous pages with helpful instructions.) What if you like the idea of using Excel to track project information but setting up a spreadsheet yourself feels daunting? You're in luck: some generous editors have provided access to templates you can use—and customize to your needs. For example, check out the templates from Louise Harnby and Katie Chamberlain.[13]

If you track projects in Excel, you might want to use the same spreadsheet to map out your work time during the week. Simply add a new worksheet to the spreadsheet, and then set it up as a calendar, with each row representing thirty or sixty minutes. At a minimum, include all hours of the day and night that you might work (I prefer to include all hours I'll likely be awake so that I can schedule in non-work activities too). Then, block out time for each project and task you need to work on during a week. For example, you might schedule to work on project 1 from 9:00 a.m. to noon on Monday and then schedule to work on project 2 from 1:00 p.m. to 5:00 p.m. In addition to listing the project name in the assigned cells, consider highlighting the cells with a specific color so it's easy to see at a glance how you've divided your time between different projects and tasks.

Track Your Time

Even if you're using a project-fee approach and therefore don't need to tell a client how many hours you spent on a project, you should track your time so you can evaluate your speed. Over time, you'll be able to identify trends in how long it takes to complete a certain type of editing for a certain type of project and perhaps even for a certain client. You can use that information to make sure you're arriving at realistic estimates when you develop project fees or tell a client how many hours you'll likely spend on a project.

---

13. Louise Harnby, "How to Schedule Editing and Proofreading Projects and Payments in Excel," *The Parlour* (blog), November 11, 2012, www.louiseharnby proofreader.com/blog/editorial-annual-accounts-template-excel#; Katie Chamberlain, "Editors' Tracking Programs," Beacon Point, n.d., accessed January 15, 2020, http://beaconpointservices.org/editors-tracking-programs.

Tracking your time might also help you become more productive. If you know that the tracker is going, you might be better able to stay focused and ignore distractions. You might also be motivated to implement new strategies to edit faster, such as by using shortcut keys and macros. Every once in a while, compare your current editing speed to your speed six or twelve months ago. (Of course, try to compare projects that are similar in difficulty.) Are you happy with the results? If they're the same or you're editing slower now, brainstorm potential reasons. Should you do something different so you can speed up (using editing tools, getting more sleep, etc.)? Or maybe you've simply reached a max editing speed. If that's the case, great! Otherwise, look for ways to be more productive.

End Each Workday by Creating a To-Do List for the Next Day

Consider ending each workday with a note about where you are on a project and anything you need to keep in mind when you start up again the next day. You might also benefit from making a to-do list of smaller items (since presumably you'll already have the bigger items scheduled in for the day). With the notes and the to-do list, you'll be able to get up to speed faster when you begin working again.

Strategies to Manage Your Project Schedule

No matter how well you apply the productivity strategies we've discussed so far, you won't be able to maximize your productivity if your clients don't send projects on time. So, consider implementing strategies that encourage your clients to stay on track. Below are some approaches that have worked for me and other editors. Try one or a combination of these strategies to see what works best for you, the types of clients you typically work with, and the kinds of projects you typically work on.

First, if you schedule projects at least a few weeks in advance, re-quire a nonrefundable booking fee. The fee might be 20–25 percent of the estimated project fee and could be applied to the amount of the project fee due when the client sends you the project to start editing. If the client needs to reschedule the submission date and doing so will negatively affect your schedule, you can require the client to pay a new nonrefundable booking fee; also make sure to renegotiate your dead-line. If you can't accommodate the client's desired deadline, then re-fer the client to other editors who might be able to meet the deadline.

Similarly, you can charge a cancellation fee. If a client cancels the project before you begin, consider charging 25–50 percent of the es-timated project fee, with the exact percentage based on whether you'll be able to fill the resulting gap in your work schedule. Of course, for this option to work, the client must have already paid a deposit for the project. You might charge 25 percent if the client cancels two weeks before the submission date, and you might charge 50 percent if the client cancels the day before the submission date. If the client cancels the project after you've started editing, make sure that the cancellation fee compensates you for the amount of work you've completed as well as for the gap you'll have in your schedule.

If you schedule projects in advance, and particularly if you don't charge a booking or cancellation fee, make sure to touch base with a client about a week before his or her project is due to you. That way, you can verify whether the client is still on target to get the project to you on time. If the client's schedule has changed, you'll have a bit of time to see whether you can tweak your schedule to accommodate the change or whether you need to reschedule the project or perhaps subcontract parts or all of the project to another editor. (Of course, you should only subcontract to individuals who you trust will per-form as well as you would on the specific project.)

Alternatively, consider accepting projects on a first come, first served basis rather than scheduling projects in advance. For example, a client might tell you that a project will be ready for you in two weeks, but you won't formally schedule the project and the turnaround time until the project comes in. If another client submits a project in the meantime, you'll prioritize that one.

Whichever methods you decide to implement, make sure you communicate them to your clients. If you choose to charge a nonrefundable booking fee or cancellation fee, explain it to your clients and include appropriate clauses in your contract. Your contract should also specify that your return deadline will change if the client submits the project to you late and that you might not be able to work on the project at all if your schedule is filled with other clients' projects. By implementing one or more of the strategies above, you'll be encouraging clients to stay on schedule and you'll also be protecting yourself when clients still run behind or cancel a project.

Strategies to Stop Procrastinating

Even if you're a highly motivated and disciplined person, you're probably hit with the procrastination bug now and then. You feel the urge to do *anything* but work on the project your schedule says you should be working on right now. You tell yourself that you'll get started in ten minutes, but thirty minutes later you still haven't started—though the shelves in your fridge are now clean, and the food is organized by color. Why does the thought of working on the project fill you with dread? And how can you overcome that feeling and get started?

The first step is to understand why you want to procrastinate. If you dig deep, you'll likely find that you're putting off the work for one of a few reasons. Often, people—and I think editors in particular— procrastinate working on an important project because they have perfectionist tendencies and fear making mistakes. I'll discuss perfectionism more in the next chapter; here, I'll just talk about the topic in relation to procrastination. The key is to acknowledge that you shouldn't expect yourself to be perfect and that your clients shouldn't either. (If they do, you need to find new clients.) Giving yourself permission to make mistakes can remove the dread that causes you to procrastinate. If you're still afraid of making errors, then reassure yourself that you can always make another pass through the document to fix any problems that you missed (or introduced) during the first pass.

Another reason you might be procrastinating is that you're not sure how to get started on a project. I've felt that way before, especially when I'm providing a new service (e.g., writing a white paper) or editing a manuscript on a topic I don't know anything about. I've found that the resulting discomfort is also related to the problem of perfectionism: because the work or topic is new, I'm afraid I won't be able to meet my expectations for providing high-quality work.

To overcome these issues, I use a few strategies. First, I'll complete a little research to better understand the topic of the manuscript or the new service. That research will likely involve scanning some publications similar to the one I'll be working on, so I can get an idea of what's standard. Next, I'll skim the materials the client has provided, so I can get a better sense of what I'll be working on. Then, it's time to start the actual work. At this point, if I still feel like procrastinating, then I tell myself I need to work on the project for only thirty minutes (I know I can endure anything for that long). If those thirty minutes are excruciating, then when the time is up I can switch to working on a different project or task. But almost without fail, after I've gotten thirty minutes into a project, I am feeling more comfortable and don't mind continuing to work on the project for an entire work block.

Giving yourself permission to switch to another project after a certain length of time can help in other procrastination situations too. For instance, maybe you're dreading a project because you find it boring. Tell yourself that you need to work on it for only XX minutes and then can take a break or switch to another work-related task, such as sending a contract for another project or cleaning off your desk. Knowing that the time is limited will make you feel that the work is less onerous. And when the time is up, you might decide that you can keep working on the project for a bit longer before moving on to something else.

Of course, other reasons can prompt procrastination, such as being physically or mentally tired or feeling overwhelmed by personal matters—such as relationship difficulties or financial problems. If you're feeling tired, evaluate whether you're getting enough sleep and taking time to relax. How can you adjust your schedule so you have time to rest and recharge? Are you following the advice to take regular breaks during the workday? And what about your diet? Are you loading up on fruits and veggies, or are you relying on processed foods for fuel?

If you're procrastinating because your thoughts are focused on a stressful personal situation, try meditating, praying, writing your thoughts in a journal, talking with a family member or friend, or using other strategies that will help you achieve a calmer mental state. Take long, deep breaths, which can help your heart rate slow down and help you think more clearly.[14] Also make sure you're exercising—it truly is a remedy for a variety of troubles. For me, exercising not only increases endorphins (feel-good hormones) but also helps me formulate ways to address stressors.[15] After I've worked my body, my mind feels more prepared to focus on work.

The next time you feel the pull of procrastination, take a moment to assess the reason. Then implement one or more of the strategies above to overcome the urge. I bet that after even just ten minutes

---

14. Marijke De Couck et al., "How Breathing Can Help You Make Better Decisions: Two Studies on the Effects of Breathing Patterns on Heart Rate Variability and Decision-Making in Business Cases," *International Journal of Psychophysiology* 139 (2012): 1–9.

15. Kathleen Mikkelsen et al., "Exercise and Mental Health," *Maturitas* 106 (2017): 48–56.

of working, you'll feel empowered and motivated to keep plowing through the project.

Key Takeaways

- The more productive you are, the more time you'll have for additional projects, other business tasks, and personal pursuits.
- Find tech tools that help you manage your time, organize your work, and edit faster and more accurately.
- Schedule your work hours and all other activities in your day. Take a short break after each focused, distraction-free work session.
- Schedule in time to exercise.
- Determine when you're most productive and what motivates you.
- When you're tempted to procrastinate, identify the underlying reason so you know what strategies to apply so that you can overcome the cause.

11 *Achieving Work/Life Balance*

Everyone's heard of work/life balance, but it seems that few people achieve it—or if they do, they don't maintain it for more than a few weeks or months. And some people believe that work/life balance is a myth. My take? You're not likely to experience this balance 100 percent of the time, but you can enjoy it often—if you have the right mindset and are committed to applying key strategies. So, this chapter will explore those topics. I'll also talk about how to address negative client feedback, perfectionism, and imposter syndrome, all three of which can obviously decrease your work enjoyment and seep into your attitude toward life overall. Though I can't guarantee that following the tips in this chapter will keep your life perfectly balanced, I am confident that you'll be closer to maintaining that balance and you'll know what to do if things start to wobble.

Balancing Work and Personal Pursuits

Adopting the Right Mindset

Those who think work/life balance isn't possible often reach this conclusion because they assume *balance* means "to make equal." Sure, that's one definition, but I prefer another of *Merriam-Webster's* definitions: "to bring into harmony."[1] For most people, it's un-realistic to think that they can spend as many hours per day on personal matters as they do on work. When your work life and personal life are in harmony, you'll feel good about the amount of time you spend on both. And you won't fall into the trap of think-ing that you need as much leisure time as work time in order to achieve balance.

Perhaps you're skeptical about *balance* not meaning "to make equal," so let's consider an example. Research indicates that people need a combination of carbohydrates, protein, and fat for overall health. We need a balance among the three, but we don't need the same amount of each for maximum functioning. Various diets rec-ommend different ratios for each macronutrient, and the optimal ra-tios for one person might differ from the optimal ratios for someone else. Likewise, one person might thrive when working more hours than are ideal for another person. So, the key is to recognize that both work and leisure are important and to then figure out the ideal ratio for you. Admittedly, some people may prefer a lower ratio of work hours than they need to log so that they can meet financial goals. Later in this chapter, I'll present strategies for making this difference feel less significant. (Also see chapters 8 and 14 for ideas on how to increase your freelance income.)

Take some time to think about your life right now. Do you cur-rently have a pretty good balance between work and the other as-pects of your life? You might want to write down a description of your ideal mix of work and personal activities and then evaluate whether you're currently close to the ideal. If you're not, do you need to make a few tweaks, or is an overhaul in order? Think about what's going well and what needs improvement. For instance, do you need to wrap

---

1. *Merriam-Webster*, s.v. "balance (*n.*)," accessed January 31, 2020, www.merriam-webster.com/dictionary/balance.

up earlier in the day so you can eat dinner with your family? Or do you need to establish boundaries with family and friends so they're not frequently interrupting you during your work hours?

In figuring out how to achieve balance, it's essential to understand that achieving balance requires making choices. When you say yes to something, you need to say no to something else. And once your schedule is filled with work and other activities, if you want to take on something additional, you need to give up something else.

Saying no can be hard, but it can be a healthy response. Don't feel guilty saying no to something—even a good thing—that you're not passionate about and that would prevent you from doing something that you value (e.g., hanging out with family, maintaining religious practices, or volunteering with an organization you support). If your work schedule is full, you don't need to accommodate potential clients who ask you to fit them in. Simply explain that you'll be available starting XX date and that if they can't wait until then, you'll be happy to recommend some other professionals who might be able to help. Sure, taking on another project may initially seem appealing because you'll be bringing in more money, but is the extra money worth giving up time you'd otherwise spend with your family and friends, on hobbies, or on sleep? If you cram extra work into your schedule more than a few times, you'll likely learn that the answer is no—and that you've likely become burned out or sick, meaning your body will force you to find more balance.

On the flip side, it's also okay to tell a friend that you can't go out to lunch this week because you need to finish a project and that if you did go, you'd need to stay up late working or you'd have to miss your niece's dance recital. Let your friend know that you do want to catch up with him or her and that you'll be available the following week (or whatever the case might be).

It's important to realize that even after you've figured out the right balance between work and personal life and you've taken steps to maintain this balance, there will be times when your balance wobbles a bit. Sometimes, family emergencies will come up that require a lot of your time and attention. Another week, you might need to put in a few extra work hours to complete a project. Those fluctuations in the amount of time you spend on work and personal life are okay. Returning to the diet metaphor, you don't have to eat the optimal ratio of carbs, protein, and fat at each meal to remain healthy. But if you consistently eat an unbalanced diet, you're eventually going to feel the effects, and the same thing will happen if you're regularly missing your target in terms of work/life balance. If you do need to focus more on work one week, aim to work a little less than the norm the following week so you can have extra time to focus on the things you gave less attention to the previous week.

Also be aware that your ideal work/life balance will likely change over time because your circumstances will change, whether in terms of family (getting married, welcoming a baby into the family, becoming an empty nester, etc.), the season (school vacations, sports schedules, etc.), or other factors. So, if you start to feel out of balance, reassess your situation and figure out what your new ideal balance is and what you need to do to achieve it.

Applying Strategies to Achieve Balance

After you've identified your ideal work/life balance, it's time to implement specific strategies to help you achieve the ideal. These strategies aren't revolutionary, but they are easy to forget or ignore, especially when you're already feeling out of balance. Without further ado, here are the strategies.

DECIDE WHAT YOUR NONNEGOTIABLES ARE

You're not likely to succeed at achieving work/life balance unless you've decided what aspects of work and life you're not willing to adjust. If you don't identify these aspects, then you'll be tempted to compromise on them when life gets busy. Then you'll feel dissatisfied but might not be aware of why. So, write down what you simply won't budge on. For me, one example is my commitment to not work on Sundays. If needed, I'll work on Saturdays—even into the night—but you'll never find me working on Sundays, not even checking my work email. Because I've decided not to violate my core value of taking Sundays off, I don't have a hard time telling clients that I won't respond to emails or phone calls on Sundays and that I can't meet project deadlines that would require me to put in hours on a Sunday.

SCHEDULE IN WORK HOURS, BREAKS, FREE TIME, DAYS OFF, AND VACATIONS

Decide how many hours you'll work each week, and then schedule those hours into your calendar, indicating which project you'll work on during each hour. With those hours penciled in, don't let yourself feel pressured to slip in a few more. Okay, I get it—you've no doubt heard of (or experienced) the feast-or-famine cycle, so you might be tempted to put in extra hours if you have the work. But if you're doing so on a regular basis, you're definitely not experiencing a famine (and you're not likely to if you follow the marketing strategies in this book). So don't get in the habit of stealing time from personal pursuits so you can put in more work time.

Once you've scheduled in your work time, note when you'll take breaks during your work hours. As I explained in chapter 10, you need these breaks in order to maintain productivity. I also believe you need to take at least one entire day off from work each week. If you're spreading your work hours over the entire week, you'll likely start to feel that work is consuming your life and that you never get a break from it. In addition, make sure to schedule in vacation time, even if you don't leave your home during that time. Taking a vacation (and unplugging from work during that period) increases health and well-being, as well as work productivity after you return from your break.[2] Before your vacation starts, let clients know how long you'll be out of the office so that they won't expect to hear from you during your time off. Also turn on an email autoresponder, and include a message explaining when you'll return emails. During your leave, resist the urge to respond to business emails or to work on business projects. You deserve—and need—a break!

MAKE TIME TO EXERCISE

As I explained in chapter 10, exercising is a key strategy for remaining productive while working. Regularly exercising can also help you avoid chronic diseases and reduce stress, whether or not related to work. Lower stress levels make your life more enjoyable and increase your ability to constructively address issues that arise. Additionally, regularly exercising increases self-efficacy—that is, the belief that you can deal with difficult situations and accomplish tasks and goals. With greater self-efficacy, you'll feel more capable of balancing work and life and resolving any challenges that come up.[3] You'll likely also feel more energetic, meaning that at the end of the workday, you'll have the energy and desire to spend time with loved ones or on hobbies. And remember, exercising doesn't have to involve a long, in-

---

2. Jessica de Bloom, Sabine Geurts, and Michiel A.J. Kompier, "Effects of Short Vacations, Vacation Activities, and Experiences on Employee Health and Well-Being," *Stress and Health* 28, no. 4 (2012): 305–318; Jana Kühnel and Sabine Sonnentag, "How Long Do You Benefit from Vacation? A Closer Look at the Fade-Out of Vacation Effects," *Journal of Organizational Behavior* 32, no. 1 (January 2011): 125–143.

3. Russell Clayton et al., "Exercise as a Means of Reducing Perceptions of Work-Family Conflict: A Test of the Roles of Self-Efficacy and Psychological Strain," *Human Resource Management* 54, no. 6 (2014): 1013–1035.

tense workout: taking a walk, gardening, and dancing to your favorite songs all count as exercise.

PURSUE YOUR HOBBIES

Even with a busy editing business and nonwork responsibilities, you should make time to pursue hobbies. And being a freelance editor doesn't mean that all your hobbies need to be related to editing or entrepreneurship. Sure, spend some personal time reading books on grammar and business—if doing so will be enjoyable. But don't stop upcycling furniture, jamming on an instrument, or taking cooking classes if any of those is your thing. Though you may need to cut back at some points, either in frequency or in your number of hobbies, you'll feel more balanced and therefore better able to manage work and other responsibilities if you take some time for yourself. Open a discussion with immediate family members so they understand why you need to keep up your hobbies and how doing so can help you be more relaxed and, as a result, more enjoyable to be around.

SET BOUNDARIES FOR CLIENTS

Setting boundaries is healthy, and communicating them to clients gives clients a better idea of what to expect when working with you. For instance, if you won't be working during the weekend, clients will know not to call you then or to expect a response to any emails that come in. This knowledge can help clients avoid a lot of unnecessary worry. (For ideas regarding what types of boundaries to set, see the "Business Standards" section in chapter 3.)

What if clients don't respect your boundaries? First, ensure that you've clearly explained them and that the clients understand them. For instance, if you'll be answering phone calls only between 9:00 a.m. and 4:00 p.m., make sure to specify which time zone you're working in. If you're sure a client understands a certain boundary but still fails to respect it, provide some patient reminders. The client likely isn't trying to overstep; rather, he or she probably is busy like you, has many things to manage, and has simply forgotten what your boundaries are. If the reminders don't fix the problem, then consider directly discussing the issue with the client, firmly letting him or her know that you expect your boundaries to be respected. If this discussion doesn't help, consider firing the client or charging the client more to compensate for the boundary breaking.

Even if a client (or potential client) is downright rude, be polite in response. If you're fuming inside, take several deep breaths and several minutes—or even hours—before responding. Talk through the issue with a family member, friend, or colleague, and ask for his or her input. Often, someone who's more removed from the situation will help you better understand where the client is coming from . . . or can confirm that your feelings aren't off base. Instead of turning the conversation into a hate fest, ask for help in crafting a response that is respectful and also conveys that you deserve respect. If a client is trying to push you to do something you don't want to do, be firm but polite in saying no.

SET BOUNDARIES FOR IMMEDIATE FAMILY MEMBERS

Clients aren't the only ones who need boundaries. For your benefit as well as the benefit of your family (or roommates, if applicable), you need to establish boundaries and expectations regarding when you'll be working, when and for what reasons it's okay to interrupt you during work hours, and what household tasks you will and will not be responsible for. For the best results, lead a discussion and be open to family members' input rather than simply laying down the law. If you're willing to compromise, they'll be more likely to support your business efforts and respect your boundaries.

Start the discussion by explaining your business goals and why your business is important—to you, your family, and your clients. Then describe how everyone will benefit when they respect your boundaries and, conversely, what the negative results will be when your boundaries aren't respected (e.g., if you're interrupted, you might have to work later instead of spending time with your family). Invite everyone to voice any questions or concerns, and then brainstorm ways to help ensure that your decision to work from home is a win-win for everyone. Assure your family that you'll set aside time to spend with them. Decide when those times will typically be, and encourage family members to list activities they want to do during those times.

After you've established boundaries and expectations, consider posting them on your office door or, if you don't have an office, somewhere in your workspace to serve as a reminder. You'll also benefit from posting your work schedule, including when you have meetings and therefore really shouldn't be interrupted. Another option is to buy a sign with "Open" on one side and "Closed" on the other. Hang the sign on your door, with the appropriate side of the sign facing out. If you have children who can't read, you could use pictures that indicate when you're available or unavailable (you might even want your children to draw the pictures). With young children, it's also a good idea to role-play various situations. For example, have your children practice knocking on your office door rather than walking in unannounced. Likewise, have them practice going to an older sibling if they need something but the sign on your door indicates you shouldn't be disturbed unless there's an emergency (and explain what counts as one).

If you have young kids, consider having older siblings or other family members babysit the young ones. Or hire a babysitter, even if

"I wear a wig while I'm working so family members can see when I'm 'at work.'"
—*Anonymous freelance editor*

for just a few hours a day or week. You'll be more productive, and the extra work could pay for most or all of the cost of babysitting. Alternatively, arrange with another parent for the two of you to take turns babysitting your kids and the other parent's kids. Maybe you'll have babysitting duty Mondays and Wednesdays, and the other parent will take Tuesdays and Thursdays. You can also arrange to alternate taking kids to and from school and activities.

If by choice or necessity you'll be the only one at home with your children during work hours, be realistic about how long you can work without needing to check on and assist them. If you have school-age kids, help them establish routines for while you're working. Perhaps when they arrive home from school, you'll greet them and spend five minutes talking about their day, and then they'll work on school assignments. After that, they can play with friends in the neighborhood, watch a TV show, or read. Also, consider putting together an activity box that your kids can pull out for times when they would otherwise come to you saying, "I'm boooored."

A few final suggestions: If the kids are loud enough that you can't concentrate (even with your office door shut), then buy a pair of noise-canceling headphones. You could also try turning on a fan or a white-noise machine. Also, keep in mind that even the best kids (and adults) will likely sometimes cross the established boundaries—after all, no one is perfect. So, try to be somewhat flexible as well as patient. After all, your family is trying to be flexible and patient with you.

SET BOUNDARIES FOR EXTENDED FAMILY AND FRIENDS

Extended family and friends also need to know what your boundaries are. Explain that just because you're home, that doesn't mean you can talk on the phone for an hour, babysit someone else's kids, or run an errand for someone. Ask relatives and friends to support you in achieving your business goals by respecting your boundaries.

Strategies to Achieve Work/Life Balance

- Identify your nonnegotiables.
- Schedule when you'll work, take breaks, and take vacations.
- Make time to exercise.
- Pursue hobbies and develop new ones.
- Establish and communicate boundaries for clients, family members, and friends.
- Outsource tasks.

OUTSOURCE TASKS

Another way to achieve greater work/life balance is to outsource tasks. Can you put a teenage son or daughter in charge of making dinner a few times a week? (If that's not possible, consider making several days' worth of meals over the weekend. Or look into a meal-delivery service.) If yard work or housework is cutting into your available time for work, family, friends, or hobbies, consider paying someone to complete those tasks. Or maybe you can outsource a business-related task. The key is to decide which tasks take up significant time but aren't ones you enjoy doing. Then, see if someone else can do the tasks for you. Even if others charge more than you earn per hour, the cost might be worth it if you'll gain greater work-life balance.

Dealing with Crises

At some point, you or someone you care about may experience a crisis that prevents you from working your normal number of hours or from focusing when you are working. In that event, you'll feel less stressed about your work if you've already created an emergency-management plan. Though some of the steps I'm going to suggest may seem intuitive, emergency situations tend to short-circuit people's ability to think clearly, so establishing your plan before a crisis strikes will help ensure that you approach business matters as logically as possible and that you don't forget anything.

First off, make sure that you're using a system to track all your projects so you can easily see what's currently on your plate. That way, you'll have an easier time figuring out whether you'll be able to meet your deadlines or will need to ask for extensions. You'll be more likely to still meet deadlines if you've made a habit of planning to finish projects a couple days before the actual deadlines.

If you need to ask for an extension, don't feel pressured to provide a lengthy explanation of the crisis and why you won't be able to meet the original due date. Simply note that an emergency will prevent you from meeting your deadline, and then state the date that you'll be able to finish the project. If the client needs the project returned by an earlier date that won't be feasible for you, then offer to subcontract the work to another editor you trust. If the client doesn't want you to hire a subcontractor, you'll need to explain that you will return the project uncompleted and will refund the client for the amount of work you didn't finish. If the client is okay with you hiring a subcontractor, then make arrangements with the other editor ASAP. Decide whether you'll completely turn the project over to the other editor or whether you'll take on a project management or quality control role. After deciding your level of involvement and the amount of work each of you will put in, determine how much of the project fee you'll keep and how much you'll give to the other editor. Also provide project information that will help the other editor get up to speed quickly. At a minimum, you'll want to explain the level of editing, identify which style guide to follow, provide the style sheet you've created for the project, and note any quirks in the author's writing style that you're retaining or revising. Also specify whether the subcontractor should correspond directly with the client or whether you'll be the main contact.

Another important step in preparing for an emergency is to ensure your files are backed up somewhere other than your computer. (If they're not, a hard drive failure could be the cause of a crisis.) You might want to regularly save your files to an external hard drive, but even if you do, also save them in a cloud storage system. That way, you'll still be able to access the files and share them with clients and subcontractors even if you won't have access to the computer you typically work on—say, if you will need to head out of town on quick notice or will be spending time in the hospital. On a related note, if you typically work on a desktop computer, it's a good idea to have a backup laptop so that you can take it with you if the emergency requires you to be away from home. Further, having a backup, even if you usually work on a laptop, will be a huge stress reliever if your primary device stops working.

You should also consider explaining to a family member, significant other, or close friend how to access your email account and work files on your computer or on the cloud in case a health challenge prevents you from doing so. Make sure to cover all the information the individual will need to know—for example, passwords for your computer, email account, and cloud storage account; the location of your electronic work folders; and the location of your project schedule. Specify what the individual should do in various circumstances. For instance, if you're too sick to check your email regularly, should the individual turn on an autoresponder and email any clients who are expecting to hear from you in the next few days?

One final tip: During a crisis, you'll likely be quite busy dealing with it, so you might feel like you don't have time to take care of your personal needs (assuming that the crisis isn't related to your own health). But keep in mind that caring for yourself is an important key in being able to handle the crisis and think clearly while working.

You'll probably need to reduce the amount of time you spend on self-care, but still strive to get an adequate amount of sleep; to exercise in some way; and to do something else to decompress, such as reading, meditating, or talking to someone. And don't be afraid to ask for support when you need it. Acknowledging that you'll benefit from help is a strength because it shows that you're self-aware, realistic, and confident enough to reach out to others.

Dealing with Negative Client Feedback

I don't know of anyone who likes receiving criticism or complaints, but maybe there's one brave soul out there who does. (If so, I'd love to learn his or her secret.) It's understandable if your stomach ties in knots when you receive negative feedback from a client. But the resulting stress won't help you achieve well-being, so what can you do to take the feedback in stride and respond in a way that will ease your tension, address the criticism, and even improve the client's opinion of you? The first and most important step is to avoid getting defensive. Instead, ask the client for details so you can better understand the situation. Consider restating the client's concerns; by doing so, you're signaling to the client that you're listening and that you acknowledge the concern.

Once you understand the situation, express empathy and, if appropriate, apologize. Apologizing isn't a sign of weakness or failure; in fact, apologizing is a sign of strength and maturity. Even if you haven't done anything wrong, it's okay to say you're sorry or to at least express regret that the client is unhappy about the situation. Simply doing so can quickly deescalate a tense situation.

Now it's time to address the negative feedback itself. When the client explained the issue, you might have realized that it resulted from miscommunication and that you can clear up the situation relatively easily. It might help to refer to information in your contract

Sample Crisis Plan

- Make sure you're using a system to track all your projects.
- If needed, ask your client for an extension.
  - Note that an emergency will prevent you from meeting the original due date.
  - State the date that you'll be able to finish the project.
  - If the client needs the project returned by an earlier date, offer to subcontract the work.
  - If the client doesn't want you to subcontract the work, explain that you will return the project uncompleted and will refund the client for the amount of work you didn't finish.
- If your client is okay with subcontracting the work, make arrangements with an editor you trust.
  - Decide whether you'll completely turn the project over to the other editor.
  - Determine how much of the project fee you'll keep and how much you'll give to the other editor.
  - Provide project information that will help the other editor get up to speed quickly.
  - Specify whether the subcontractor should correspond directly with the client or whether you'll be the main contact.
- Ensure that your files are backed up, preferably in a cloud storage system.
- Give a family member, significant other, or close friend access to your email account and work files, and explain what to do in various circumstances.
- Don't forget to take care of your personal needs, such as getting adequate sleep and decompressing.
- Ask for support when you need it.

or in an email conversation. Or maybe you need to explain why ending a sentence with a preposition isn't wrong. As tempting as it may
be to respond with a snarky comment (e.g., "If you'd actually read the
contract, you'd know that we agreed to XYZ"), channel all the zen
you can so that your tone is friendly. You want to convey that you're
an ally, not an enemy.

If you realize that you have made a mistake, admit it and explain
how you'll address the problem. For instance, if you missed or introduced an error in a manuscript you edited, you can offer to fix the error and to email the client the updated file. Of course, if the error
wasn't caught until after the manuscript was published, you need to
take a different tack: apologize and explain how you'll avoid the error
in the future. Whatever the case, it's typically best to avoid making an
excuse, even if it's legitimate, such as being distracted by a family
emergency. Giving an excuse can suggest that you're trying to avoid
blame, but what you really want to do is show that you are willing to
take responsibility and will do better in the future. With that being
said, if the client asked you to complete a rush job, then you can remind the client that the tight deadline meant you couldn't edit to
your typical standards. And if you made a single error in a multipage
document, kindly educate your client that commonly accepted accuracy rates are in the range of 80–95 percent.[4]

Even if you feel incredibly bad about any errors you made, don't
overapologize. Apologizing profusely can actually be a turnoff.
And don't immediately agree to review the entire document again
for free or to refund some of what the client paid you. The client
probably isn't expecting either option. (As a precaution, include
in your contract a clause specifying what you'll do if the client finds
errors.)

---

4. See, for example, Amy Einsohn and Marilyn Schwartz, *The Copyeditor's
Handbook*, 4th ed. (Oakland: University of California Press, 2019), 5.

If you follow the suggestions in this section, you likely won't lose your client's business. In fact, if you handle the situation respectfully and maturely, you might increase your client's loyalty to you. After all, most clients don't expect an editor to be perfect; rather, they expect the editor to accept feedback, take responsibility for mistakes the editor made, and strive to avoid the mistakes in the future.

Dealing with Perfectionism

I briefly touched on perfectionism in the previous chapter, and I want to cover the topic in more depth here because perfectionism can have a significant effect on your well-being and work/life balance. Not all editors are perfectionists, but I feel pretty confident in saying that the majority of copy editors are.[5] I haven't been able to find any research confirming this assumption, but the topic comes up frequently in online editing forums, in blog posts and articles for editors, and even in copy editor job descriptions. Perfectionist qualities can help you be good at your craft, but the pursuit and pressure of perfection can also lead to paranoia and poor performance—ultimately decreasing your feeling of well-being.

So, how can you balance perfectionist tendencies with the realities of editing? How can you cope with the fact that time and budget constraints mean you can't review a document over and over and *over* again even though you just know you missed something during your previous passes? The first step is to accept that you're not perfect and, even more important, that you don't need to be. Accepting this

---

5. I definitely fall into this category. Earlier in my career, there were times that I realized I'd made an error and would then tell myself that I wasn't skilled enough to be an editor and that I should quit the profession. Thank goodness I had supportive colleagues and I don't like to quit after I've started something.

fact can be very freeing. You won't feel the pressure to achieve an outcome that isn't possible (as frustrating as that impossibility might be). Of course, accepting imperfection doesn't mean that you're throwing your high standards out the window. Rather, it means that you're striving to do your best—and to become even better—but you're not a stress case each time you're about to hit Send when emailing a client your edited document.

In addition, make sure you're regularly engaging in activities that help you improve your skills. Read books on grammar and writing, participate in editing forums (in which you'll have the opportunity to learn from what other members post), and complete in-person and online courses on topics related to editing. Also, take note of specific areas you're weak in (e.g., determining whether to use *lay* or *lie*); whenever you come across one of those items in a document, pay particular attention to it and go to a credible source to ensure you've addressed the issue correctly. Make a list of items you often forget to check in a document, and then complete a separate pass in which you look only for those items (Find and Replace is your friend here). Additionally, see if you can use macros to help you identify errors that you're likely to miss on your own. By implementing these practices, you'll get closer to achieving the accuracy you aspire to.

When you do make mistakes, don't tell yourself you failed. Instead, remind yourself that mistakes provide an opportunity to grow and improve. Sure, that's easy for me to write, but it may be harder for you to actually believe. When you can't seem to forgive yourself for making a mistake—or when you're afraid a client won't—take several slow, deep breaths. Acknowledge that you're letting your perfectionism be your enemy rather than helping you to perform to the best of your abilities. Make a list of reasons that your negative thoughts and fears are inaccurate or exaggerated. For instance, think of all the times you've received praise for your high-quality work. (Tip: file this praise in a physical or email folder, and then read through it when you need a pick-me-up.) Then, make a plan for how you'll avoid the mistake in the future, and move on.

Avoiding Imposter Syndrome

Whether or not you battle with perfectionism, you've likely experienced imposter syndrome. In fact, 70 percent of people have, including incredibly successful people such as Tina Fey, Tom Hanks, Facebook executive Sheryl Sandberg, and Nobel Prize winners.[6] As the term implies, imposter syndrome involves thinking that you don't have the skills needed to complete your job—and that someone is eventually going to call you out as a fraud. As a freelancer, you might be prone to imposter syndrome for multiple reasons. For one, you don't work in the same office as others, including those who evaluate your performance, so you might not receive positive feedback that often. You might also feel imposter syndrome if the number of project requests you receive drops or if you don't win a project you provided a bid for.

Whatever the reasons, you can keep imposter syndrome at bay through taking a few steps—many are the same as for addressing perfectionism. Here's one strategy: when you feel inadequate or afraid (about not getting enough work, not doing well enough, etc.), acknowledge the thoughts and then identify any evidence that confirms or contradicts them. Let's consider an example: You presented

---

6. The statistic is from Jaruwan Sakulku, "The Imposter Phenomenon," *International Journal of Behavioral Science* 6, no. 1 (2011): 73–92. For information on successful people with imposter syndrome, see Holly M. Hutchins, "Outing the Imposter: A Study Exploring Imposter Phenomenon among Higher Education Faculty," *New Horizons in Adult Education and Human Resource Development* 27, no. 2 (2015): 3–12; W. Brad Johnson and David G. Smith, "Mentoring Someone with Imposter Syndrome," *Harvard Business Review*, February 22, 2019, https://hbr.org/2019/02/mentoring-someone-with-imposter-syndrome.

two project bids this week, and both were rejected; now you're afraid that no one will ever hire you again or that you'll have to drastically lower your fees. Put that thought on trial. What's the evidence for and against your dismal thought? Evidence supporting the thought is the two project bids from this week—and maybe a few bids over the last several months. Evidence contradicting the thought is that during the last three weeks, four of your project bids were accepted. And you're also in talks with two other potential clients. Clearly, the evidence that contradicts the thought is more substantial, and you need to convict that negative thought.

But what if the evidence for and against the thought is relatively balanced—or the evidence for is stronger? That just means it's time to implement a plan to address the issue. For instance, spend more time marketing your business, especially to individuals and companies that typically are willing to pay the rates you charge. If you're worried that your editing skills are weak, then complete training that will help you improve. By taking action, you'll likely feel empowered, which will help you cure the imposter syndrome.

Here are a few more tips: Don't compare yourself to others, because "comparison is the thief of joy" and isn't productive.[7] (However, do consider selecting role models who inspire you to improve.) Compare your current performance, in terms of editing quality, income, and the like, to your past performance. Quantify the progress you've made, and take satisfaction in even small improvements. After all, even the fastest, most successful runners in the world are typically improving only by seconds from race to race. When you start to feel doubts creep in, repeat self-affirmations (see chapter 3) and adopt the persona of someone who's self-confident and skilled. As research shows, faking it till you make it really does work.[8]

---

7. Quote attributed to Theodore Roosevelt.
8. Carney, Cuddy, and Yap, "Power Posing."

Key Takeaways

- You can achieve balance between work and personal life by adopting the right mindset and applying key strategies.
- Make time for yourself—to relax, exercise, pursue hobbies, and spend time with family and friends.
- Set boundaries for family members, friends, and clients.
- When you receive negative feedback from a client, respond respectfully and empathetically.
- Strive to provide high-quality service, but remember that no one is perfect.
- When you have negative thoughts, challenge them and also look for ways to continue to improve.

12 *Overcoming the Fear of Taxes*

Taxes. If you didn't just flinch, groan, or feel your stomach drop, congrats—you're probably one of few. I certainly don't love taxes (does anybody?), but I also don't fear them. I don't want you to fear them either. Since fear often results from a lack of knowledge, my goal in this chapter is to give you the information you need in order to understand the basics of federal taxes in the United States. By the end of the chapter, you probably still won't like the thought of taxes, but hopefully you also won't feel dread every time you hear or see the word.[1]

The Basics

If you earn $400 or more in a year from freelancing, you need to file a federal income tax return. Why such a low number? Because as a freelancer, you're responsible for paying not only income tax but also self-employment tax, which is currently 15.3 percent of your income

---

1. As a reminder, I'm not a certified accountant or tax preparer. The advice I give in this chapter is exactly that: advice. For more information on various tax topics, check out www.irs.gov. The website contains a wealth of information (as well as tax forms and instructions), and a lot of the content is pretty straightforward and easy to understand.

up to a threshold amount. (I'll explain more about self-employment tax in the next section.)

Because you'll be paying self-employment and income taxes, you should set aside approximately 30 percent of every payment you receive so that you're prepared when tax day comes. Note that 30 percent is just an estimate. To get a more targeted estimate, you'll need to consider your specific financial situation. For example, if you have a lot of deductions and credits and are in a low tax bracket, you won't need to earmark as high a percentage as someone who can't claim as many deductions and credits and is in a higher tax bracket. Also, if you live in a city that taxes you (hello, New York City), you'll probably want to set aside 40 percent. To make sure you're really setting aside the money, consider opening a savings account just for taxes. At the end of each month, total how much you earned freelancing that month, and then transfer the appropriate percentage to the savings account.

You're probably wondering whether you should file taxes on your own or whether you should pay a tax preparer. My answer: if you're doing just a little freelancing on the side, you might be okay preparing your tax return, with or without a program like TurboTax. But be aware that you'll probably miss out on some ways to lower your tax liability—and using a tax-filing program isn't foolproof (I know from personal experience). You might qualify to get free tax help through the IRS's Volunteer Income Tax Assistance program, but there's no guarantee the volunteers in your area will have much experience helping freelancers. And for the maximum tax benefits, you'll want to work with someone who's well versed in what tax deductions you can take and in other ways to (ethically) keep your tax liability as low as possible.

As you earn more through freelancing, and especially if you decide to file your taxes as an S corporation, you'll definitely benefit from paying a professional to complete your tax return. Sure, you

"You need to shop around and interview different accounting firms. What can you do for me? For what price? What can I do to prepare my materials for you so that I can afford your service? We used a large accounting firm for a few years but found that a small one focused on helping small businesses was much better for our needs."

—*Virginia McGowan, freelance editor*

might pay a tax preparer a couple hundred dollars to file your taxes, but you'll likely reduce your tax liability by more than that amount if you have an expert do the work for you rather than if you do it yourself. Plus, paying a tax preparer is an approved tax deduction, and you can work on paying projects during the hours you'd otherwise be working on your taxes. So, spend a little money to save more money.

Self-Employment Tax

The self-employment tax contains two components: 12.4 percent for Social Security and 2.9–3.8 percent for Medicare. There's a maximum income amount subject to the Social Security portion ($142,800 in 2021), so if you earn more than the maximum, you'll be taxed only the Medicare portion on any income above the max. (The Medicare portion is 2.9 percent for net income of up to $200,000, then 3.8 percent on any net income above $200,000.) When you're employed by a company, the company pays half of the self-employment tax, but if you're a freelancer you're responsible for the entire amount. Thankfully, 50 percent of what you pay in self-employment tax is deductible on your income tax return. (Oh, the complexities of the federal tax code!)

The easiest way to estimate how much you'll owe for self-employment tax is to use an online calculator. (Google will lead you to a lot of options.) If you want to manually calculate the amount, you can use Schedule SE. Basically, you start by multiplying your net income (i.e., earnings minus expenses) by 0.9235. Then, you multiply the resulting number by 0.153. For example, if Jane Grammar's net income is $100,000, she'll multiply that number by 0.9235, for a total of $92,350. Then, she'll multiply that number by 0.153 for a total of $14,129.55. That's the estimated amount she'll pay in self-employment tax. The nice thing about online calculators is that they'll take into account whether you've earned more than the threshold amount for the Social Security portion of the tax. If you calculate the tax manually, you'll need to calculate income above the threshold separately. The takeaway: online calculators are your friend! True, you'll have to complete Schedule SE when you file your annual tax return, but using an online calculator is a great tool for getting an informal estimate.

Quarterly Payments

If you're earning money as a freelancer, the IRS wants you to pay taxes quarterly rather than just on April 15. Not that I love quarterly taxes, but they do actually make sense. For one, federal taxes are designed to be a pay-as-you-go system. If you're an employee, taxes are taken out of every paycheck, and the IRS wants freelancers to pay as they go too. (Fortunately, we don't have to pay more often than once every three months.) Also, having freelancers pay every quarter increases the likelihood that they'll have the money to pay the amount owed. Some people just aren't good at saving money, even if they know they'll need it for taxes later on.

Before we tackle how to pay quarterly taxes, let's talk about some cases in which you can avoid paying every three months. First, you don't need to pay quarterly if you'll owe less than $1,000 in income taxes for the year. (To get an idea of how much you'll owe, look at your previous year's tax return.) Second, you can avoid quarterly payments if you're also employed at a company and you increase the tax withheld from paychecks to cover at least 90 percent of what you'll owe in income taxes for the year. (As I mentioned before, estimate that around 30 percent of your freelance earnings will go toward taxes, so keep the equivalent dollar amount in mind when deciding how much extra money to have withheld from your paychecks. You can also use the Tax Withholding Estimator at https:// apps.irs.gov/app/tax-withholding-estimator/results for an idea of how much extra you should have withheld from paychecks.) Third, you can avoid paying quarterly taxes if you have a spouse, you are filing jointly, and your spouse has extra money withheld from his or her paycheck to cover the taxes you'd need to pay on your freelance income.

Unless one of these three cases applies, you need to pay taxes quarterly—or else you'll face a payment penalty come April 15. (More on that later.) Now let's get into the details of figuring out how much to pay and how to make the payments. Start by filling out Form 1040-ES. To complete the form, you'll need to estimate how much self-employment income you'll earn this year. Don't worry too much about getting the estimate just right. Simply calculate what you expect to earn based on the number of hours you plan to work this year multiplied by what you expect to earn per hour. Later in the year, if you realize your estimate was too low, you can complete Form 1040-ES again and adjust the amount you pay the remaining quarters. If you initially didn't pay enough, you may be expected to pay a penalty when you file your return in April. You can find out by completing Form 2210. If you do owe a penalty, you can indicate on the form that you're requesting a waiver for one of the approved reasons, such as that your income varied throughout the year.

After you've completed 1040-ES, you'll know how much to pay each quarter. You can make the payment online by going to www.irs .gov/payments, and you'll have the option to authorize a bank transfer, to pay via debit or credit card, or to initiate an electronic fund withdrawal. You can also pay by phone, mail, or bank wire. If you

Quarterly Tax Information

- January 15
- April 15
- June 15
- September 15

HOW TO FILE AND PAY

- Form 1040-ES
- Payment via www.irs.gov/payments, bank transfer or wire, debit or credit card, electronic fund withdrawal, phone, or mail

SITUATIONS IN WHICH QUARTERLY PAYMENTS AREN'T REQUIRED

- You'll owe less than $1,000 in income tax for the year
- You're employed at a company and the amount of taxes withheld from paychecks will cover at least 90 percent of the amount you'll owe in income taxes (on employee and freelance income) for the year
- You're filing jointly with your spouse, and your spouse has enough money withheld from his or her paycheck to cover at least 90 percent of the combined amount you and your spouse will owe

want to pay in cash, you can visit a participating retail store (after you've registered for this option).

Quarterly payments are due April 15, June 15, September 15, and January 15 of the following year, unless any of those dates falls on a weekend or legal holiday; if that's the case, the payment is due the following date that isn't a weekend or holiday. Make sure to submit each payment by the due date or you'll likely be charged a late penalty. It's a good idea to add reminders to your calendar, say, on the first Monday of each due-date month.

Annual Tax Return

Whether you decide to file your taxes yourself or to hire a tax preparer, you should know the basics regarding annual returns. If you're a sole proprietor or an LLC filing as a sole proprietor (and not as an S corp), you'll fill out Form 1040 as well as Form 1040 Schedule C. Schedule C is where you'll report your business income and expenses.

If during the year you earned $600 or more from a company, the company should send you a 1099 by February of the following year, and the form will document the amount you earned. When the form arrives, check it against your records to ensure the amount is correct. If it's not, ask the company for a corrected version. Why? Because the company also submits a copy of your 1099 to the IRS, so you'll want to make sure the IRS has the right information. What if you don't receive a 1099? You don't need to ask the company to give you one. On Schedule C, you'll record all freelance earnings on one line; you won't list 1099 amounts separately. Any 1099s you receive are more of a formality for you, and the IRS uses the forms to help ensure that people pay taxes on what they earn.

On Schedule C, you'll also record all business expenses, which will reduce your total tax liability. (See the section "Tax Deductions for Freelancers," later in this chapter, for a list of deductions you can take.) You'll also need to fill out Schedule SE. As I mentioned earlier, by completing this form you'll know exactly how much you owe in self-employment tax.

If your business is an LLC, you can file your taxes as an S corporation. The main benefit is that you can reduce your tax liability because you can reduce the amount you owe in self-employment tax. Here's how it works: From your business income, you pay yourself a reasonable wage (based on the number of hours you work, common rates in the industry, etc.).[2] Your remaining earnings are considered shareholder dividends. Your reasonable wage is subject to self-employment taxes, but your shareholder dividends aren't.

Consider this example: Jane Grammar earned $90,000 last year freelancing full-time, and a reasonable wage for the type of editing she does in her geographic area is $50,000. So, she takes $50,000 as her reasonable income, and she pays the 15.3 percent in Social Security and Medicare taxes on that amount, totaling $7,650. She takes the remaining $40,000 of her earnings as shareholder dividends, so she doesn't have to pay the self-employment tax on that amount, which saves her $6,120.

Sounds nice, right? Well, it is, but there are some potential downsides that you need to consider: First, we're talking only about savings on self-employment taxes; you'll still have to pay income tax on your total net profit. Second, the income you designate as your reasonable wage will affect the Social Security benefits you'll receive when you retire. Social Security benefits are calculated in part by looking at the thirty-five years in which you reported the highest income—and that income won't include the earnings you designated as shareholder distributions. So your retirement benefits per month will be lower (by perhaps several hundred dollars) than if you designated all of your business earnings as your income.

Another downside is that you'll have more administrative responsibilities: you'll need to run payroll at least once a year because you're considered an employee of the LLC, you'll have to file at least one quarterly payroll return with the IRS per year, and you'll need to complete bookkeeping tasks (e.g., recording when you pay yourself). And you'll have to complete additional tax forms every year (e.g.,

_____

2. To determine a reasonable wage, conduct some research and talk with an accountant.

Form 1120-S, Schedule K-1, and Form 941). You'll probably want to pay someone to file your tax returns for you, meaning you'll reduce the amount of money you save by electing to be an S corp. My recommendation is to talk with a CPA who specializes in helping one-member LLCs. Your CPA will look at your overall financial situation and the rules in your state (some states don't offer tax benefits to S corps) to determine whether filing as an S corp makes sense for you, as it does for me. As a final note, if you're an S corp, you need to file your annual tax return by March 15, not April 15.

How to Avoid Tax Penalties

As if paying taxes wasn't bad enough, the IRS will add salt to the wound by charging a penalty if you don't pay enough in taxes throughout the year and instead wait until the April 15 deadline. Obviously, it can be tricky to know how much to pay during the year, since a freelancer's income can vary (sometimes significantly) from month to month. Thankfully, the IRS isn't completely oblivious to the fact and allows you to avoid payment penalties in the following situations:

- During the year, you paid 90 percent of the year's tax liability.
- During the year, you paid 100 percent of last year's tax liability (or 110 percent if your adjusted gross income last year was more than $150,000).
- The amount you owe for the year (after subtracting any with-holdings) is less than $1,000.
- You didn't have any tax liability last year.

Even if you are hit with a payment penalty, it's a low percentage of the amount you underpaid. The IRS sets the rate every quarter, and in

Filing as a Sole Proprietor versus an S Corp

Category	Sole proprietor	LLC filing as S corp
Annual return deadline	April 15	March 15
Annual tax return	File as an individual	File as an individual and as an S corp
Self-employment tax	15.3% on all income up to $142,000; 2.9% on income of $142,000–$200,000; 3.8% on income above $200,000*	15.3% on reasonable wage
Income tax	Applies to all income	Applies to all income
Additional responsibilities	Bookkeeping	Bookkeeping, payroll, and payroll taxes

*Dollar amounts are for 2021.

recent years the percentage has ranged from 3 to 6 percent.[3] With a percentage in this range, if you underpaid by $500, you'd have to pay a penalty of $15–$30. So, though you'll want to avoid the penalty, it's not something you should have nightmares about. And the penalty is the worst thing that'll happen if you underpay—you won't be thrown in jail (something I was very relieved to find out!).

Tax Deductions for Freelancers

Perhaps one of the few positive aspects of taxes for freelancers is that a lot of business expenses are tax deductible. Keep in mind that a tax deduction isn't a dollar-for-dollar reduction in the amount you owe. For example, if you spend $300 on marketing, taking the deduction won't lower your tax liability by the full $300, but something is better than nothing, right? Also note that you don't have to use items solely for business purposes in order to claim them as business deductions; simply estimate the percentage of use that's for your business, and then take that percentage of the cost as a deduction. As an example, if 50 percent of your cell phone use is for business purposes, then you can claim 50 percent of your annual cell phone costs as a business deduction.

And now for a list of common deductions you can take:

- Marketing and advertising costs (business cards, print and online ads, etc.)
- Banking fees
- Health insurance not subsidized by an employer
- Computer, printer, other business equipment, printer ink, paper, and other supplies

---

3. Intuit, "IRS Penalty and Interest Rates," accessed February 21, 2020, https://proconnect.intuit.com/articles/federal-irs-underpayment-interest-rates.

- Depreciation of business equipment
- Computer programs
- Style manuals, other reference works, and other publications that will help you in your craft
- Office furniture
- Fees for professional conferences, meetings, and training (including for transportation and lodging if the event lasts more than a typical workday and isn't in your general geographic area)
- Professional association memberships
- A home office (You can take this deduction only if the space is set aside for your business; you can't count the space if you also use it for nonwork activities, such as watching TV. You get a deduction not only for the space itself but also for a percentage of any property taxes, mortgage interest, home maintenance, home depreciation, homeowners or renters insurance, and utilities you pay. For example, if your office accounts for 10 percent of your home, then 10 percent of these costs is deductible.)
- Phone service
- Internet service
- Website (design, domain, etc.)
- Business meals with clients (Typically, only 50 percent of the total cost is deductible.)
- Accounting fees
- Tax preparation fees
- Self-employment tax paid (Half the amount you pay is deductible.)
- Contributions to retirement plans such as solo 401(k)s, traditional IRAs, and SEP IRAs (See chapter 13 for information on retirement-account options.)

Another deduction you can likely take is the pass-through deduction included in the Tax Cut and Jobs Act of 2017, which will be in effect until 2025 (and could be extended). With this provision, you can deduct 20 percent of your "qualified business income" from your income taxes. Qualified business income is your net income—that is, the amount you earned after subtracting business expenses. Of course, as with so many tax provisions, there's a threshold on how much you can earn per year and still qualify for this pass-through deduction. In 2021, you can earn up to $164,900 and receive the full 20 percent deduction. If you earn more than that, you will need to meet additional qualifications and might be able to deduct a smaller percentage.

During the year, keep track of your expenses in all tax-deductible categories (I use an old-school Excel spreadsheet). You'll be glad you did when it's time to file your annual return. You'll also want to save receipts for any purchases. You won't submit the receipts with your tax return, but you'll need them if you're ever audited by the IRS (unlikely but possible). Since the IRS can typically audit you up to six years after you've filed a specific return, save your receipts for that number of years.

Pick a receipt filing system that works for you. Maybe you save all electronic receipts in an email folder (since electronic receipts are typically emailed to you) and you store all paper receipts in a large manila envelope. If you don't want to hold on to paper receipts, you can scan or take a photo of the receipts and then email them to yourself. You can also use online programs and apps such as Shoeboxed and Evernote Scannable to assist in digitizing receipts.

Using a business checking account and business credit card can help you track your business income and expenses, but your monthly account statements won't cut it if you're audited. That's because bank and credit card statements list only the total amount spent at a particular place, whereas receipts list each item you purchased and its amount. In an audit, you'll need the itemized information to show that your purchases truly were business related.

Key Takeaways

- As a freelancer, you typically need to pay income and self-employment taxes quarterly.
- Hiring a tax preparer to file your annual tax return can save you a lot of time and money—and prevent a lot of stress. If you decide to go it on your own, read up on various requirements for the self-employed. The IRS's website contains all the forms you'll need, as well as information that explains the forms and how to complete them.
- To avoid tax penalties, make sure to pay taxes quarterly and to submit your annual income return on time. Also, make sure to pay enough quarterly that you won't owe more than $1,000 at the end of the year. Alternatively, pay enough quarterly that your total tax payments equal 100 percent of your tax liability the previous year.
- Make sure to take advantage of all tax deductions available to the self-employed. Track all your expenses during the year so you don't forget to include them on your tax return.

13 *Becoming a Financially Savvy Freelancer*

Talking finances can be fun—or scary. It's fun when you see that you're making a healthy profit, you have the funds for required and discretionary costs, and you're saving for the future. It's scary if you're struggling to make ends meet, if you haven't learned the basics of budgeting and bookkeeping, or if you're not sure which decisions to make about insurance and retirement plans. The first step to removing the fear and getting on firm footing is to establish a strong foundation of financial knowledge. With this foundation, you'll be on the way to managing your money so that you can cover your costs, protect yourself against risks, prepare for the future, and have a great time along the way. This chapter will help you feel more in control of your finances and financial decisions, rather than feeling that you're always one step behind or not even taking steps.

Personal and Business Budgets

In chapter 8, I covered the basics of developing a budget so you know how much you need to charge for your work. I'll provide a recap here. Using your tool of choice (e.g., Excel spreadsheet, phone app, or software), create a budget containing all your income and expenses for the month. You'll want to list both personal and business expenses, including the tax you'll need to pay on your income, but also make sure to distinguish between the two types of expenses. Doing so will make life easier come tax time and if you're ever audited.

In looking at your budget, how do your expenses compare to your earnings? Are you able to put money in a savings account and a retirement account each month? If you're spending more than you're earning, what costs can you reduce or eliminate? Alternatively, how can you earn more money?

I've always been a saver, but I realize that many people are spenders. If they know they have money in the bank, they feel compelled to spend it. If that description fits you, don't assume you can't change. You might never be frugal, but you can learn to be disciplined with money. Set a goal of keeping a monthly budget and hitting or even exceeding your financial targets. And as motivation to achieve your goal, create some incentives (see chapter 3).

As another way to help rein in your spending each month, set a limit on how much you'll spend on items in a certain category, such as entertainment or clothes. Track your spending during the month, and if you hit the limit, don't purchase more items in the category until the next month. Additionally, think about items you might want to buy in a category in coming months; if the item is more than your monthly max, figure out how much less you should spend in that category in the meantime so that you won't go over your budget when you make the purchase. Also keep in mind necessary expenses that come up less than monthly, and budget for them. For example, if you'll be renewing your membership in a professional organization, divide the total cost by twelve to determine how much money to set aside each month so you'll have the funds to pay for the renewal. Additionally, don't forget about things that are unnecessary but nice to have, and make sure you're setting aside money for them.

Another strategy is to pay yourself a set salary each month from your business earnings. The salary should cover your personal expenses—necessities as well as any discretionary purchases you've allocated in your budget. Transfer that amount to a personal checking account. Leave enough of the remainder in your business account to cover recurring costs and to maintain any minimum balance required to avoid bank fees. Then move any remaining money to one or two savings accounts (more on that below). By paying yourself a set salary each month, you'll be less tempted to spend extra money when you have a particularly profitable month in your business.

I strongly believe that each month you should put at least 10 percent of your income into a savings account. Ideally, you should always have enough in savings to cover at least six months' worth of living costs. Consider this money a safety net; you shouldn't touch the funds unless an emergency strikes (and I'm talking a true emergency). The larger the amount of savings you have, the less stress you'll feel if an unexpected cost does come up, if you lose a regular client, or if you're unable to work for a while. Further, the more money you've saved, the less likely you are to feel guilty about turning down a project you're not interested in, investing in yourself or your business, taking a vacation, or even retiring early.

In addition to having an emergencies-only savings account, you might want to open a second account to hold any money that you don't need in your checking account or your emergency account. By having the two savings accounts, you'll be able to easily see how much discretionary money you have and how much more you need in order to make a planned purchase. You'll also be less tempted to take money from your emergencies-only account to pay for the nice but nonessential items.

Cash Flow Management

In business speak, *cash flow* refers to whether you have the funds to pay expenses that are due. With a freelance editing biz, you don't have

Sample Monthly Personal and Business Budget

Expense	Amt.	Income	Amt.	Date received
PERSONAL		Project A pymt 1		
Mortgage/rent		Project A pymt 2		
Home/rental insurance		Project B pymt 1		
Health insurance		Project B pymt 2		
Food		Project C pymt 1		
Utilities		Project C pymt 2		
Phone		Project D pymt 1		
Internet		Project D pymt 2		
Car payment				
Car insurance				
Gas				
Savings				
Retirement account				
Miscellaneous				
Expense 1				
Expense 2				
Expense 3				
Expense 4				
Total				
BUSINESS				
Website hosting				
MS Office subscription				
CMOS Online subscription				
Office supplies				
Self-employment tax				
Income tax				
Total				
EXPENSE TOTAL		INCOME TOTAL		
		INCOME MINUS EXPENSES		

too many expenses, but you do have regular personal expenses, so you can have cash flow problems if you don't bring in enough income or you don't receive client payments before you need to pay personal bills. So, it's always important to be aware of the amount of money in your personal and business accounts. Let's look at some ways to help ensure that you don't get in a cash flow bind.

- As I mentioned earlier, before you rely entirely on freelance income to cover your living costs, ideally you should have six months' worth of living costs saved; if that amount isn't possible, then shoot for a minimum of three months' worth. That way, if the strategies below don't work perfectly, you still won't be cash-strapped.
- Secure multiple clients; don't rely on one client for more than 35 percent of your total monthly income.
- Secure your next project before you finish your current one.
- Be willing to take on new types of projects, whether in terms of genres or services. That being said, realize that at first you'll likely work slower because you'll need to look up more information to know what's standard. Particularly if you're offering a new service (e.g., indexing or ghostwriting), you'll benefit from completing some training first—or finding a client who's okay with you learning on the job and making some mistakes in exchange for your charging a discounted fee.
- Require all clients to pay you 50 percent of the project price before you start working on the project.
- For long projects, break the remaining 50 percent into multiple payments (e.g., a payment each month).
- Require that clients make the final payment within fifteen days after you've completed the project.
- Encourage regular clients to put you on a retainer.

Bookkeeping

To track whether you have more cash flowing in than out, you need to engage in regular bookkeeping. You might be asking what bookkeeping is (and thinking that you don't want anything to do with it). But bookkeeping isn't that complex or time-consuming for freelance editors. You can handle it yourself, even though a lot of articles say that freelancers and small-business owners should hire a bookkeeper. You don't need one unless you have employees or subcontractors or for some reason have a complex flow of money in and out of your business. Though bookkeeping isn't that hard, don't assume you can put it off for months and then quickly catch up without any negative results. Bookkeeping isn't necessarily enjoyable (not for me, at least), but it's essential for keeping tabs on your business and personal financial health and for filing your tax return accurately.

Now, just how often do you need to engage in bookkeeping? Some people like to set aside a chunk of time once a week for bookkeeping, while others prefer to work on bookkeeping more often for a smaller amount of time. You might be able to complete bookkeeping tasks less than weekly if you typically work on longer projects and therefore don't have as many to keep track of. At a minimum, you should be bookkeeping monthly so you know how your business performed during the month and how your income compared to your expenses.

As for the actual process of bookkeeping, you have some options. You can be like me and take the old-school approach of using Excel (it's a step up from the paper notebook I used until 2011). If you've already created an Excel spreadsheet to track your projects (see "Use a System to Track Your Projects" in chapter 10), then you can use that same spreadsheet for bookkeeping purposes. Just make sure to track all income and expenses, including taxes and insurance, so you can get an accurate picture of your net profit for the month.

Another option is to use a bookkeeping program. Some of these, such as QuickBooks, will cost you money. Others, such as Wave, include free versions that have limited features but that will still probably meet your needs. For example, the free version of Wave lets you track invoices, when they're paid, which payments are overdue, how much money is in your bank account, and what your business expenses are. You can also scan receipts and connect your account to PayPal to receive client payments (though you'll be charged a transaction fee). A bookkeeping program might be your best option if you lack confidence in your math or Excel skills, you don't want to take the time to create a tracking system of your own, or you don't want to customize exactly what you'll track.

Whatever method you use for bookkeeping, it's important to understand two concepts: *accrual basis accounting* and *cash basis accounting*. With accrual basis accounting, you record income when you earn it and expenses when you incur them. In other words, when you finish a project, you record the amount you're being paid for the project, even if you haven't received the money yet. Similarly, if you ask a designer to create a logo for your business and arrange to pay after you receive the finished design, you record the amount when you agree to make the purchase, not when you pay. With cash basis accounting, you record income when you receive it and you report expenses when you pay them. So, if you charge 50 percent up front for a project and then the other 50 percent after you complete the project, you'll record each amount separately, when you receive the amount. And you'll record the expense for logo design when you actually pay the designer.

Accrual basis accounting is the more common method for recording income and expenses. This method can give you a better idea of your earnings and income during a specific period. Additionally, using accrual basis accounting can save you a bit of time because you'll record the total amount you earn for a project and won't need to document when you receive each portion of the total payment. However, I think the cash basis method is a better option for freelance editors. Sure, you'll spend a few more minutes on bookkeeping, but you'll also have a better idea of your cash flow. And you need to keep track of payment installments anyway, to ensure you receive all the money that you're due. Another benefit is that with cash accrual accounting, you aren't taxed on your earnings until you actually receive them. So, cash basis accounting is definitely the way to go. Be aware that if you've been using the accrual method and want to switch to the cash method, you'll need to fill out IRS Form 3115.

Insurance

As a freelancer, you have many choices to make regarding insurance—and not just health insurance. Let's take a look at the most common types of insurance, the most common options for each, and whether you even need the insurance.

Health Insurance

The federal government no longer requires you to have health insurance, but of the various types of insurance we'll discuss, health insurance is the most important to have. Health insurance can make preventive care more affordable, which may encourage you to get the regular checkups that'll help you avoid more serious and costly health conditions later on. For those who already have health concerns, health insurance may help you receive the ongoing treatment you require. Perhaps even more important, health insurance can help you avoid a staggering medical bill if you need to be hospitalized or receive other significant medical treatment, perhaps even on a regular basis. As a personal example, in my late twenties I got a severe concussion and was hospitalized. The total medical bill reached tens of thousands of dollars, but I was responsible for a much smaller amount because I had health insurance. As with having any type of insurance, having health insurance helps you minimize your risk when the unexpected happens. The insurance can give you some reassurance that you'll be financially okay even if you have a health emergency. For me, the reduced risk and the peace of mind are worth the monthly premium.

That said, the monthly premium can get your heart pumping—and the premium never fails to increase each year. So, you have a right to be frustrated. I think of health insurance premiums much as I do income tax: not something I enjoy paying but nevertheless something that's in my best interest to pay (of course, you won't be breaking the law by not paying for health insurance).

Though health insurance is typically more expensive than you'd like, you do have some options in terms of how much you'll pay. Likely the least expensive route is to get coverage through the employer-subsidized policy of someone else in your household. Of course, you won't have that option if you're in a household of one or if no one else in the household has a job with medical benefits. In that case, you might opt for a plan with a high deductible (around $1,500 or more for an individual), meaning that your monthly premium will be relatively low but that you'll have to pay more for any health services you use before your insurance will start paying for anything. If you choose a high-deductible plan, you can also have a health savings account. The money you contribute to the account isn't taxed, so you'll be saving more of your hard-earned dollars.

If you have a solid amount of money in savings—and therefore could pay for medical expenses out of pocket if you haven't already reached your deductible—then you'll probably be okay with a high-deductible plan. If you have a smaller emergency fund, you might want to choose a plan with a higher monthly premium but a lower deductible.

Where exactly do you find health insurance plans? You've probably heard of the Health Insurance Marketplace (www.healthcare .gov), but it's not the only resource. You can also check out the websites of specific insurance companies, and you can work with an insurance broker. The latter is often a good choice because the broker will help you decide what type of plan is best for your situation and then will search across policies at multiple insurance companies to find the best deal for you. You might also be able to find policies—and receive discounts—through professional organizations you're a member of (e.g., Freelancers Union and the National Association for the Self-Employed). Be aware, however, that the membership fee to join such an organization can wipe out any savings you'd get on insurance. So, make sure to examine all the associated costs.

In addition to the private health insurance options offered by companies such as Aetna and United Health Care, you might want to look into health care sharing ministries. In these organizations, health care costs are shared among all members. Members pay a certain amount each month, and the money goes into a pool from which funds are withdrawn to pay for members' health care costs. Typically, members pay considerably less per month than they would if they had a standard health insurance policy, and this savings is a huge draw for many people. Also, the deductible can be much lower.[1] But you also need to know about some potential downsides. For one, membership is sometimes limited to people of a certain religion or to people who agree to live by guidelines such as not smoking, abusing alcohol, or having extramarital sex. It's also important to understand that health care sharing ministries are nonprofits rather than insurance companies; as such, these ministries aren't

---

1. Carolyn Schwarz, "Thrifting for More: Savings and Aspirations in Health Care Sharing Ministries after the Affordable Care Act," *Medical Anthropology Quarterly* 33, no. 2 (2019): 226–241.

state regulated and aren't legally bound to pay a member's medical claims, cover preexisting conditions, or limit out-of-pocket costs.[2] Further, monthly payments aren't tax deductible because they're technically not insurance payments.

If you decide to consider enrolling in a health care sharing ministry, make sure you understand exactly what's involved. Read online reviews of the ministry, and check whether it's been investigated and fined by any states for inappropriate operations.[3] Also talk with people who are current or previous members of the ministry. Of the people I've heard from, some have had great experiences and have saved huge amounts a month, while others have shared tales of woe. Of course, bad experiences aren't limited to members of health care sharing ministries: many people with private health insurance have had negative experiences too. Some insurance companies and some ministries are better than others—and sometimes it depends on a person's specific situation. Moral of the story: before making a decision, do your research.

Life Insurance

Having life insurance is a good idea if you financially support others in your family. If you pass away, the policy will provide your beneficiaries with funds to cover funeral expenses, the monthly mortgage payment, educational costs for children, and other kinds

---

2. James R. Salzmann, "Statutory Millennialism: Establishment and Free Exercise Concerns Arising from the Health Care Sharing Ministry Exemption's 1999 Cutoff Date," *Southern California Law Review* 93, no. 303 (2018): 304-338.

3. Regulatory agencies in some states have fined ministries that misrepresent themselves as insurance companies and therefore imply that they guarantee coverage of medical claims. See, for example, Reed Abelson, "It Looks Like Health Insurance, but It's Not. 'Just Trust God,' Buyers Are Told," *New York Times*, January 2, 2020.

of expenses. You have two options when it comes to life insurance: term policies and whole-life policies. Let's explore each type.

With a term policy, you select how long you want the policy to last—typically from ten to thirty years. You also choose how much you want the policy to be worth (more on that in a minute). Then, if you pass away during the time the policy is valid, your beneficiaries will receive the policy amount. If you pass away after the policy expires (because the term has ended or you're no longer paying the monthly premium), your beneficiaries won't qualify to receive funds.

The thinking behind a term policy is that you need the financial protection only when you have dependents or others relying on your income; after dependents are self-sufficient or you've built a large nest egg, you don't need the protection a term policy provides. Therefore, select a term based on how long you think you'll need to financially support your beneficiaries.

Now for the question of what policy amount (i.e., "death benefit") to choose. Common advice is to choose a policy that's worth ten to twelve times your annual income. You can base the number on last year's tax return or on what you expect to earn this year in freelancing. The death benefit amount and the term of the policy will largely determine what your monthly premium is. The higher the death benefit and the longer the term, the higher the premium.

The monthly premium for a term policy is typically less expensive than for a whole-life policy because a term policy has an end date, whereas a whole-life policy doesn't (as long as you keep paying your premium). That's the main difference between the two types of policies.[4] Another difference is that whole-life insurance has a savings component. A portion of your monthly premium is put in a tax-deferred investment account, meaning your policy's cash value increases over

---

4. With either option, you'll select a policy amount and pay a monthly premium, and your beneficiaries will receive a payout when you die.

time. You can borrow against the cash value and use the funds for education or retirement. The particulars of when and how you can use the accumulated cash, as well as the interest rate you'll be charged, can be complicated, so be sure to talk with an insurance professional if you're considering a whole-life policy. Personally, I don't think this type of policy is the best financial choice—you'll get a better ROI with other investment options. So, before choosing a whole-life policy, ensure that it really is the best option for your long-term needs.

Short- and Long-Term Disability Insurance

Now on to short- and long-term disability insurance. I'm discussing these options because many websites focused on insurance and small businesses claim that having such policies is essential. However, I tend to disagree, particularly when it comes to short-term disability insurance. If you have a few months' worth of savings, then don't spend your money on a short-term policy; instead, just continue to sock away funds. A long-term disability policy makes more sense, but I still have reservations. One reason is that editors aren't at as great a risk of becoming disabled as are people who have physically strenuous or risky occupations. Also, if you were to break a leg or for some other reason needed to stay in bed, you could still complete your work on a laptop. True, editors aren't completely without risk—for example, eye damage or carpal tunnel syndrome could make it difficult to edit. But because there's only a small chance of experiencing a disabling condition, long-term disability insurance isn't worth the monthly premium for most people. I'm not alone in this opinion: in a poll I conducted, less than 2 percent of editors who responded had short-term disability insurance and less than 11 percent had long-term disability insurance. A long-term policy *might* be worth considering if you are the only income earner in your household and are the provider for dependents.

With that long caveat, let's dive into what disability insurance is all about. The purpose of this type of insurance is to cover a portion of your income if a medical condition prevents you from working. With a short-term disability policy, your benefit period will start within fourteen days after you've submitted your claim (as long as your health issue is covered by your policy). The benefit period will last for the length of time you've purchased your policy for (typically three to six months) or until your disability ends, whichever is shorter. During this period, you'll receive a percentage of your typical monthly income—you'll select the percentage when you purchase the policy, and 60 percent is a common choice. Your insurance premium will be based largely on how quickly your benefit period starts (the "elimination period"), how long the period lasts, and the percentage of income you'll receive. Other factors can include your health at the time you purchase the policy, your age and sex, and your occupation.

Now let's talk about long-term disability policies. As with short-term policies, you can choose when the benefit period will start, how long it will last, and what percentage of income you'll receive per month. And, of course, these decisions will affect how expensive your monthly premium is. Typically, people have the benefit period start thirty to ninety days after the disability begins, and the period can last from a few years up until retirement age. As with short-term disability policies, people typically choose an income benefit of 60 percent.

Some long-term disability policies include a residual, or partial, disability benefit. With this option, if you can't work full-time but can work part-time, you'll still receive a benefit payout (though the amount will be lower). Another policy component to be aware of is the own-occupation clause. During the period specified in the clause, you'll receive your monthly benefit if your disability prevents you from working in your occupation. After that period ends, you'll receive your benefit only if your disability prevents you from working in any job, even if not related to your profession or skills. To prevent this situation, you can purchase own-occupation coverage at an extra cost. If you do decide you want long-term disability insurance, talk with several insurance agents to help you figure out which plan is best for your situation.

Business Liability Insurance

A number of editors have asked me whether they need business liability insurance, and my answer is no. The reason: editing simply isn't that risky of a profession. I don't know of any editors who've been sued for work-related reasons (and I've asked a lot of editors and done a fair amount of research to find cases). But since a lot of sources say that *all* freelancers should have liability insurance, I'm going to cover the basics here. Then you'll be ready to decide whether to dole out the cash for a policy.

The most common types of business liability insurance for freelancers are general liability and professional liability. General liability covers your legal expenses if you're sued for property damage or for physical injury or harm. You're at little risk of such lawsuits because you'll likely work from home and won't have clients visiting you there. General liability also covers you if you're sued for personal injury. In legal terms, *personal injury* refers to issues such as libel, slander, and copyright infringement. Professional liability insurance, often also called errors and omissions insurance, covers you if you're sued for allegedly making errors in your work or otherwise being negligent. Sometimes these policies also cover you in personal injury lawsuits.

Both types of policies might be beneficial if you're a writer in addition to an editor, since writers are more at risk of being accused of copyright infringement and libel. Additionally, writers are more likely to be blamed for informational errors, which could cause people physical harm (e.g., a pharma writer stating the wrong dose for a drug). Though authors have been sued for errors and negligence, editors are at low risk since they're typically not responsible for a document's content but, rather, only for whether the content is grammatical and understandable. If an editor does make a mistake, he or she is typically simply informed of it and perhaps asked to fix it. At worst, the editor loses the client but isn't sued.

You can also purchase home-based business insurance, which covers business equipment in your home. However, many standard home insurance policies will cover business equipment up to a certain amount. Since editors don't require a lot of expensive equipment, your standard home insurance policy will probably cover your needs. Check your policy, and decide whether you want additional coverage.

If you freelance for businesses, once in a while you might be asked to sign a contract that requires you to have liability insurance. Is purchasing the insurance your only option? Nope. Typically you can simply explain why you don't need liability insurance (e.g., no risk of physical injury), and the company will be willing to strike out that clause. If the company won't budge, then you'll need to decide whether the amount you'll earn from the company is enough to make liability insurance worth the cost.

"I've always gotten institutions to waive their requirement that independent contractors hold liability insurance. Those policies for contractors are usually boilerplate and are meant to apply to vendors who operate vehicles or serve alcohol on a university campus, for example. I've found that if I explain that I'll be doing extremely low-risk editing work on my own premises—sometimes it helps to explain over the phone if I can speak to someone that way—the administrator will usually amend the contract to waive the insurance requirement."
—Laura Portwood-Stacer, freelance editor

Retirement Savings

Considering all the tasks involved in running a freelance business, it can be easy to forget about saving for the retirement years. But setting aside money for retirement is one of the most important things to do—unless you love your business so much that you'll never want to retire *and* you won't ever face circumstances that require you to limit your work hours. If you don't have a retirement account or aren't contributing to it regularly, seriously consider setting up an account and/or scheduling automatic contributions ASAP, as in first thing tomorrow morning. As you probably know, the sooner you start contributing, the more time your savings will have to compound; waiting even one year can have a considerable effect on how big your nest egg is at retirement time.

I bet that at this moment, some of you are saying you simply don't have a spare penny to deposit in a retirement account. A few freelancers might truly be in such dire straits, but most really can regularly contribute at least a small amount, even if only $20 each month. Go back to your budget and look for what expenses you can cut out or lower. Or decide to work two extra hours a month. Sure, either option will require you to sacrifice, but you'll be very grateful you did when retirement time comes and you have enough money to meet your financial needs.

As you continue to expand your editing business and earn more money, increase your contributions to a retirement savings account. Don't assume that as long as you're contributing something, you'll have the needed funds when you're ready to retire. To figure out how much to contribute each month, use one of the many calculators online. You might also want to speak with a financial adviser, who can give you guidance tailored to your specific situation. Whatever type of retirement account you choose to contribute to, make sure to consider all maintenance and other types of fees, which will cut into the amount of money your account amasses. Also keep in mind that you don't have to limit yourself to one type of account. Each type has different rules and benefits, so you might want to open multiple kinds of accounts to reap various advantages and to diversify your investment mix. Now, let's cover the types of accounts you can choose from.

Traditional and Roth IRAs

You've likely heard of traditional and Roth IRAs, but let's still go over the basics. With both types of retirement plan, in 2021 you can contribute a maximum of $6,000 (or $7,000 if you're at least 50 years old), and you can roll over money from a 401(k) into an IRA. The main difference between a traditional IRA and a Roth IRA is that with a traditional account, you pay taxes when you withdraw the money during retirement, whereas with a Roth account you pay taxes before contributing the money, so you don't pay taxes on the money when you withdraw it. With both types, you typically can't start withdrawing money until you're 59½. With a traditional IRA, you must start taking distributions at age 72, but a Roth IRA doesn't have this requirement. If you want to withdraw money before you're 59½ years old, you'll likely have to pay a penalty. With a Roth account, you'll likely also have to pay taxes on withdrawals if you're not yet 59½ or you haven't had the account for at least five years.

If your freelance income is relatively low right now but you expect it to increase over the years, then you'll likely benefit from opening a Roth IRA account; if you're already making a healthy amount, a traditional IRA is probably the better choice. Of course, you could open both types of account and contribute to both (up to the combined max of $6,000). Both types do have some restrictions regarding individuals with high income, so review the guidelines to determine whether you qualify for either type of account.

Simplified Employee Pension (SEP) IRA

You're eligible to open a SEP IRA account if you're at least 21, you've earned at least $600 in business income in a year, and you've operated your business for at least three of the past five years. With a SEP IRA, you can contribute more than is allowed for traditional and Roth IRAs. In fact, each year you can contribute up to $58,000 (in 2021) or 25 percent of your net income—whichever is lower. As with a traditional IRA, you pay taxes on SEP IRA funds when you withdraw them upon retiring. The potential downside of a SEP IRA is that if you have employees who meet certain criteria, you're required to contribute the same percentage to their accounts as to yours. Of course, this requirement is a nonissue for most freelance editors, since they don't have employees. As with most other types of retirement accounts, you'll likely have to pay a penalty if you make withdrawals from your SEP IRA before age 59½ and you must start taking them by age 72.

Solo 401(k)

A solo 401(k) is similar to a 401(k) account available through an employer, and you're eligible for a solo account as long as you earn money through freelancing and don't have any full-time employees (aside from yourself, of course). A solo 401(k) allows you to make large contributions each year because you can contribute as an employer and an employee in your business. As an employer, you can contribute 25 percent of earned income, up to $58,000 (or $64,500 for those 50 and older) in 2021. As an employee, you can contribute up to an additional $19,500 or 100 percent of earned income (whichever amount is lower), and the amount increases to $26,000 if you're at least 50 years old. *Earned income* is defined as your net self-employment earnings minus (1) any retirement contributions you make and (2) 50 percent of your self-employment tax. You won't pay any taxes on the money in

Comparison of Retirement Savings Accounts

Account type	Max. annual contribution (in 2021)	Min. withdrawal age w/o penalties	Age when you must start taking distributions	When taxes are assessed	Penalties	Notes
Traditional IRA	$6,000 (or $7,000 if age 50+)	59½	72	When withdrawing	If funds withdrawn before age 59½	
Roth IRA	$6,000 (or $7,000 if age 50+)	59½	No requirement	Before contributing	If funds withdrawn before age 59½ or before account has been open for 5 years	Can roll over funds from Roth 401(k) accounts
Simplified employee pension (SEP) IRA	$58,000 or 25% of net income, whichever is lower	59½	72	When withdrawing	If funds withdrawn before age 59½	If you have employees who meet certain criteria, you're required to contribute the same percentage to their accounts as to yours

Comparison of Retirement Savings Accounts *(continued)*

Solo 401(k)	As employer: $58,000 (or $64,500 if age 50+) or 25% of net income, whichever is lower As employee: $19,500 (or $26,000 at age 50+) or 100% of earned income, whichever is lower	59½	72	When withdrawing	If funds are withdrawn before age 59½
Roth 401(k)	As employer: $58,000 (or $64,500 at age 50+) or 25% of net income, whichever is lower As employee: $19,500 (or $26,000 at age 50+) or 100% of earned income, whichever is lower	59½	72 (unless rolled over to Roth IRA account)	Before contributing	If funds are withdrawn before age 59½ or before account has been open for 5 years	Can roll over funds to Roth 401(k) accounts

your account until you withdraw funds after retiring. To avoid a penalty, you won't be able to withdraw money until you're 59½, and you have to start taking distributions by age 72.

Roth 401(k)

The main difference between a solo 401(k) and a Roth 401(k) is that with a Roth account, you make your employee-side contributions with after-tax dollars (the same as with a Roth IRA). In other words, you'll pay taxes only on the employer-side contributions. Another difference between the two types of 401(k) accounts is that with a Roth account, you'll typically have to pay a penalty if you withdraw funds before you've had the account for five years, even if you've reached retirement age. As with a traditional 401(k), you're required to start taking Roth 401(k) distributions by age 72. However, you can get around this rule by rolling your Roth 401(k) into a Roth IRA, since the latter doesn't require you to start taking distributions at a specific age.

Key Takeaways

- To effectively manage your personal and business finances, establish and follow a budget.
- Use a bookkeeping system that will help you track your income and expenses and keep tabs on your cash flow.
- Of all the types of insurance policies freelancers might think about purchasing, health insurance is the most essential. Before purchasing life insurance, disability insurance, or business insurance, consider your situation and determine whether these types of policies will be beneficial for you.
- Don't forget to save money for retirement. You have a lot of options, and a financial adviser can help you decide which types of account(s) to contribute to.

Conclusion

We've covered a lot of territory in this book, and you likely have a lengthy list of action items. (Bonus points if you've already started implementing them!) You might also be feeling a little overwhelmed when you think of everything you need or want to do for your business. Take a deep breath, and remind yourself that your business doesn't need to be perfect in order for you to enjoy it and earn a living. Start by implementing the most important concepts, such as setting up a business bank account and creating a contract for every new project you receive (see appendix A for a list of key action items addressed in this book). Then move on to the strategies that'll help you expand your business, increase your earnings, and achieve your ideal work/life balance. Enjoy the process of improving your business bit by bit, according to a pace that's comfortable for you.

Enjoying the process is important so that you don't burn yourself out, but it's also important to push yourself a bit. You'll be surprised at how much you can achieve through hard work. Recognize that you'll experience some disappointments and discouragement along your freelancing journey, but if you learn from your mistakes and keep working at your business, you *will* succeed. Half of the equation in reaching success is pushing through the difficult times. Too often, business owners give up when the going gets a little rocky. Be confident that the challenges don't define you and that they won't limit you if you don't allow them to. Have the determination to work past the difficulties so that your business can become what you want it to be.

Even when things are going well, look for additional ways—even if quite minor—to continue improving your business. Ask yourself whether you can make a process more efficient or whether you can make a connection that will help you break into a type or genre of editing that excites you. By always working on your business, you'll remain engaged and feel satisfaction with each win, whether large or small.

Keep in mind that you don't have to take this journey alone. Plenty of people are willing to share what's worked for them in their businesses. Establish meaningful connections with other freelancers—and not just those who edit. Ask questions and contribute your own answers when you have relevant information to share. Fostering relationships with people can be one of the most rewarding parts of building your business.

By cultivating these relationships, you'll become a more skilled freelancer, you'll be able to help others increase their skills, and you'll likely gain insights that will enrich your life outside of work. After all, the purpose of this book is to help you run a successful freelance editing business that will enhance your life overall. I want your business to work for you, not the other way around. Remember, with the right mindset and tools, you truly can thrive, not just survive, as a freelance editor. Best of wishes on your freelance editing journey!

Most Important Action Items for Establishing a Freelance Editing Business

This book highlights a lot of steps to take in establishing and ramping up your freelance business. Especially if you're just starting out as a freelancer, you'll benefit from prioritizing the following action items. After you've crossed these items off your list, move on to the other suggestions in the book, particularly the ones that you haven't explored at all in the past.

- Develop a business plan.
- Decide on a business entity.
- Get a business license.
- Set up a business bank account and a credit card account.
- Establish a marketing plan.
- Develop or expand your business network.
- Create a website for your business.
- Set up a LinkedIn profile.
- Determine your rates.
- Develop a contract and an invoice.
- Create a schedule identifying which hours and days of the week you'll work.
- Create a project schedule and tracking system.
- Determine how much to pay in taxes each quarter, and add reminders to your calendar regarding when you need to submit payments.
- Create a personal and business budget.
- Set up a retirement account.

Improving Editing Skills through Using Editing Programs and Other Resources

If you're just entering the field of editing, you'll greatly benefit from completing formal training. I speak from experience. As a kid, I loved reading and also enjoyed writing, and both activities helped me learn basic principles of grammar, punctuation, and so forth. But it wasn't until I started taking editing courses in college that I really developed my editing skills. I learned exactly when commas are needed—and when they aren't—and that the "rule" about never ending a sentence with a preposition is hogwash. Without training, I wouldn't have known that there was a lot I didn't know and that I had areas of weakness. Let me be clear: my intent isn't to criticize editors who haven't completed formal training. But in the thirteen years that I've hired and trained editors (whether in the corporate world or at a university), I've seen a great deal of evidence that professional training can make a huge difference in editors' skills and performance.

Of course, initial training isn't enough if an editor wants to excel; continued professional development is essential. Just one reason is that language and conventions evolve. What was considered okay a few decades ago might be considered taboo today—or vice versa. I believe that the best editors regularly participate in professional development. Perhaps once a year, they enroll in a class or attend a conference. On a monthly, weekly, or maybe even daily basis, they might participate in a forum, listen to a podcast episode, or read a blog post or book chapter related to editing. By engaging in a variety of types of professional development, editors learn from a broader range of perspectives and learn about a broader range of topics.

To help you start or continue your training and professional development, below I've listed university programs related to editing, professional organizations that provide relevant training, and professional organizations that hold conferences for editors. I've also listed some editors' forums that I've found to be particularly beneficial to participate in. I've chosen not to list blogs, podcasts, and YouTube channels because they can be short-lived and, particularly in the case of blogs, there are numerous ones to choose from (more than I've personally reviewed). That being said, do check out some of these resources, and then subscribe to the ones you find the most helpful.

Colleges and Universities Offering Courses/Programs

- Boston University Editorial Institute (various courses)
- California State University (Certificate in Literary Editing and Publishing)
- Emerson College (Copyediting Certificate)
- Macquarie University (Graduate Certificate of Editing and Electronic Publishing)
- New York University School of Professional Studies (Certificate in Professional Copyediting, Proofreading, and Fact-Checking)
- Pace University (Certificates in Book Publishing, Digital Publishing, Magazine Publishing, and Business Aspects of Publishing; Master of Science in Publishing)
- Portland State University (Master of Arts or Science in Book Publishing)
- Queen's University (Editing in Academic and Professional Contexts course)
- Ryerson University (Certificate in Publishing)
- Simon Fraser University (Editing Certificate)
- UC Berkeley Extension (Professional Sequence in Editing)
- UC San Diego Extension (Copyediting Certificate)
- University of Alberta Faculty of Extension (courses in writing and editing)
- University of Chicago Graham School (Editing Certificate)
- University of Cincinnati College of Arts and Sciences (Copyediting and Publishing Certificate)
- University of Denver (Denver Publishing Institute)

- University of Melbourne (Master of Creative Writing, Publishing, and Editing)
- University of Southern Queensland (Graduate Certificate of Editing and Publishing)
- University of Washington (Certificate in Editing)

Professional Organizations Offering Training

- ACES: The Society for Editing
- Chartered Institute of Editing and Proofreading
- Editcetera
- Editorial Freelancers Association
- Editors Canada
- Institute of Professional Editors
- National Association of Independent Writers and Editors
- Publishing Training Centre

Organizations Hosting Conferences for Editors

- ACES: The Society for Editing
- Chartered Institute of Editing and Proofreading
- Communication Central
- Editors Canada
- Institute of Professional Editors
- National Association of Independent Writers and Editors

Editors' Forums

- Business + Professional Development for Editors (Facebook group)
- Copyediting-L (website and email list)
- EAE Backroom (Facebook group)
- Editors' Association of Earth (Facebook group)
- Editors Lair (website)

Further Reading and Bibliography

Further Reading

Adin, Richard, with Jack Lyon and Ruth E. Thaler-Carter. *The Business of Editing: Effective and Efficient Ways to Think, Work, and Prosper.* Waking Lion Press, 2013.

Beverley, Paul. *Macros for Editors.* Archive Publications, January 18, 2021. www.archivepub.co.uk/book.html.

Cather, Karin, and Dick Margulis. *The Paper It's Written On: Defining Your Relationship with an Editing Client.* New Haven, CT: Andslash Books, 2018.

Editorial Freelancers Association. "Editorial Rates." www.the-efa.org/rates.

Fuller, Barbara. *How to Start a Home-Based Editorial Services Business.* Guilford, CT: Globe Pequot, 2013.

Harnby, Louise. *How to Earn Passive Income.* N.p., 2020.

Kellett, Ann. *A Freelancer's Guide to Difficult Clients.* New York: Editorial Freelancers Association, 2018.

Lyon, Jack. *Macro Cookbook for Microsoft Word.* West Valley City, UT: Editorium, 2011.

———. *Wildcard Cookbook for Microsoft Word.* West Valley City, UT: Editorium, 2015.

O'Moore-Klopf, Katharine, comp. "Copyeditor's Knowledge Base." KOK Edit. www.kokedit.com/ckb.php.

Slaunwhite, Steve, Pete Savage, and Ed Gandia. *The Wealthy Freelancer.* New York: Penguin/Alpha, 2010.

Virag, Karen, and Editors' Association of Canada. *Editorial Niches: A Companion to Editing Canadian English.* 3rd ed. Toronto: Editors Canada, 2015.

Sources Cited

Abbot, Lydia. "10 Tips for Picking the Right LinkedIn Profile Picture." *LinkedIn Talent Blog*, August 5, 2019. https://business.linkedin.com/talent-solutions /blog/2014/12/5-tips-for-picking-the-right-linkedin-profile-picture.

Adaval, Rashmi, and Robert S. Wyer Jr. "Conscious and Nonconscious Comparisons with Price Anchors: Effects on Willingness to Pay for Related and Unrelated Products." *Journal of Marketing Research* 48 (April 2011): 355–365.

Baillie, Phon. "How to Choose a Niche as a Proofreader or Copy Editor." *Art of Proofreading Blog*, March 2019. www.artofproofreadingblog.com/choose -niche-proofreader-copy-editor.

Bastian, Mathieu. "Your Skills Are Your Competitive Edge on LinkedIn." *LinkedIn Official Blog*, October 16, 2014. https://blog.linkedin.com/2014 /10/16/your-skills-are-your-competitive-edge-on-linkedin.

Bawa, Kapil, and Robert Shoemaker. "The Effects of Sample Promotions on Incremental Brand Sales." *Marketing Science* 23, no. 4 (2004): 345–363.

Berthon, Pierre, Leyland Pitt, and Colin Campbell. "Addictive De-Vices: A Public Policy Analysis of Sources and Solutions to Digital Addiction." *Journal of Public Policy and Marketing* 38, no. 4 (2019): 451–468.

Bond, Samuel D., Stephen X. He, and Wen Wen. "Speaking for 'Free': Word of Mouth in Free- and Paid-Product Settings." *Journal of Marketing Research* 56, no. 2 (2019): 276–290.

Bowker. *Self-Publishing in the United States, 2013–2018*. Bowker, 2019. https://media2.proquest.com/documents/bowker-selfpublishing -report2019.pdf.

Brumby, Duncan P., Christian P. Janssen, and Gloria Mark. "How Do Interruptions Affect Productivity?" In *Rethinking Productivity in Software Engineering*, edited by Caitlin Sadowski and Thomas Zimmerman, 85–107. Berkeley, CA: Apress, 2019.

Carney, Dana R., Amy J. C. Cuddy, and Andy J. Yap. "Power Posing: Brief Nonverbal Displays Affect Neuroendocrine Levels and Risk Tolerance." *Psychological Science* 21, no. 10 (2010): 1363–1368.

Chamberlain, Katie. "Editors' Tracking Programs." Beacon Point. Accessed January 15, 2020. http://beaconpointservices.org/editors-tracking -programs.

Chartered Institute of Editing and Proofreading. "Standards in Proofreading." Accessed February 7, 2020. www.sfep.org.uk/standards/standards-in -proofreading.

Clayton, Russell, Christopher H. Thomas, Barjinder Singh, and Doan Winkel. "Exercise as a Means of Reducing Perceptions of Work-Family Conflict: A Test of the Roles of Self-Efficacy and Psychological Strain." *Human Resource Management* 54, no. 6 (2014): 1013–1035.

Coulson, Joanne C., Jim McKenna, and Matthew Field. "Exercising at Work and Self-Reported Work Performance." *International Journal of Workplace Health Management* 1, no. 3 (2008): 176–197.

Creswell, J. David. "Neural Reactivation Links Unconscious Thought to Decision-Making Performance." *Social Cognitive and Affective Neuroscience* 8, no. 8 (2013): 863–869.

Creswell, J. David, Janine M. Dutcher, William M. P. Klein, Peter R. Harris, and John M. Levine. "Self-Affirmation Improves Problem-Solving under Stress." *PLOS ONE* 8, no. 5 (2013): e62593.

Curtin, Melanie. "11 Great Jobs for Introverts." *Inc.*, March 29, 2019. www.inc .com/melanie-curtin/11-great-jobs-for-introverts.html.

Dalton, Amy N., and Stephen A. Spiller. "Too Much of a Good Thing: The Benefits of Implementation Intentions Depend on the Number of Goals." *Journal of Consumer Research* 39, no. 3 (2012): 600–614.

de Bloom, Jessica, Sabine Geurts, and Michiel A. J. Kompier. "Effects of Short Vacations, Vacation Activities, and Experiences on Employee Health and Well-Being." *Stress and Health* 28, no. 4 (2012): 305–318.

De Couck, Marijke, Ralf Caers, Liza Musch, Johanna Fliegauf, Antonio Giangreco, and Yori Gidron. "How Breathing Can Help You Make Better Decisions: Two Studies on the Effects of Breathing Patterns on Heart Rate Variability and Decision-Making in Business Cases." *International Journal of Psychophysiology* 139 (2012): 1–9.

Dodgson, Lindsay. "The Psychology behind Why We're So Bad at Keeping New Year's Resolutions." *Business Insider*, January 7, 2018. www.businessinsider .com/the-psychology-behind-why-we-cant-keep-new-years-resolutions -2018-1.

Eckel, Catherine C., and Ragan Petrie. "Face Value." *American Economic Review* 101, no. 4 (2011): 1497–1513.

Edwards, Chad, Brett Stoll, Natalie Faculak, and Sandi Karman. "Social Presence on LinkedIn: Perceived Credibility and Interpersonal Attractiveness Based on User Profile Picture." *Online Journal of Communication and Technologies* 5, no. 4 (2015): 102–115.

Einsohn, Amy, and Marilyn Schwartz. *The Copyeditor's Handbook*. 4th ed. Oakland: University of California Press, 2019.

Ferrari, Joseph R., Catherine A. Roster, Kendall P. Crum, and Matthew A. Pardo. "Procrastinators and Clutter: An Ecological View of Living with Excessive 'Stuff.'" *Current Psychology* 37 (2018): 441–444.

Friedman, Ron. "Schedule a 15-Minute Break before You Burn Out." *Harvard Business Review*, August 4, 2014. https://hbr.org/2014/08/schedule-a-15 -minute-break-before-you-burn-out.

Gee, Laura K., Jason J. Jones, Christopher J. Fariss, Moira Burke, and James H. Fowler. "The Paradox of Weak Ties in 55 Countries." *Journal of Economic Behavior and Organization* 133 (2017): 362–372.

Gregg, Melanie J., Jenny O, and Craig R. Hall. "Examining the Relationship between Athletes' Achievement Goal Orientation and Ability to Employ Imagery." *Psychology of Sport and Exercise* 24 (2016): 140–146.

Harackiewicz, Judith M., Elizabeth A. Canning, Yoi Tibbetts, Cynthia J. Giffen, Seth S. Blair, Douglas I. Rouse, and Janet S. Hyde. "Closing the Social Class Achievement Gap for First-Generation Students in Undergraduate Biology." *Journal of Educational Psychology* 106, no. 2 (2014): 375–389.

Harnby, Louise. "How to Schedule Editing and Proofreading Projects and Payments in Excel." *The Parlour* (blog), November 11, 2012. www.louise harnbyproofreader.com/blog/editorial-annual-accounts-template-excel#.

Hauser, Marc D. "The Mind of a Goal Achiever: Using Mental Contrasting and Implementation Intentions to Achieve Better Outcomes in General and Special Education." *Mind, Brain, and Education* 12, no. 3 (2018): 102–109.

Heim, Bradley T., Gillian Hunter, Ithai Z. Lurie, and Shanthi P. Ramnath. "The Impact of the ACA on Premiums: Evidence from the Self-Employed." *Journal of Health Politics, Policy, and Law* 40 no. 5 (2015): 1061–1085.

Hills, Laura. "The Medical Practice Employee's Guide to Establishing Worthwhile Professional and Personal Goals." *Journal of Medical Practice Management* 27, no. 3 (2011): 159–163.

Hogan, Candice L., Jutta Mata, and Laura L. Carstensen. "Exercise Holds Immediate Benefits for Affect and Cognition in Younger and Older Adults." *Psychology and Aging* 28, no. 2 (2013): 587–594.

Holloway, Daniel, and Thomas Schaefer. "Practitioner Perspectives on Leadership in Small Business." *International Journal of the Academic Business World* 8, no. 2 (2014): 27–36.

Holmes, Paul S., and David J. Collins. "The PETTLEP Approach to Motor Imagery: A Functional Equivalence Model for Sport Psychologists." *Journal of Applied Sport Psychology* 13, no. 1 (2001): 60–83.

Horcajo, Javier, Borja Paredes, Guillermo Higuero, Pablo Briñol, and Richard E. Petty. "The Effects of Overt Head Movements on Physical Performance after Positive versus Negative Self-Talk." *Journal of Sport Exercise Psychology* 41, no. 1 (2019): 36–45.

Hutchins, Holly M. "Outing the Imposter: A Study Exploring Imposter Phenomenon among Higher Education Faculty." *New Horizons in Adult Education and Human Resource Development* 27, no. 2 (2015): 3–12.

Intuit. "IRS Penalty and Interest Rates." Accessed February 21, 2020. https://proconnect.intuit.com/articles/federal-irs-underpayment-interest-rates.

Johnson, W. Brad, and David G. Smith. "Mentoring Someone with Imposter Syndrome," *Harvard Business Review*, February 22, 2019. https://hbr.org/2019/02/mentoring-someone-with-imposter-syndrome.

Kaiser Family Foundation. "Premiums and Worker Contributions among Workers Covered by Employer-Sponsored Coverage, 1999–2019." September 25, 2019. www.kff.org/interactive/premiums-and-worker-contributions-among-workers-covered-by-employer-sponsored-coverage-1999-2019.

Kim, Ji Young, Spiro Kiousis, and Juan-Carlos Molleda. "Use of Affect in Blog Communication: Trust, Credibility, and Authenticity." *Public Relations Review* 41, no. 4 (2015): 504–507.

Knight, Craig, and S. Alexander Haslam. "The Relative Merits of Lean, Enriched, and Empowered Offices: An Experimental Examination of the Impact of Workspace Management Strategies on Well-Being and Productivity." *Journal of Experimental Psychology* 16, no. 2 (2010): 158–172.

Kühnel, Jana, and Sabine Sonnentag. "How Long Do You Benefit from Vacation? A Closer Look at the Fade-Out of Vacation Effects." *Journal of Organizational Behavior* 32, no. 1 (January 2011): 125–143.

Kumar, Ashish, and Jari Salo. "Effects of Link Placements in Email Newsletters on Their Click-Through Rate." *Journal of Marketing Communications* 24, no. 5 (2018): 535–548.

Kushlev, Kostadin, and Elizabeth W. Dunn. "Checking Email Less Frequently Reduces Stress." *Computers in Human Behavior* 43 (2014): 220–228.

Lee, Jung Eun, and Jessi H. Chen-Yu. "Effects of Price Discount on Consumers' Perceptions of Savings, Quality, and Value for Apparel Products: Mediating Effect of Price Discount Affect." *Fashion and Textiles* 5, no. 1 (2018): 1–21.

LinkedIn. "Statistics." 2019. https://news.linkedin.com/about-us#statistics.

Locke, E. A., K. N. Shaw, L. M. Saari, and G. P. Latham. "Goal Setting and Task Performance: 1969–1980." *Psychological Bulletin* 90, no. 1 (1981): 125–152.

Lu, Serena Changhong, Dejun Tony Kong, Donald L. Ferrin, and Kurt T. Dirks. "What Are the Determinants of Interpersonal Trust in Dyadic Negotiations? Meta-analytic Evidence and Implications for Future Research." *Journal of Trust Research* 7, no. 1 (2017): 22–50.

Mark, Gloria, Shamsi T. Iqbal, Mary Czerwinski, Paul Johns, Akane Sano, and Yuliya Lutchyn. "Email Duration, Batching, and Self-Interruption: Patterns of Email Use on Productivity and Stress." In *Proceedings of the 2016 CHI Conference on Human Factors in Computing Systems*, 1717–1728. New York: ACM, 2016.

McFeely, Shane, and Ryan Pendell. "What Workplace Leaders Can Learn from the Real Gig Economy." Gallup, Workplace, August 16, 2018. www.gallup.com/workplace/240929/workplace-leaders-learn-real-gig-economy.aspx.

Mickiewicz, Adam. "Facets of Imagery in Academic and Professional Achievements: A Study of Three Doctoral Students." *Studies in Second Language Learning and Teaching* 3, no. 3 (2013): 397–418.

Mikkelsen, Kathleen, Lily Stojanovska, Momir Polenakovic, Marijan Bosevski, and Vasso Apostolopoulos. "Exercise and Mental Health." *Maturitas* 106 (2017): 48–56.

Morton, Jennifer M., and Sarah K. Paul. "Grit." *Ethics* 129, no. 2 (2019): 175–203.

Nasdaq. "The Gig Economy: 2020 Freelance Workforce Predicted to Rise to 43%." June 14, 2017. www.nasdaq.com/article/the-gig-economy-2020-freelance-workforce-predicted-to-rise-to-43-cm803297.

Nguyen, Thi Thao Duyen T., Thomas Garncarz, Felicia Ng, Laura A. Dabbish, and Steven P. Dow. "Fruitful Feedback: Positive Affective Language and Source Anonymity Improve Critique Reception and Work Outcomes." In *Proceedings of the 2017 ACM Conference on Computer Supported Cooperative Work and Social Computing*, 1024–1034. New York: ACM, 2017.

Niles, Frank. "How to Use Visualization to Achieve Your Goals." *HuffPost*, June 17, 2011. www.huffpost.com/entry/visualization-goals_b_878424.

Norcross, John C., Marci S. Mrykalo, and Matthew D. Blagys. "Auld Lang Syne: Success Predictors, Change Processes, and Self-Reported Outcomes of New Year's Resolvers and Nonresolvers." *Journal of Clinical Psychology* 58, no. 4 (2002): 397–405.

O'Connell, Ann. "50-State Chart of Small Claims Court Dollar Limits." Nolo, Legal Topics, January 24, 2020. www.nolo.com/legal-encyclopedia/small-claims-suits-how-much-30031.html.

Overall, Jeffrey, and Sean Wise. "The Antecedents of Entrepreneurial Success: A Mixed Methods Approach." *Journal of Enterprising Culture* 24, no. 3 (2016): 209–241.

Owen, Neville, Geneviève N. Healy, Charles E. Matthews, and David W. Dunstan. "Too Much Sitting: The Population-Health Science of Sedentary Behavior." *Exercise and Sport Sciences Reviews* 38, no. 3 (2010): 106–113.

Ozimek, Adam. "Freelancing and the Economy in 2019." UpWork, press release, 2019. www.upwork.com/press/economics/freelancing-and-the -economy-in-2019.

Pattison, Kermit. "Worker, Interrupted: The Cost of Task Switching." *Fast Company*, July 28, 2008. www.fastcompany.com/944128/worker-interrupted -cost-task-switching.

Peck, Frances. "Introverted Networking: Not an Oxymoron." *The Editor's Weekly* (blog), Editors Canada, December 1, 2015. https://blog.editors.ca/?p=3284.

Pencavel, John. "Recovery from Work and the Productivity of Working Hours." *Economica* 83 (2016): 545–563.

Powers, Brian W., Ashish K. Jha, and Sachin H. Jain. "Remembering the Strength of Weak Ties." *American Journal of Managed Care* 22, no. 3 (2016): 202–203.

Puig-Ribera, Anna, Judit Bort-Roig, Maria Giné-Garriga, Angel M. González-Suárez, Iván Martínez-Lemos, Jesús Fortuño, Joan C. Martori, et al. "Impact of a Workplace 'Sit Less, Move More' Program on Efficiency-Related Outcomes of Office Employees." *BMC Public Health* 17, no. 1 (2017): 455–466.

Reedsy. "The Lean Publisher." *Reedsy Blog*, May 1, 2020. https://reedsy.com /publishers/the-lean-publisher.

Roster, Catherine A., and Joseph R. Ferrari. "Does Work Stress Lead to Office Clutter, and How? Mediating Influences of Emotional Exhaustion and Indecision." *Environment and Behavior* 50 (2019): 86–115.

Rovello, Jessica. "5 Ways Katie Ledecky, Michael Phelps, and Other Olympians Visualize Success." *Inc.*, August 23, 2016. www.inc.com/jessica-rovello /five-steps-to-visualize-success-like-an-olympian.html.

Rudolph, Stacey. "Understanding the Importance of E-mail Subject Lines." Business 2 Community, March 27, 2016. www.business2community.com /infographics/understanding-importance-e-mail-subject-lines-infographic -01492127#za6tqbgOJuwElo71.97.

Sakulku, Jaruwan. "The Imposter Phenomenon." *International Journal of Behavioral Science* 6, no. 1 (2011): 73–92.

Salzmann, James R. "Statutory Millennialism: Establishment and Free Exercise Concerns Arising from the Health Care Sharing Ministry Exemption's 1999 Cutoff Date." *Southern California Law Review* 93, no. 303 (2018): 304–338.

Sander, Elizabeth, Arran Caza, and Peter J. Jordan. "Psychological Perceptions Matter: Developing the Reactions to the Physical Work Environment Scale." *Building and Environment* 148, no. 15 (2019): 338–347.

Schwarz, Carolyn. "Thrifting for More: Savings and Aspirations in Health Care Sharing Ministries after the Affordable Care Act." *Medical Anthropology Quarterly* 33, no. 2 (2019): 226–241.

Shannon, Vanessa R., Noah B. Gentner, Ashwin Patel, and Douglass Muccio. "Striking Gold: Mental Techniques and Preparation Strategies Used by Olympic Gold Medalists." *Athletic Insight* 4, no. 1 (2012): 1–11.

Slaunwhite, Steve, Pete Savage, and Ed Gandia. *The Wealthy Freelancer*. New York: Penguin/Alpha, 2010.

Stamp, Pauline, Theodore Peters, and Andrew Gorycki. "In Spite of Technology: A Failure in Student Project Ownership." *Organization Management* 17, no. 1 (2020): 36–42.

Talarico, Donna. "From Inbox to Enroll: Email Marketing Tips." *Recruiting and Retaining Adult Learners* 18, no. 11 (2016): 2–3.

Turner, Susan, and Al Endres. "Strategies for Enhancing Small-Business Owners' Success Rates." *International Journal of Applied Management and Technology* 16, no. 1 (2017): 34–49.

Willits, Liz. "2019 Email Marketing Statistics: We Analyzed 1,000 Emails from Today's Top Experts." *AWeber Blog*, January 9, 2019. https://blog.aweber .com/email-marketing/2019-email-marketing-statistics.htm.

Wood, Wendy, and David T. Neal. "Healthy through Habit: Interventions for Maintaining Health Behavior Change." *Behavioral Science and Policy* 2, no. 1 (2016): 71–83.

Wright, David J., Caroline J. Wakefield, and Dave Smith. "Using PETTLEP Imagery to Improve Music Performance." *Musicae Scientiae* 18, no. 4 (2014): 448–463.

Zhu, Ze, Lauren Kuykendall, and Xichao Zhang. "The Impact of Within-Day Work Breaks on Daily Recovery Processes: An Event-Based Pre-/Post -experience Sampling Study." *Journal of Occupational and Organizational Psychology* 92, no. 1 (2019): 191–211.

Index

268, 269–270, 271, 305; forms, 271,
273, 274–275, 288; Medicare, 274;
payment of, 271–272; penalties, 271,
272, 275, 277, 280; reduction of
liability, 39, 52, 279–280; resources,
267n, 268, 279; schedule of
payments, 270–271, 272, 275, 305;
for S corporation, 36, 37, 52,
268–269, 273–274, 276; self-employment tax, 12, 267–268, 269–270,
278; setting aside money for, 12,
268, 271, 282; Social Security, 270,
274; for sole proprietorship, 34, 35,
36, 273, 276; tax preparers, 268–269,
275, 280; use of Employer Identification Number (EIN), 38, 52. *See
also* expenses; finances; income
templates, 179–181, 200, 222, 223. *See
also* website: design
time management: need for in
freelancing, 17–18, 239–240;
strategies, 227, 231–232, 240,
241–242; tools, 223, 245. *See also*
deadlines; outsourcing; procrastination; productivity; projects;
schedule, work
training: conferences, 95–96, 278, 307,
309; from editing organizations,
94, 95–96, 113, 121, 278 (*see also*
Editorial Freelancers Association;
Facebook; LinkedIn; social media);
editing quizzes, 17, 45, 220; from
forums, 45, 309, 263; need for,
26–28, 72–75, 307–309; opportunities to provide, 74, 118; as tax
deduction, 278. *See also* education;
work experience
Twitter. *See* social media

unique selling proposition (USP),
104–107, 108, 120–121, 130, 145

vacations, 12, 45, 159, 250–251
vision statement, 42, 53–58, 74. *See
also* goals
visualization, 62–64, 71, 75

weaknesses, 43, 67–68. *See also*
confidence; mistakes; training
website: blog, 138–140, 141; communication of niche, 80, 128, 137, 139;
communication of unique selling
proposition (USP), 120–121;
content, 123, 128–138, 140; creation
of, 124–125, 138, 305; design,
127–128; domain name, 33, 51, 125,
126–127, 138; establishment of
credibility through, 123, 132–133,
136, 140; link to, 84, 91, 117, 135;
need for, 122–123, 133, 140;
promotional pieces on, 116, 121, 123,
137–138. *See also* search engine
optimization (SEO); social media
Word. *See* Microsoft Word
work experience: establishment of
credibility through, 24, 186; what to
share on LinkedIn, 145–146, 148,
150; what to share on website, 132,
136–137. *See also* credibility; letter of
introduction; résumé
work-life balance: achievement of,
246–256; and health, 248, 251–252,
258–259. *See also* family; friends;
prioritization; roommates

YouTube, 118–119. *See also* social
media

Founded in 1893,
UNIVERSITY OF CALIFORNIA PRESS
publishes bold, progressive books and journals
on topics in the arts, humanities, social sciences,
and natural sciences—with a focus on social
justice issues—that inspire thought and action
among readers worldwide.

The UC PRESS FOUNDATION
raises funds to uphold the press's vital role
as an independent, nonprofit publisher, and
receives philanthropic support from a wide
range of individuals and institutions—and from
committed readers like you. To learn more, visit
ucpress.edu/supportus.